MW01225516

Close Calls

Close Calls

Managing Risk and Resilience in Airline Flight Safety

By

Carl Macrae

palgrave
macmillan

First published 2014 by
PALGRAVE MACMILLAN

Palgrave Macmillan in the UK is an imprint of Macmillan Publishers Limited, registered in England, company number 785998, of Houndmills, Basingstoke, Hampshire RG21 6XS.

Palgrave Macmillan in the US is a division of St Martin's Press LLC, 175 Fifth Avenue, New York, NY 10010.

Palgrave Macmillan is the global academic imprint of the above companies and has companies and representatives throughout the world.

Palgrave® and Macmillan® are registered trademarks in the United States, the United Kingdom, Europe and other countries.

ISBN 978–0–230–22084–3

This book is printed on paper suitable for recycling and made from fully managed and sustained forest sources. Logging, pulping and manufacturing processes are expected to conform to the environmental regulations of the country of origin.

A catalogue record for this book is available from the British Library.

A catalogue record for this book is available from the Library of Congress.

Typeset by MPS Limited, Chennai, India.

Contents

Foreword

I am delighted to be given the opportunity to write this Foreword. Furthermore, I do so with some measure of pride. Carl Macrae chose to be an undergraduate student of psychology during my time teaching at the University of Manchester. Indeed, he was my tutorial student during his first and final years. I remember writing at the bottom of one of his early essays: 'More psychology, Carl, and less philosophy, please'. Fortunately that did not constrain his talents, as this book goes to show.

Safety science is one of the toughest games in town. Unlike the natural sciences, it is not enough for an idea to be read, quoted and tested. It has to work in practice as well. There are not enough trees in the rainforest to write a set of procedures that will guarantee freedom from harm. To progress in this most difficult of areas needs a subtle combination of modern psychology, human factors and a deep understanding of the philosophy of technology. In my view, Carl's discussion of the nature of safety is one of the best I have ever read. And I have spent a professional lifetime trying to unravel its complexities.

A large part of my work has examined the nature of error and risk in safety critical systems, and yet I have always had difficulty with the meaning of the term 'risk'. That it is said to be a function of both likelihood and severity has never been entirely satisfactory. The argument that runs through this book that interrelates risk, safety and resilience – what Carl terms 'risk resilience' – clarified my thinking. I had a true 'Aha' feeling when reading this. Risk resilience is about an organisation's ability to protect its operations from the potential of minor mishaps combining into major catastrophes. In short, it is about the effectiveness of the practices that produce defences, barriers and safeguards rather than about the actual or predicted outcomes of reported (and usually minor) events. This is an observation of major theoretical and practical importance.

The main thrust of this book is to elucidate the processes and practices by which the risks of airline flight safety incidents are understood, identified and acted upon by very experienced flight safety investigators. These practices are analysed with regard to three important and innovative organisational concepts: risk resilience, interpretive vigilance and participative networks. These concepts are grounded in richly detailed data from an in-depth ethnographic study of the work that is actually done in airlines to analyse safety and manage risk or, more precisely, 'risk resilience'.

I have long argued for the importance of understanding the practical contexts and conditions in which people work, and this book wonderfully exemplifies and extends that idea. It demonstrates the value of closely analysing the practical work of safety management, and the important and practical insights that can result. This is an area with which I am well acquainted; nonetheless, the insightful and original exposition developed in this book cast fresh light for me upon familiar ground. I confidently predict that this work will have a major impact upon the way safety professionals and academics think and do research. This impact should be felt particularly in healthcare, where Carl is currently focusing much of his efforts and where there remains so much work to do.

No doubt we have all experienced the 'I-wish-I-had-written-that' feeling. I certainly felt it many times when reading this. It is a joy to read something that I wish I could have written. Especially when the writer was once my student, and amongst the best of them. Would he have been so good had he not been a Manchester psychology graduate? Almost certainly, yes. But he may have exercised his talents in some other less demanding (but more professionally appreciated) domain, such as experimental psychology – if you can control the variables, it has to be trivial. But that's my personal prejudice after having been an academic psychologist for nigh on forty years.

Jim Reason
Professor, Department of Psychology
University of Manchester

Preface

As I type this sentence I am sat sipping a glass of wine while watching a beautiful sunset of mauve and umber, waiting for dinner to be served before settling down a little later to watch a movie. A small screen tells me that, although I would not know it, the temperature outside is a brisk fifty two degrees below freezing and I am travelling at nearly nine hundred kilometres an hour, suspended ten kilometres above the Earth. Outside, a few centimetres to my right, there is so little oxygen that I would pass out in seconds. But the only indication of any of this is a slight tremor on the surface of my drink and the low rumble of the four giant turbofans that are propelling me at such startling speeds across the sky.

The experience of modern aviation is now so commonplace that its most remarkable feats pass unnoticed, a mere interruption – and usually a discomfort – in our busy daily lives. Mass travel on the lower edge of the stratosphere at speeds close to the speed of sound seems normal, routine, simple, even. Yet it is anything but. This single aircraft is made of millions of individual components that must all work in perfect harmony for the next eleven and a half hours. This single flight is the result of the coordinated efforts of not just the crew onboard, but of thousands of individuals. Many of those individuals are charged with thinking about one thing only: flight safety. This book is about one particular breed of those safety professionals – airline flight safety investigators, and the ways they see and make sense of the complex, ambiguous world they inhabit.

Aviation stands out amongst modern industries for its scale and complexity, its deep preoccupation with reliability and its sophisticated infrastructure for improving and enhancing safety. This is an industry in which one major airframe manufacturer has been known to boast that their airliners achieve on-time departure reliability of 99.67% – compared to their competitor's presumably woeful 99.35%. This is also an industry renowned for routinely achieving seemingly astonishing levels of safety. In 2012 fatal airline accidents occurred at the lowest rate since the dawn of the jet age. Nearly forty million flights resulted in just 21 fatal accidents. Yet even that statistic was greeted in the industry as a sign that they might just have been lucky and must try harder next time. The timeless quote of Alfred G. Lamplugh, an aviation insurer speaking in 1931, is still found on the walls of airline offices around the world and echoes in the minds of many in the industry: "Aviation in itself is not inherently dangerous. But to an even greater degree than the sea, it is terribly unforgiving of any carelessness, incapacity or neglect".

Even all those years ago, Lamplugh was merely channelling those who had gone before. "In flying I have learned that carelessness and overconfidence are usually far more dangerous than deliberately accepted risks", wrote Wilbur Wright to his father, a full two years before he and his brother Orville piloted the very first powered, controlled and heavier-than-air flights in December 1903, traversing barely a hundred feet across a small field near Kitty Hawk, North Carolina. That first flight could now easily take place within the confines of terminal buildings at any number of airports around the world. Yet carelessness, overconfidence and neglect still rank amongst the greatest fears of those who monitor and oversee flight safety – whether exhibited in the activities of airline operations, or in their own activities of safety oversight.

Echoing those first faltering, tentative experiments in the air, aviation has largely advanced through failure. The infrastructure of safety improvement in aviation is really an infrastructure for experiencing, cataloguing, understanding and learning from failure: it is an infrastructure of resilience, in one way or another. Accidents provide some of the most potent and visible sources of knowledge and improvement, but the routine activities of safety improvement are now more commonly driven by far less costly and visible events: incidents, errors, anomalies, near misses, disruptions, defects and close calls all challenge, in small ways, the industry's sense of control and mastery, and open up new arenas of ignorance and uncertainty to marshal and explore.

How organisations learn from failure and how they harness incidents to drive improvement remain some of the most pressing and fundamental questions in the field of risk and safety management. They are questions that are of immediate and direct relevance to those working in hospitals, banks, oil refineries, mines, railways, nuclear power stations, ships and many of the other complex sociotechnical systems that modern society depends upon. The airline industry most certainly does not hold all the answers. But it has spent decades thinking about the questions, and for that reason – amongst others – it is the focus of this book. Learning from incidents and close calls is one of the founding strategies of safety improvement in aviation. Despite the emergence of impressive new technologies of risk modelling and predictive analysis, looking back to learn from incidents and errors still sits at the core of modern airline safety management systems. It is also one of the most widely emulated but deceptively complex and least well-understood strategies of risk and safety management. By focusing on airline flight safety investigators, this book looks beyond principles and generalisations to examine the practical work that is actually involved in learning from failure, and the particular analytical and interpretive challenges that must be confronted when organisations attempt to improve safety by transforming moments of risk into sources of resilience.

This book has been a long time coming. The field of risk management has evolved dramatically in the years between its tentative inception and its final delivery. When I first began the research on which this book is based back in 2001, the concepts of resilience, latent risks and ignorance were still relatively arcane and technical terms confined to small corners of academic study. Since then we appear to have entered a world besieged by crises, disasters and uncertainties. The outright collapse of much of the financial sector in 2008 suddenly brought the intersections of risk, ignorance and complex organisation firmly into the public eye. As it happened I found myself working in the risk management group of a large financial institution during that period and was able to watch those events, and the debates that surrounded them, play out first hand. My brief spell in the high towers of financial risk was undoubtedly the most interesting time to work in the City of London in the last seventy-five years, perhaps ever. I am – perhaps slightly morbidly – pleased to have had that opportunity.

As a seeming magnet for crises, I was also working in the National Health Service as a special advisor at the pioneering National Patient Safety Agency when, quite abruptly, it was abolished by a new government keen to reorganise. Much of my time at the NPSA was devoted to redesigning the National Reporting and Learning System: the patient safety incident reporting system for the NHS in England and Wales that is almost certainly the largest safety incident reporting system of its kind in the world. The NRLS offers an astonishingly rich resource that remains, for the large part, hidden from and inaccessible to those on the front-line of patient safety improvement. Many of the ideas and principles explored in my prior research and in this book underpinned a future vision for the NRLS, and I hope this important improvement work is able to continue once the dust of reorganisation settles. The NHS is now in the midst of learning from a further crisis of patient safety, following two inquiries into gross failures of safety management, oversight and regulation at a healthcare organisation in Mid Staffordshire. Despite all this, it is nonetheless heartening to see the sorts of cultures and practices I describe in this book being reinvented – and in places being radically improved upon – in pockets throughout our healthcare system.

This book is, I hope, richer for those intervening adventures in risk and safety. But in writing it I have been careful to remain true to the original ethnographic and empirical research that I conducted in a small number of airlines and state air safety agencies. In preparing this book I have seemingly produced, and discarded, enough material for several others; perhaps they will follow another day. This book is ultimately an account of the analytical, investigative and improvement practices of the highly specialised and largely unknown profession of airline flight safety investigators. Safety incident investigation is increasingly seen as an old and outdated approach to enhancing safety, particularly as new and fashionable risk management technologies and improvement models sweep through organisations. Safety investigators and the work that they do are certainly not considered to be in the vanguard of safety improvement. This is a shame. The practitioners of this craft address head-on some of the most fundamental challenges that risk management faces; they have been doing it daily, and for a long time. Complexity, ignorance, improvement, resilience: these cumbersome words are rarely used by flight safety investigators, but they represent what this small professional community has been grappling with for over a hundred years.

As might be expected of a book so long in the making, I have built up an extraordinarily broad and deep range of debts in its production. First and foremost, I remain deeply indebted to the flight safety investigators and their employers who welcomed me so wholeheartedly into their world. They provided me with unrestricted and open access not only to themselves and their daily work, but also to huge volumes of safety data, to their operations centres and offices, to management and committee meetings, not to mention the occasional opportunity to wander amongst hangars and aircraft. The investigators themselves – at all the airlines, regulators and state agencies involved in this work – should individually remain anonymous, but they have my heartfelt and continuing thanks. I am also particularly deeply indebted to Jim Reason for both sparking my interest and setting this particular ball rolling so comprehensively back in Manchester in the late 1990s. His generosity with his ideas, time and wisdom appear to have set me on a professional and, I suspect, lifelong search for safety. I consider myself privileged to have gained a deeply erroneous and accidental education – in the best possible of senses – from Jim and remain grateful for his support over the years.

This work began at the University of East Anglia's Centre for Environmental Risk in 2001, and the core funding came about thanks to a collaboration between Nick Pidgeon and Mike O'Leary, both of whom were my doctoral advisors and to both of whom I remain grateful for the freedom and support they offered me. My time at UEA in 'ENV' would not have been the same without Finlay Scott, Tracey Holley, Miguel de Franca Doria, Kat Haynes, Tom Lowe and Duncan Russell – all now scattered across the globe. In 2004 I spent three enjoyable, engaging and productive months at the Australian National University in Canberra with Andrew Hopkins. I am indebted to him for hosting me there and for taking such an interest in my work: that time proved pivotal for this research. At ANU I also benefited immensely from Mike Smithson's knowledge of ignorance and Fiona Keer's firsthand experience of the trials – and more than occasional humour – of flight safety oversight.

The people and place of the Centre for Analysis of Risk and Regulation at the London School of Economics have been deeply influential in shaping this work, both during my doctoral studies and later when I worked there as a researcher. I am particularly indebted to the support of Bridget Hutter and Mike Power, who both strongly encouraged me to first start – and then finish – this volume. At CARR, where I remain a Research Associate, I have benefited from seminars, workshops, conferences and conversations with a range of international visitors and colleagues; those with David Demortain, Sally Lloyd-Bostock, Sarah Dry, Jakob Vestergaard, Clive Jones, Javier Lezaun, Will Jennings and Martin Lodge were always good fun. John Downer deserves a special mention, not only for being a great colleague and friend, but for our countless conversations on safety and accidents which have challenged and refined my thinking enormously.

This book is about airlines, but the underpinning ideas have latterly benefited from a number of years spent percolating in healthcare. I remain indebted to Sir Liam Donaldson, Donald Berwick, Peter Pronovost and Roger Resar, whose early interest in this work ensured that my recent attention has quite dramatically refocused from passengers to patients. I am particularly grateful to Martin Fletcher, former Chief Executive of the National Patient Safety Agency, for inviting me in as a special advisor and offering me such a wide-ranging role and remit. It was a pleasure and an education to develop some of these ideas in practice and to work closely with Suzette Woodward, Kevin Cleary and Peter Hibbert. I also benefited from insightful conversations with Tara Lamont, Linda Matthew, Frances Healey, Joan Russell, Mike Surkitt-Parr, Dagmar Luettel, Donna Forsyth, Amar Shah and many others who are now dispersed around the healthcare system. More recently, taking up a Health Foundation Improvement Science Fellowship has provided me the space to finally complete this manuscript, and in particular has allowed me to work closely with my fellow fellows Julie Reed, Tim Draycott and Davina Allen, as well as Bill Lucas and Fiona Reed – all of whom, in different ways, have greatly influenced my thinking on safety improvement and the work that underpins it. The fellowship has also provided opportunities for extensive discussions on the nature of quality, safety and improvement with many generous luminaries in the field and I am grateful to the vision and energy of Paul Batalden, Martin Marshall, Nick Barber and Helen Crisp for starting and continuing to support such an important programme of work on improvement science – and for allowing me to be part of it.

Mary Dixon-Woods and Charles Vincent kindly welcomed me to their respective research groups as I completed this manuscript and both have entertained a wide range of valuable and helpful conversations on safety – patient and otherwise. Also due my gratitude are Graham Braithwaite at Cranfield University Safety and Accident Investigation Centre, Paul Schulman at Mills College, and Karlene Roberts and Tony Hare at UC Berkeley who have allowed me to vicariously join their seminars on high reliability over several years. Thanks are importantly due to my editor, Virginia Thorp, for her remarkable patience as I slowly fitted this manuscript around – or, more often, had to entirely set it aside due to – my myriad other commitments, transitions and responsibilities that have filled the past few years. And thanks are also due to Kiran Bolla and Geetha Williams for organising the final production of this manuscript.

This book would not have been possible without the generous funding I received from the Economic and Social Research Council, award numbers S42200134055 and PTA-026-27-0984, a collaborative industry partner in the airline industry who shall remain nameless (though anonymity does not belie gratitude), and an Improvement Science Fellowship from the Health Foundation, an independent charity working to continuously improve the quality of healthcare in the UK. I am grateful for all of this support.

Much closer to home, Amelie is due an extraordinary thank you. Amelie has long been a huge source of resilience in my life, and has had to put up with errors, accidents, risk and incidents – not to mention safety of one flavour or another – for pretty much our entire history. This research, and later this book, have been permanent guests in our lives, and she has been an extraordinarily patient and gracious host. None of this would have made any sense without her. It would also be remiss of me not to mention the role of my two other life partners, though they walk on four legs and have had all of their energetically typed contributions to this manuscript tracked down and, I hope, entirely removed. Finally, this book is rightly dedicated to my parents, Lynne and Ian. It is also for my mother's parents, Dennis and Ada Shuker, who lost their lives in the Tenerife air disaster of 5th May 1965.

1
Searching for Risk and Resilience

"Close Call". The term is redolent of the lucky escape, the close brush with disaster, the narrowly avoided catastrophe. Close calls don't come much closer than on the morning of 21st November 1989, at London's Heathrow airport. Flying blind in thick cloud and fog, relying on instruments and struggling with bouts of food poisoning and the notoriously tricky old 'Sperry'-type autopilot, the crew of a Boeing 747 began their final approach. Breaking through heavy cloud just seconds before touch down, they made the gut-wrenching realisation they had drifted way off the runway centre-line, out over the airport's perimeter fence. Punching the engines to full go-around power to abort the landing, the aircraft lumbered away, clearing the luxury Penta Hotel with little more than twelve feet (3.65 metres) to spare, sending staff and guests screaming into the street. Near-misses don't come much closer. Nothing but providence and a few feet separated hundreds of people from an horrific catastrophe.

Dramatic events that place hundreds of lives in the balance are rare in commercial aviation. But thanks in part to striking moments such as this, the idea of learning from close calls and near-miss events has become deeply embedded in the culture and practice of airline safety management. It is an idea that has spread far and wide. Analysing and learning from near-miss events and operational incidents is now a central component of risk management practice in industries as diverse as healthcare, nuclear power and banking. At one time, only the most costly and harmful accidents were subjected to intense investigation. Now all manner of procedural mishaps, human errors and operational defects are routinely catalogued and submitted to in-depth analysis and investigation. Well-established incident reporting programmes can collect tens or even hundreds of thousands of reports each year, each one capturing a fleeting encounter with risk. These provide organisations with countless opportunities for uncovering risks in their operations and for improving safety. But, in practice, investigating, analysing and learning from incidents is rife with complications and difficulties. Transforming incidents into improvements confronts some of the deepest and most fundamental challenges of risk management.

When organisations take safety seriously, risk managers can soon find themselves awash with reports of errors, anomalies, near-misses and failures that are diligently filed by personnel from around the organisation. Some of those incidents may have very serious implications for safety, but many will not. Most operational incidents reported to risk managers involve only minor defects and fleeting disruptions: the occasional mishaps, complications and fluctuations that are inherent to all organised human activity. But in some cases, the underlying risks and the potential consequences can be catastrophic. Analysing incidents is therefore challenging and consequential work: the stakes are high and signals of risk are weak and ambiguous. Failures to identify and address risks at this early stage of risk management are particularly insidious. They allow risks to remain dormant and hidden deep within an organisation. When early warning signs are missed, people simply may not realise that certain risks exist in the first place – until they are dramatically and catastrophically realised. Interpreting and learning from incidents therefore depends on close calls of another kind: fine-grained judgements to determine where safety is satisfactory and where it is troubling, and which weak signals of risk matter most and should be investigated, and which should not. The art of risk analysis is not simply knowing what to look for, it is also the art of knowing what to overlook.

This book is about the practical work of risk management and the practical challenges that are inherent to analysing and learning from incidents, errors, failures and close calls. Specifically, this book is about the practices of airline flight safety investigators. Flight safety investigators are responsible for overseeing the safety of airline operations and ensuring that risks to flight safety are properly identified, understood and addressed. They are a special breed of risk manager and belong to a distinct technical and professional community with roots stretching back over a hundred years to the earliest days of formal air accident investigation. Nowadays, most flight safety investigators work in commercial airlines and much of their work focuses on assessing and investigating relatively minor flight safety events, reports of which are submitted in their thousands by airline personnel.

This role places flight safety investigators at the sharp end of risk management. They work in a context in which the deep interpretive challenges of risk management are particularly pronounced. In large airlines, front-line operational personnel can report tens of thousands of safety incidents each year. Each of those incident reports is extremely brief – often little more than a one-line description with some additional geographical and technical data. Typical incident reports merely highlight, for instance, that "flights A2490, A2940 and A2840 all operate from the same station at the same or similar departure times, which causes call-sign confusion". Or that, "during pre-flight checks, the wrong departure route was entered into the flight computer and the error was only noticed and corrected after take-off". By definition, these are reports of transient and fleeting events that have typically resulted in limited – and usually no – adverse outcome. A defect was discovered or an error was made, and then corrected. Investigators must trawl through these incidents to work out what they mean and what their implications might be for flight safety, all the while looking for new risks and remaining attentive to the early and weak signs of emerging threats. This work requires extensive and deep technical expertise. It also requires creative thinking, a deep index of suspicion and a healthy – or perhaps unhealthy – dose of curiosity.

Close calls involving jumbo jets and luxury hotels provide clear signals of risk, and naturally provoke intensive investigation and improvement efforts. But such events are extremely rare. The routine stuff of close calls is no longer a dramatic brush with catastrophe. Instead, the majority of events reported to investigators appear, at first blush, to be rather humdrum and mundane moments of organisational life. 'Distant misses' or 'far calls' might be more appropriate descriptors. The consequence of near-miss events becoming more distant and risk management becoming more precautionary is that warnings get weaker and more equivocal. The early signs of emerging risks are rarely self-evident, and the most serious and challenging risks typically lie at – or just beyond – the limits of current knowledge. Signs of new and emerging risks must be actively interrogated, pieced together and made sense of by investigators. To complicate matters further, safety investigators, like most other risk managers, have no executive control or direct authority to address risks. They provide independent oversight and impartial guidance, and so are separated from operational and executive functions. As a result, investigators' practical strategies for managing and addressing risks are almost as subtle and nuanced as their strategies for identifying and assessing them.

This book, then, is about the practical work that is done to analyse, learn from – and make – close calls in safety improvement. It explores how operational incidents, failures and errors are interpreted and analysed in practice and how some come to be defined as risky whilst others are deemed acceptably safe. It examines how the earliest and most tentative signs of risk are identified and extracted from a mirky sea of anomalies and defects. And it analyses how knowledge is produced and practices are improved by transforming small moments of organisational life into signals of risk, around which wide-ranging activities of investigation and improvement are then organised. Flight safety investigators engage in a continual search for risk and resilience: this is the story of that search.

Making sense of safety

Risk has become an organising feature of modern industrial life. Ideas and ideals of risk management are embedded in a proliferation of risk management standards, safety improvement models and error analysis methods. Whilst risk is a staple of both professional and academic discourse, the practical nature of the work actually involved in interpreting and managing risk is more often assumed than explored. The practical work of analysing and addressing risk can remain largely invisible to the regulators and executives who are responsible for assuring the safety of their organisations. It often remains invisible in much of the research literature, too. Yet if organisations are to improve their ability to manage risk and safety, it is first necessary to understand the practices and the practical work that underpin these tasks. This requires up-close, prolonged and in-depth study of the situated practices, practical theories and analytical tactics that are employed by risk managers to make sense of and address organisational risks. We need to make sense of the practical work that risk managers do when they themselves make sense of risk and safety – and that was my purpose when I began this research.

Over the course of four years I observed, interviewed and worked with a group of airline flight safety investigators to understand the work they did and the shared knowledge and conceptual tools that they found useful. My focus was on understanding how flight safety investigators monitor, identify, analyse and manage risks to airline flight safety. My principle aim was to understand the interpretive work that is involved in identifying and understanding risks and organising safety improvement. I wanted to understand how flight safety investigators interpret the masses of safety incidents that are reported to them, how they use those incidents to identify and uncover potential risks to safety, how they analyse those risks and monitor safety and how they work to coordinate investigations and oversee improvements. As such, my attention focused on the cultural practices, the cognitive work, the conceptual frameworks and the shared social representations, ideas and models that underpin and shape how investigators analyse risk and improve safety. That is, my focus was on making sense of safety.

How experts interpret and make sense of safety is central to how risks get managed – and whether certain risks are even noticed and understood in the first place. When the interpretation and analysis of risks goes awry in organisations, risks can be inadvertently neglected or ignored. Effective risk management is the art of continually identifying and addressing the most pressing set of problems threatening safety. It is also the art of knowing what to overlook. Or, to put it another way, the most fundamental challenge of risk management practice is knowing "which aspects of the current set of problems facing an organisation are prudent to ignore and which should be attended to, and how an acceptable level of safety can be established as a criterion in carrying out this exercise" (Turner, 1976a, p. 379).

Investigators, like all risk managers, are confronted with masses of safety-relevant information and are faced with the imperative to act early and often, before risks are revealed by major organisational failures. But data on risk do not interpret themselves. In modern, complexly hazardous organisations like airlines, risks are rarely self-evident. One of the core challenges facing safety investigators is therefore interpreting and making sense of incidents and identifying the underlying risks that these may point to – challenges that are amplified and particularly pronounced in the setting of airline flight safety oversight. In the course of their daily work, "managers literally must wade into the ocean of events that surround the organisation and actively try to make sense of them" (Daft and Weick, 1984, p. 286). Risk managers face this challenge in the extreme, and this book is about how flight safety investigators work to meet this challenge.

To understand how investigators analyse, improve and make sense of safety, I focused on understanding their situated practices of risk management as they actually conducted their day-to-day work. Studying practical work in its organisational setting is notoriously challenging. It requires detailed analysis of the organisational context, social structures and conceptual and material resources used in practice. It also requires attentiveness to the cultural, cognitive and interpretive processes that underpin routine activities (Hutchins, 1996). Moving away from front-line personnel such as – in aviation – pilots and engineers, practical work takes on a less visible form, being more about analysing and interpreting than operating and acting. Studying how investigators analyse, make sense of and act on risks is particularly challenging due to the subtle nature of interpretive work. Interpretation and sensemaking involve active, effortful processing and social interaction. Sensemaking – literally the processes of making sense of situations, data and events – involves building a coherent account by combining the information, evidence, theories and knowledge at hand (Weick, 1995; Maitlis, 2005). Active processing and interpretation are typically occasioned by things that are out of the ordinary: "sensemaking begins with the basic question, is it still possible to take things for granted? And if the answer is no, if it has become impossible to continue with automatic information processing, then the question becomes, why is this so? And, what next?" (Weick, 1995, p. 14).

The work of risk management is focused on understanding failures and uncertainties: two common triggers of sensemaking. Efforts to make sense are commonly provoked by problems, gaps, puzzles, novelty, ambiguity and surprises – when things can no longer be taken for granted and when people's sense of the familiar and routine has been shaken. At core, sensemaking is a process of identifying, bracketing and labelling certain things as relevant and worth attending to and then relating those things to existing concepts, knowledge and broader frames of reference to work out what they mean. Those broader frames of reference may be past experiences, memories, stories, professional standards, formal models or company procedures. Interrelating moments of experience with frameworks of knowledge is at the heart of how people interpret events and make data meaningful. These processes are inevitably social – if only because the frames of reference that people draw on are the products of previous collective activities, social communities, organisations and prior interactions (Wenger, 1999). The nature of expert practice, then, needs to be understood as more than merely doing, behaving or acting. Rather, practice "is doing in a historical and social context that gives structure and meaning to what we do" (Wenger, 1999, p. 47). To understand how professionals work, it is important to understand what knowledge they draw on and how they put that knowledge in practice. Put another way, "if you want to understand the essentials of what accomplished engineers know, you need to look at what they do as well as what they possess" (Cook and Brown, 1999, p. 387).

In this book, my focus is on what flight safety investigators do, what they know and how they put that knowledge into practice to manage risk and improve safety. This study took me deep into the practical world of flight safety investigators and allowed me to lift the lid on their work. To explore this world I used a range of methods over several phases of fieldwork. These ranged from short interviews, critical incident reviews, structured group discussions, in-depth interviews and working with investigators day-in, day-out for months at a time. During this time I spent some 400 hours systematically observing their practice, observed and discussed the analysis of 464 flight safety incidents, sat in on five different forms of safety meeting, including board meetings, team meetings and operational reviews, and conducted 39 lengthy and iterative in-depth interviews (Macrae, 2007; 2009). I studied the work of 26 flight safety investigators, at various levels of seniority, working across seven different organisations. My work was iterative. Each stage contributed to an emerging and evolving picture of practice, which set the focus for future stages of work. These methods allowed me to conducted research "in close rather than from the armchair" (Weick, 1995, p. 173). I listened to investigators' conversations, observed their work, questioned their assumptions and worked with them to refine and elaborate my emerging explanations of their practice. I came to learn about the challenges they faced, the tactics they employed to deal with those challenges and the fundamental assumptions, conceptual tools and practical theories that shaped their work, their thinking and their management of risk. My analysis rigorously followed the tenets of the constant comparative grounded theory method, which seeks to produce useful, relevant and coherent theories of organisational life that are well-grounded in empirical evidence (Glaser and Strauss, 1967), and my methodology was ethnographic (Emerson, Fretz and Shaw, 1995; Crotty, 1998) in which, quite simply, I sought "to conduct informal interviews in industry, to participate in industrial life, and to 'be around' as industrial life unfolds" (Turner, 1971, p. 136).

My work was conducted in five airlines and two state air safety agencies, though I primarily focused on the work of flight safety investigators in large international airlines. All of these organisations employed specialist flight safety investigators whose primary responsibilities were analysing and responding to flight safety incidents. Five of these organisations were based in the UK and two of them in its linguistic and cultural cousin, Australia. These organisations were chosen to allow me to challenge, test and elaborate my emerging theoretical account of investigators' practice. They were selected both for their similarities and differences in terms of the safety management principles and tools being used, their operational activities and the linguistic and regulatory frameworks they operated within. My focus was on producing well-grounded theory that was recognisable and useful to the practitioners involved, so I regularly engaged with flight safety investigators to invite challenge and comment on my emerging explanation of their practice. Nonetheless, as with all ethnographic explanation, this account is necessarily my working theory of their working theory.

Well-grounded theory interrelates the particular and the general, the practical and the theoretical. Throughout this book I liberally show the practical thinking and the work of flight safety investigators in order to richly illustrate both their working theory – and mine – and to deeply ground my analysis in the practical world of flight safety management. When the direct words of investigators are presented they are either indented and set apart from the main text, or are marked in "double quotation marks", and referenced with an anonymous safety investigator (Si) code. These codes provide a degree of transparency regarding the relative sources of the fieldwork data being presented, while ensuring anonymity: each code refers to a participant involved in a specific phase of my research, and not to a specific individual investigator. Throughout my analysis in the chapters that follow, quotes in 'single quotation marks' are indirect quotations, being either common terms used by investigators or comments that were not recorded verbatim in my fieldnote or interview transcripts (e.g. Emerson, Fretz and Shaw, 1995). To provide further anonymity to the investigators and the organisations involved in this research, a range of technical details and names have been altered or disguised in all of the examples, vignettes and incidents presented.

A reasonable question at this juncture might be – why airline flight safety investigators? There are a number of reasons. Airlines represent one of the most technologically advanced and one of the least forgiving operational environments that exist. But they are also extraordinarily safe. This is in large part due to a well-developed infrastructure of safety oversight that spans regulation, design, manufacture and operation. It is also because so much effort is put into analysing and learning from failures. Accident investigation has been formally conducted for over a century and incident analysis has been deeply established in aviation for decades. Flight safety investigators have been at the forefront of these movements. Investigators represent a long tradition of safety management and a well-established professional community. Yet there is also surprisingly little wider understanding of the practices and the practical work of flight safety investigators. This is despite airlines having become something of a touchstone in the world of safety and reliability. Aviation is commonly held up as an exemplary case, and models and metaphors from airline flight safety are being increasingly and widely applied in other industries. Many of those models and metaphors are unfortunately rather fragile: they are not always built on a deep or rigorous understanding of the practical work and the cognitive, social and organisational processes that contribute to the extraordinary levels of safety that the passenger air transport system routinely achieves. A better grounded understanding of flight safety management therefore seems important, both to explain this challenging arena of risk management and as a route to producing better theories and exemplars for other areas of industrial life.

Ultimately, this book is about a small number of airlines and the role of one particular type of risk manager that works within them. But the reach and implications are much broader. This book is about the practical work of managing risk in complex, challenging and dynamic organisations, where the opportunities for failure are manifold, the consequences of accidents are extremely costly but the actual incidence of adverse outcomes is surprisingly low. The work of risk management is always unique and specific to the context it operates in. But many of the underlying principles, approaches and practices of interpreting risk and improving safety described here are relevant to many other risk management domains, from hospitals to oil rigs to trading floors. So while this book is about airlines and airline flight safety investigators, the implications and aspirations reach beyond the specifics of the airline industry: this analysis aims to help make sense of the practical work that is involved in managing risk and improving safety in all complex, dynamic and unforgiving organisational settings.

Bracketing the problem

The work of flight safety investigators represents the sharp end of risk management. Investigators are responsible for monitoring, analysing and interpreting reports of flight safety incidents to identify any emerging risks, as well as overseeing and organising any required investigation and improvement activities to address those risks. This work brings many of the most pressing challenges of risk management into sharp relief. In particular, this work raises three important sets of questions that have implications and relevance to both the theory and practice of risk management.

First is perhaps the most fundamental issue of all. What is risk management trying to achieve? What does safety look like in organisational settings where errors occur frequently, risks are potentially catastrophic, systems are complex, but adverse outcomes are relatively rare? The meaning of safety is both deeply problematic and deeply consequential in practice. How safety is understood determines how risks are analysed and managed. Practical theories of safety provide idealised benchmarks against which safety is judged and risks are assessed. How investigators understand safety, and how those understandings influence their assessments of risk, are deeply consequential and complicated questions.

Second, how are weak signals of threat and the early signs of emerging risks first identified? How do investigators interpret and bracket indications of potential problems? Managing risks and improving safety depends on first recognising that a risk might exist. What do the formative and earliest moments of risk identification look like, and what analytical strategies and interpretive tactics are used to identify those early signs of potential risks? Identifying new and emerging risks is a critical element of risk management, and is a key purpose of incident reporting programmes more broadly. In a complex, messy and noisy world, distinguishing signal from noise and uncovering the early signs of risk are some of the most pressing challenges in risk management.

Third, how is new knowledge produced and change effected in response to operational incidents and disruptions? How is safety improved? Investigators are responsible not just for assessment and analysis, but for coordinating improvement and overseeing changes to practise throughout an organisation. Yet, as is the case for most safety oversight functions, they are independent and removed from operational activities. They work at a distance. How, then, do they influence and drive change with no executive capacity? How do they determine what changes are needed and where to focus resources? And how do they ensure resources are organised to deliver improvements? These are persistent challenges in all of risk management and issues that need to be negotiated by all risk managers.

Investigators confront these questions afresh each day. How they answer them in practice is centrally important both to our understanding of risk management and safety improvement, and to our efforts to support and improve risk management itself. As such, this book engages with these three core issues. How is organisational safety understood and analysed in practice? How are early signals of risk identified and interpreted? And how are errors and incidents used to drive improvement, shape culture and improve practice? At core is the question of how close calls and safety incidents are used by risk managers to understand safety, produce knowledge and improve practice in complex sociotechnical systems – and what the particular practices of flight safety investigators can reveal for current theories and models of risk management.

Organisations, risk and knowledge

This book is about the practical work of managing risk: what it looks like, why it takes certain forms and how it can be improved. It is also a book about the practical work involved in overseeing and improving safety in complex systems. And it is a book about how experts think about safety, analyse error and interpret and respond to weak signals of risk. The focus is on describing and explaining the practical work of flight safety investigators, to understand the cultural practices of this professional group and the key characteristics of their approach to risk analysis and safety management. The point is not only to describe these practices, important though that is. The purpose is also to contribute to our theoretical understanding of risk management and the practical theories that underpin it: to produce new conceptual insights and in so doing elaborate, challenge and extend existing theories of safety and risk. And theories there are aplenty.

At first blush the range of ideas and theories that have been advanced to explain risk management, safety improvement and resilience in organisations is quite startling. The field of risk management has undergone something of an explosion (Hutter, 2001; Power, 2007). Issues that were once the preserve of niche academic sub-disciplines are now mainstream issues in both academic and popular discourse. Risk, complexity, resilience, failure, ignorance: popular as well as professional attention has seen a dramatic turn to these issues in recent years (e.g. Sheffi, 2005; Harford, 2011; Zolli and Healy, 2012; Hutter and Power, 2005), on top of the work of an already packed landscape of regulators, standard setters, government agencies, professional bodies and advisors all seeking to define and impose a variety of risk and safety management models.

Despite this cacophony of voices, two strong undercurrents run through the dominant ideas and discourses of risk management. One is a deep assumption embedded in many of these ideas. The other is a broad theme that characterises and frames many debates in this field. The deep – and often hidden – assumption is that social and technological systems always exist in a degraded and imperfect state, and that much of the work of risk management is therefore a continual process of uncovering and dealing with the errors, imperfections and surprises inherent to the sociotechnical systems that we create. Safety is an ongoing process: "a dynamic non-event" (Weick, 1987, p. 118) that requires ongoing effort, invention and adaptation to produce a seemingly stable non-outcome – where bad things constantly don't happen. Entropy and ignorance are continual sources of organisational risk, and safety must be actively managed and "continuously reaccomplished" (Wildavsky, 1988, p. 209) in the face of changing and unknown risks and the gradual degradation of systems. Or, to put it more bluntly, "Risk management, like life, is 'one damn thing after another'" (Reason, 1997, p. 36). This assumption underpins and informs a broad theme that runs through much of this field: that the most fundamental challenges of risk management arise from the complex and problematic relationship between knowledge and practice in complex sociotechnical systems. How do organisations remain cognisant of the risks they are responsible for both manufacturing and managing? How do we generate effective knowledge of risks? And how can practice be informed and improved by that knowledge?

Both this deep assumption and this broader theme run throughout many of the dominant theories of organisational accidents and sociotechnical failure. They also animate and frame many explorations of the social and organisational sources of safety. These issues can be seen in the original work on accidents and disasters that has shaped this field, and they resonate in current debates on the nature of safety, resilience and improvement. They also define and delineate the core concerns of this book.

Organisational risk

Much of our knowledge of risk and safety is derived from the analysis of past accidents and failures. A variety of theories have been developed to explain the causes of accidents and the organisational sources of risk. Each provides a different image of organisational failure and focuses on different aspects of organisational life: activity and error, knowledge and ignorance, and values and deviance. Or, perhaps more pithily, the unintended, the unexpected and the unaccepted. Taken individually, each of these provides a partial theory of organising and its inherent risks. Taken together, they offer a rich conceptualisation of how risks and accidents are generated in complex sociotechnical systems – and specify the malign forces arraigned against those tasked with managing risk and improving safety.

Perhaps the most popular and widespread theory of organisational accidents – amongst practitioners working in the field, at least – focuses on the activity of humans in their organisational context and how both those activities and that context can go awry. Led by Reason's (1990,

1995, 1997) influential work, in this view organisational risks have two primary sources. The first is human error, or 'active failures': human actions gone wrong. The notion of error "is intimately bound up with the notion of intention" (Reason, 1990, p. 17). Errors are deviations or departures from intended actions and are viewed as an inevitable feature of human action. They must be managed by efforts to address error-provoking local conditions, such as poorly designed equipment. And they must be protected against by creating organisational mechanisms that can catch and contain errors when they do occur. These mechanisms are the second defining feature of Reason's model: the safety defence or barrier that represents any aspect of an organisation that is intended to deal with errors or other threats to operational safety.

Organisations can be conceived as being designed with numerous layers of diverse defences – 'defences in depth' – that protect against individual errors and failures. The defences take the form of, for instance, procedures, supervision, training or simply physical protections. Of course, it is fallible humans who design, maintain, operate and manage these defences, and therefore defences are always partial and incomplete. Holes in safety defences, or 'latent conditions', are "an inevitable part of organisational life" (Reason, 1997, p. 11), and can lie dormant and undiscovered in an organisation until they interact with some set of unsafe acts, at which point the defence is breached. Slices of Swiss cheese, full of holes, provide the common image for this model – and if enough holes line up, a sequence of errors can breach all the defences and cause a catastrophic accident. But defences are a double-edged sword. Introducing new defences – such as a new protocol or a checklist – adds complexity and opacity to a system. It becomes harder to understand the interactions that can occur between errors and defences, introduces new opportunities for error and makes it harder to identify where errors are occurring, as they may be being compensated for by multiple defences. Organisational risks are therefore produced through an "insidious build-up of latent conditions" (Reason, 1997, p. 8), and these hidden defensive weaknesses threaten to combine with active failures to bring about catastrophic accidents.

Swiss cheese is a common item on the menu when safety professionals meet, and the principles and tools developed by Reason and his colleagues have proved popular and productive in practice (e.g. Maurino et al., 1997; Australian Transport Safety Bureau, 2004; Vincent et al., 2000). The problematic relationship between risk, practice and knowledge is at the heart of this theory of organisational accidents, though how or why latent conditions become – or remain – latent is relatively unexplored. We must look to other theories for those explanations. Themes of organisational complexity and hidden interactions are also central to Perrow's (1984, 1999) thesis of normal accidents. While Reason argues that active failures and latent conditions are inevitable in organisations, Perrow argues that accidents themselves are inevitable, or normal, in certain types of organisation, namely those in which operational activities are both highly complex – and therefore hard to comprehend – and tightly coupled, where failures in one area can quickly propagate to others. Perrow's analytical focus is on the structure of sociotechnical systems rather than the social processes that produce them, but the underlying implications are clear. Accidents can be incomprehensible, unpredictable and appear 'impossible', particularly to the managers and operators working on the organisational front-line (Sagan, 1995; Wagenaar and Groeneweg, 1987). And the designers and regulators of complex systems face deep and persistent epistemic challenges in their efforts to monitor, understand and assure safety (Downer, 2009). In some form or other, accidents are therefore impossible to eradicate.

A broader body of work attempts to explain the social, cultural and organisational processes through which signs of threats and risks are misunderstood or entirely missed by people and through which pockets of organisational ignorance can emerge and persist. The work of Barry Turner (1976a, 1978) was both seminal (Weick, 1998a) and eloquent. It has been developed and drawn on by a range of organisational scholars (e.g. Weick and Sutcliffe, 2001; Hopkins, 1999, 2000, 2005; Vaughan, 1996, 2005; Pidgeon, 1991, 1997; Turner and Pidgeon, 1997; Smithson, 1990). Turner adopted an explicitly cultural approach, and viewed organisations as systems of shared beliefs and collective assumptions that influence what information is attended to and how it is interpreted and communicated – and importantly, what is overlooked and ignored. Organisational cultures are not monolithic, and organisations are populated by numerous sub- or "micro-cultures" (Turner, 1971, p. 2) based on locally distinct patterns of knowledge (Turner and Pidgeon, 1997). Communication between these different organisational groups or "silos" (Hopkins, 2005, p. 41) can be problematic, resulting in different interpretations of the same situation emerging: the "variable disjunction of information" (Turner and Pidgeon, 1997, p. 40).

Organisational risks can both arise from and be perpetuated by unevenly distributed knowledge, partial communication and assumptions that blinker and limit perception. Turner describes how, over time, events and circumstances that are discrepant with peoples' currently held knowledge and beliefs can accumulate in organisations. This insidious process of incubation sees the gradual build-up of organisational conditions and practices that are at odds with current knowledge: a sprawling "incubation network" (Turner and Pidgeon, 1997, p. 74) of discrepant and misunderstood or hidden problems that are at odds with the current collectively held picture of the world. Simply put, this represents "the management system losing touch with its operational realities" (Turner, 1994, p. 216). If uninterrupted, this incubation network gradually develops into disaster, when an initiating or "precipitating incident produces a transformation, revealing the latent structure of the events of the incubation period" (Turner and Pidgeon, 1997, p. 75). Disasters arrive with considerable surprise along with a "cultural collapse" (Turner and Pidgeon, 1997, p. 72), as the limits of the previously held norms, assumptions and beliefs are laid bare. As such, accidents are defined culturally – as a catastrophic breakdown in the collectively held knowledge of risk.

How does such a situation develop? Through "false assumptions, poor communications, cultural lag, and misplaced optimism" (Turner, 1976a, p. 395) that produce a "collective ignorance" (Turner and Pidgeon, 1997, p. 116) or "collective neglect" (Turner, 1976a, p. 385) of risks. These processes have been reframed as cultural mechanisms of risk-blindness and risk-denial, that prevent risks being noticed or fully appreciated (Hopkins, 2005, p. 61). They underpin the emergence of a mismatch between how organisational practices are understood and the way they actually are. 'Practical drift' can see local work activities evolve away from established ways of working, leaving gaps in the way people do and understand things in different areas of an organisation (Snook, 2000; Snook and Connor, 2005). Organisational practices can 'migrate' away from the originally specified and designed ways of doing things, and move towards – and sometimes beyond – the limits of safe performance (Rasmussen, 1997; Amalberti et al., 2006). Dianne Vaughan (1996) explains the social processes through which accepted norms and boundaries of safety can gradually shift over time: events that were once considered deviant gradually and incrementally come to be seen as normal. This normalisation of deviance progresses simply and subtly, by groups "redefining evidence that deviated from an acceptable standard so that it became the standard" itself (Vaughan, 1996, p. 65) – typically because people don't appreciate or understand the full implications of that evidence.

At the heart of these cultural theories is the idea of ignorance and the deep problems associated with generating effective knowledge about organisational technologies, practices and associated risks (e.g. Smithson, 1989, 1990; Weick, Sutcliffe and Obstfeld, 1999;

Weick, 1998b; Pidgeon, 1998; Downer, 2011). Ignorance is primarily a social creation (Smithson, 1990, p. 208), and efforts to understanding the sources of organisational risk are in many ways efforts to understand the organisational sources of ignorance. The catch, of course, is that ignorance is inherent to social organisation. Organisations are based on presumptions of selective ignorance and limited attention (Turner, 1971; Weick, 1998a): with the division of labour comes specialisation, expertise and the variable distribution of knowledge – and ignorance. The challenge in risk management practice is to differentiate between those things that can be safely ignored and those that must be attended to, and to develop practices that can identify, uncover and smoke out ignorance.

Sources of safety

Safety is a troublesome notion. Traditionally it has been associated with the avoidance of harm. A solid granite sign stands outside the headquarters of the UK's Civil Aviation Authority Safety Regulation Group at Gatwick airport. It reads, 'Safety is no accident'. This is true, in both senses. But it is only part of the picture. The absence of harm, or the avoidance of accidents, is a necessary but not sufficient signifier of safety (Braithwaite, 2001). Few would claim that the occupants of that jumbo jet were safe purely because it didn't hit a hotel and they came to no harm. Adverse or harmful outcomes point to the absence of safety, but the avoidance of harm does not equate directly with a state of safety. There is a deep asymmetry of meaning here that underlies many of the analytical and interpretive challenges in this area: "while high accident rates may reasonably be taken as indicative of a bad safety state, low asymptotic rates do not necessarily signal a good one" (Reason, 2000, p. 6). Our knowledge of what contributes to safety, what a safe organisation looks like and what characterises effective risk management is therefore coloured with ambiguity. This is because it is hard to determine how effective organisational risk management is when its ultimate achievements are things that do not happen. Nonetheless, we must try – and many have.

A wide range of theory has been developed to explain the organisational sources and characteristics of safety. All of these are open to the legitimate challenge that you cannot prove a negative: that it is not possible to establish that these characteristics and processes will prevent accidents. But the ambitions of many of these theorists are often more nuanced. Much of the theory seeks to describe practices observed in organisations that operate under very trying conditions, facing high-tempo, complex, uncertain and risky situations and organising themselves accordingly. Other frameworks have been developed that aim to define the strategies and deep principles that appear to underlie effective safety management – based both on organisational practices that appear effective at responding to and addressing risks, and by holding up a mirror to our theories of organisational accidents. Two broad schools of thought frame thinking in this area, and each represents an idealised approach to dealing with the challenges of managing knowledge, practice and risk in organisations. These strategies are resilience and anticipation.

Originally delineated as risk management strategies by Wildavsky (1988), and recently experiencing a surge of interest, these strategies and their implications are being energetically explored in theory and practice (Hood and Jones, 1996; Royal Society, 1992; Weick, Sutcliffe and Obstfeld, 1999; Collingridge, 1996; Comfort, Boin and Demchak, 2010; Hollnagel et al., 2006, 2008, 2011). The strategy of anticipation aims at the prediction and, literally, anticipation of risks, and is based on preventative action taken to stop adverse events from occurring. This is summed up, for instance, in Hollnagel's (2004, p. 185) assertion that "in order to prevent incidents and accidents it is necessary to predict them". Resilience, in contrast, aims for a flexible and adaptive capacity to respond to, cope with and learn from adverse events and to develop an ability to deal with an unknown future. Resilience does not require prediction because, as Hopkins (2001, p. 67) argues, "it is not necessary to predict the precise trajectory of an accident in order to be able to prevent it". So, while normative risk analysis methods and guidelines are based on anticipatory, predictive methods, organisational and cultural theories of safety have latterly focused on ways of achieving resilience.

A huge number of standards, guidelines, frameworks and methods have been produced to prescribe how formal risk and safety management systems should be designed and operated. These are typically described in a profusion of flow charts. At base, risk and safety management systems provide formalised organisational structures and processes for thinking about, predicting, communicating and addressing risks. They have been conceptualised in numerous ways (e.g. Cox and Tait, 1991; Koorneef and Hale, 1997; Hale, Wilpert and Freitag, 1998). Normative frameworks prescribe a series of analytic steps through which risks are predicted and actions chosen. Risk management is treated as decision-making: "acceptable-risk problems are decision problems; that is, they require a choice among alternative courses of action" (Fischhoff et al., 1981, p. 2).

Terminology and detail, again, differ widely across different models (e.g. Royal Society, 1992; Interdepartmental Liaison Group on Risk

Assessment, 1996; Cabinet Office, 2002; British Standards Institute, 1996; Standards Australia, 1999; Health and Safety Executive, 2001; Institute of Risk Management, 2002; National Infrastructure Protection Centre, 2002), but there are three essential steps in all these frameworks. First, the threats faced by an organisation and their possible consequences are identified and catalogued. Second, risk levels are calculated for each threat by assessing the likelihood and the severity of the harmful consequences or outcomes that might result. Third, these risk levels are compared to a predetermined criteria or level of acceptability, and unacceptable risks are selected for action or 'treatment'. The process is then to be repeated as an ongoing cycle.

The key challenges here arise from the assumptions embedded in these normative and anticipatory models in relation to organisational knowledge and practice. Risk management is treated primarily as a 'decision problem'. As such, acquiring knowledge of risks is considered largely unproblematic, as is translating this knowledge into practical organisational improvements; the challenge is measuring risks and deciding which to address. In contrast, in the organisational and cultural theories of safety discussed shortly, knowledge of risk is considered deeply problematic: the emphasis is firmly on how organisations can find out about risks, address gaps in their knowledge and use that knowledge to improve practice. This distinction is perhaps best summed up as between normative models that aim to 'predict and decide' and more cultural and organisational theories that focus on how to 'diagnose and learn' about safety and risk.

Current organisational theories typically focus on the cultural practices that support safety. A growing body of work examines the social processes and cultural characteristics of organisations that tend to achieve high levels of reliability in complex and hazardous operations, such as nuclear aircraft carriers and nuclear power plants (e.g. Roberts, Rousseau and La Porte, 1994; Rochlin, 1989, 1996; La Porte, 1994; Rijpma, 1997, 2003; Roberts, 1990, 1993). One of the defining characteristics of these organisations is how they monitor for disruptions and surprises and then rapidly organise resources to analyse and address them. In this way, high-reliability organisations (HRO) achieve reliable operational outcomes through continual adaptation to and correction of deviations and disruptions as they occur (Weick, 1987). Underpinning this are diverse social practices for communicating about what is going on, checking and cross-checking performance, and monitoring for problems or deviations from normal operations (Rochlin, 1989). When anomalies are identified, informal networks of experts form around them – "experiential epistemic networks" (Rochlin, 1989, p. 169) that temporarily transcend formal authority structures and put those with the most experience in charge of resolving a problem, rather than those with the highest rank. High-reliability depends both on dealing with errors and problems when they are still small, and on developing alternative means to trial-and-error learning. HROs are "coloured by efforts to engage in trials without errors, lest the next error be the last trial" (La Porte and Consolini, 1991, p. 20). These efforts include story telling, fostering diverse perspectives, mental simulation, imagination and learning vicariously from other organisations (Weick, 1987, 1989; Schulman, 1993; Pidgeon and O'Leary, 1994; Pidgeon, 1998). HROs aim to avoid the illusion that no bad events occuring means that there is nothing more to know, and instead aim to foster a "chronic suspicion that small deviations may enlarge" (Weick, 1987, p. 18). These observations share much with the core tenets of resilience, which Wildavsky (1988, p. 93) argues is a process of "interrogating the unknown" through a process of trial and error and which offers "a discovery process that discloses latent errors so we can learn how to deal with them . . . Trial and error samples the world of as yet unknown risks" (Wildavsky, 1988, p. 37). Analysis of errors and surprising events should be collective, "variegated – decentralised, participatory" (Wildavsky, 1988, p. 93), to provide different perspectives on the meaning of errors and to facilitate learning. These decentralised processes of trial and error are, when viewed in practice, considered to be based on the improvisational, inventive – and at times messy and chaotic – activities of groups and networks that respond in the face of failures (Boin and van Eeten, 2013).

To counter gaps in knowledge caused by specialisation, personnel in HROs are expected to be both specialists and generalists. Specialist knowledge is required, due to the complex technologies involved. But this tends to be tempered by generalist knowledge, as so much interdependent action is necessary in complex organisations (Roberts, 1990). The social interrelating that takes place within and between groups of professionals in HROs has been characterised as heedful and attentive: activities through which individuals work to understand, represent and adapt to the activity of others, contributing to the formation of a "collective mind" (Weick and Roberts, 1993, p. 364). Ultimately, many of the social processes in HROs appear designed to reduce opportunities for ignorance and avoid "thoughtless action or mindlessness" (Schulman, 1993, p. 367). These insights have been integrated into a set of principles of "collective mindfulness" (Weick, Sutcliffe and Obstfeld, 1999; Weick and Sutcliffe, 2001) that aim to conceptualise how organisations can work to notice problems early and then "enlarge what is known about what was noticed" (Weick, Sutcliffe and Obstfeld, 1999, p. 91). The core objective of mindful organising is to find and deal with unexpected problems by focusing on small moments of surprise. That is, to use surprising and unexpected events to identify where currently held expectations are wrong or flawed (Weick and Sutcliffe, 2001).

Five idealised social-cognitive processes are proposed to support safety and define the principles of collective mindfulness that maintain organisational knowledge and continually improve practice. First is a preoccupation with organisational failures, errors and near-misses. Small failures are generalised to the organisation as a whole, and so people "treat any lapse as a symptom that something is wrong with the system" (Weick and Sutcliffe, 2001, p. 10). Second is a reluctance to simplify interpretations regarding how the organisation operates. People aim to create "more complete and nuanced pictures" of the organisation (Weick and Sutcliffe, 2001, p. 11). Schulman (1993, p. 364) calls this "conceptual slack . . . a divergence in analytical perspectives among members of an organisation". The third principle is sensitivity to operations. People in all areas and levels of the organisation are "attentive to the front line, where the real work gets done" (Weick and Sutcliffe, 2001, p. 13). They are less interested in broad abstractions and more interested in "details and particulars" (Weick, 2001a, p. S74). Fourth is a commitment to resilience. HROs depend on organisational processes that can respond to and bounce back from error, as well as prevent it in the first place: "the signature of an HRO is not that it is error-free, but that errors don't disable it" (Weick and Sutcliffe, 2001, p. 14). And fifth is an under-specification of organisational structure and deference to expertise. Specialist knowledge and experience takes precedence over hierarchy in problem solving: "authority migrates to the people with the most expertise, regardless of rank" (Weick and Sutcliffe, 2001, p. 16).

The idea of continually reorganising knowledge and practice around unexpected events has a long history. The basis of this approach was present, in all but name, in Turner's (1976a, 1978) original work on disasters as cultural collapse. He detailed how, following disaster, organisations go through a period of "cultural readjustment" (Turner and Pidgeon, 1997, p. 83) – literally "the restructuring of understanding" (Turner and Pidgeon, 1997, p. 130) – during which time beliefs about risks and ways of acting are revised in light of experience. Turner's theory was about major disasters, but he proposed that similar mechanisms of cultural readjustment might be possible as a means to avoid catastrophe, by learning from minor disruptions. This could be achieved, he argued, not by considering incidents in terms of the severity of their consequences "but according to their unexpectedness in the view of prevailing institutionally accepted models of the world" (Turner, 1976b, p. IX 26). That is, learning and cultural change could be provoked by cultural disruption alone – materially adverse outcomes were sufficient, but not necessary.

Similar ideas are found in more contemporary perspectives on safety culture. In Reason's (1997, 1998) conception, "a safe culture is an informed culture, one that knows continually where the 'edge' is without necessarily having to fall over it" (Reason, 2000, p. 3) – the edge in question being between relative safety and unacceptable risk. The emphasis in this definition is on the knowing. Informed cultures are ones in which personnel "have current knowledge" (Reason, 1997, p. 195) about the determinants of organisational safety "and then translate this knowledge into enhanced resistance" (Reason, 1997, p. 116) to threats. In this view, the key is not to try and prevent latent conditions arising – an impossible task – but to identify them and "make them visible" (Reason, 1997, p. 36) so they can be addressed. Developing an informed culture depends on diagnosing organisational weaknesses in order to direct attention and improvement efforts into those areas. Ideally, identifying new risks requires creatively using information and imaginatively thinking through different scenarios that may arise from minor incidents (Pidgeon and O'Leary, 1994; O'Leary and Chappell, 1996) and maintaining "an openness that views every facet of an incident as a potential warning to some as yet unappreciated hazard" (Pidgeon, 1988, p. 362).

These observations and principles paint a rich and compelling picture of the cultural and organisational sources of safety, and attempt to grapple with the deep challenges of producing knowledge about risk and using that knowledge to improve practice. But these theories are not without their problems. These problems largely emerge when considering how these principles can be operationalised in specific practical contexts. Foremost amongst these are defining exactly what a highly reliable or collectively mindful organisation is and establishing that these processes do, in fact, underpin safe performance. Some of the proposed processes of safety even seem close to the processes implicated in analyses of major accidents – what is termed here the 'reluctance to simplify', or 'conceptual slack', sounds like the disjunction of information (Turner, 1978) and the conditions underlying the collapse of sensemaking (Weick, 1993a; Carroll, 1998).

Further, a degree of confusion persists around the concept of error and its relationship to knowledge production and organisational safety.

Learning from errors is commonly conceived as a primary source of safety and resilience (e.g. Weick and Sutcliffe, 2001), as Wildavsky (1988) holds. For instance, Rochlin (1989, p. 164) notes that "many of the organizational strategies we observed were designed in response to previous serious accidents". But at the same time, it is commonly argued that, in HROs, risks "must be mastered by means other than trial-and-error learning, since in many cases the first error will also be the last trial" (Weick and Sutcliffe, 2001, p. 21). Similarly, researchers in this area often describe and prescribe that people always fear and imagine the worst from every small error. But in practice, this is intractable, and is a central criticism of anticipatory approaches to risk management. As, while "the human imagination can concoct infinite modes of destruction" (Wildavsky, 1988, p. 92), resources are not available to address them all, and may be expended on imagined risks that never materialise. Wildavsky (1988, p. 6) calls these the risks that result from "unconsequent anticipations"; Turner calls it the "decoy problem" (Turner and Pidgeon, 1997, p. 48).

The problematic relationship between organisational knowledge and organisational practice defines many of the most fundamental issues in managing risk and improving safety – both in the many theories that have been developed to explain risk and safety and in daily organisational practice. While theorists work to explain how organisations can become aware of and remain cognisant of risks, how current and effective knowledge of risks can be generated and how that knowledge can then inform and shape organisational practices, those working at the sharp end of risk management must confront and resolve those challenges every day.

A bird's eye view

At the heart of this book is a theoretical account of the cultural practices, collective assumptions, shared concepts and practical theories that structure and underpin the risk management practices of airline flight safety investigators. The next chapter, Chapter 2, sets the scene. A series of short but detailed vignettes are presented to capture the richness and complexities of investigators' practical work in airline flight safety oversight. The broader processes and challenges of managing risks in airlines are then described, along with a detailed account of the organisational systems and types of work that underpin analysing and learning from incidents. The focus here is heavily on the particularities of airlines and flight safety, but the types of work that investigators engage in are equally representative of safety oversight activities in many other industries. The next five chapters then develop a theoretical account of investigators' work, presenting an empirically rich description of the cultural practices of this professional community. Each chapter examines a different aspect of risk management practice and presents an explanation and exemplification of one element of flight safety investigators' work. Each of these chapters, and each of these explanations, relates to and builds on the others. Readers can dip into each of these chapters depending on their interest, but those who take in the whole book will find a more cohesive, multifaceted and integrated view of the work of risk management than is offered by the single analytical focus of each individual chapter.

Chapter 3 characterises the key features of investigators' understandings of safety and risk: their interpretive framework or collectively held 'theory in practice' of organisational safety. In this chapter I explore and explain the practical theories and ideas used by flight safety investigators to understand safety and assess risk, along with the deep assumptions and concepts that underpin these. Examining these practical theories reveals how organisational safety is defined by investigators working in inherently hazardous, complex and unpredictable domains. Chapter 4 continues this analysis, and explores the organisational attributes and characteristics that are used by investigators to assess and analyse risk. This chapter focuses on the organisational components of safety that are routinely attended to and assessed by investigators, and reveals the conceptual structures that support the practical work of risk analysis. An idea that is central to investigators' practical theories of safety is resilience, and the analytical work of investigators reveals a complex and nuanced understanding of organisational safety that reframes traditional notions of both risk and resilience.

Chapters 5 and 6 characterise the approach that investigators take to monitoring and overseeing safety, and the interpretive tactics that they employ to identify risks. These two chapters examine how investigators' deep assumptions about their own fallibility and ignorance shape their practices of risk identification. In Chapter 5, I explain the aspirations and ideals of safety oversight that drive investigators' work and the risks that they face in this work. Investigators aim to remain continually vigilant to weak signs of emerging risks, to adopt a bird's eye view of safety and to produce an integrated picture of risk. And, they expect to fail. In Chapter 6 I examine the subtle and creative interpretive processes through which signs of potential risks are pieced together and through which investigators work to identify new and previously unrecognised risks. Investigators attempt to actively construct gaps in knowledge – that is, they work to actively create ignorance – and use incidents to interrogate, test and challenge current understandings of safety in an effort to uncover latent risks.

Chapter 7 characterises how investigators work to address and manage risks and how they judge where those efforts are best focused. I analyse how investigators aim to coordinate and organise safety improvement and shape organisational culture. Given that safety investigators, like all risk managers, typically have limited authority to mandate or enforce action, this chapter analyses the alternative ways that investigators work to influence, shape and improve safety. These include framing questions, circulating warnings and holding people to account for safety improvements. Given that risks often span several departments – or even several organisations – this chapter also considers how investigators work to bring together widely distributed networks of specialists to reflect on and participate in the analysis and management of risks.

To conclude, Chapter 8 draws together the different strands of investigators' work and considers the key implications for our current theories of safety and risk. This discussion considers how investigators use operational incidents to first identify gaps in their own and their organisation's collective knowledge of risk, then construct and circulate warnings that disrupt currently accepted beliefs about safety, and ultimately use those moments of symbolic disruption as a focal point for organising improvement and coordinating reflection and change. Investigators are involved in the manufacture, as much as the analysis, of close calls and near-misses. They use minor operational incidents to demonstrate how the organisation came close to something it should desperately seek to avoid, and they use those disruptions to organise and enact resilience. This book argues that, when viewed from the sharp-end, organisational practices of risk management can be explained through the enactment of three core processes: resilience, vigilance and participation. Each of these three processes needs to be properly considered in the design and operation of any risk management system – and particularly those dealing with complex, consequential and potentially catastrophic risks such as airlines.

2
Airlines, Incidents and Investigators

Airlines, and the activities that they perform, are integral parts of our modern lives. They are one of the many sprawling sociotechnical systems that modern societies both depend upon and take largely for granted. They also reflect the dramatic shifts that have occurred in the past few decades towards ever greater levels of complexity, specialisation, technology and innovation in organisations. These trends are felt in industries as diverse as banking and healthcare, and are accompanied by increasing imperatives to understand, manage and control the risks and the reliability of complex organisational systems. Airlines offer a striking example of managing complex risks and assuring high reliability. It has become entirely unremarkable to be served dinner, catch up with some work, have a nap or settle down to watch a movie while travelling at nine hundred kilometres an hour, ten kilometres above the surface of the Earth, cocooned in a life-sustaining cabin wrapped in panels of material barely a few millimetres thin, entirely oblivious to the extremes of speed, pressure, temperature and lack of oxygen that exist in the lower reaches of the stratosphere, where airliners spend much of their time.

The achievements of modern aviation are common place and routine. It seems simple and entirely normal to book a flight, check your bags, accelerate to close to the speed of sound and travel thousands of miles around the globe in a single sitting. Yet the mechanics and the social organisation required to achieve this – and to achieve it safely, reliably and routinely on a massive scale – are anything but simple. A large airliner like a Boeing 747 or Airbus A380 is made up of some six million components, is threaded with 170 miles of wiring and routinely carries around 100 tonnes of highly flammable fuel. Large international airlines can easily employ two to three thousand pilots and seven or eight thousand engineers. A single flight concentrates the collective efforts of thousands of people: from the handful of pilots and cabin crew on board, to the staff working on the ramp loading cargo and fuel; to the teams of engineers maintaining the electronics, the engines and the airframe; to the dispatchers, technical managers, air traffic controllers, designers, manufacturers, regulators and a whole host of other highly specialised personnel. At this very moment, there are likely to be around 6,000 commercial aircraft in the air around the globe, carrying at least half a million souls at startling speeds across the sky. And yet despite these challenges of enormous scale, complexity and specialisation, delicate and technologically advanced equipment, and an extraordinarily unforgiving operational environment, the international aviation system has achieved astonishing levels of safety. In 2012 there were nearly 40 million commercial airline flights around the world but only 21 fatal accidents, the equivalent of one fatal accident per 2.3 million flights (Learmount, 2013). This was the safest year ever recorded for commercial airlines – at least since the year before, when 2011 held that crown.

Airlines have not always been so safe. The history of aviation is littered with the wreckage of past accidents. These accidents have acted as one of the primary sources of new knowledge and safety improvement within the industry. Issues of safety, and of analysing and managing the risk of accidents, have been with the industry since its inception. In Britain, the first fatality of powered flight occurred in 1910 and involved a Wright Flyer, the same aircraft type in which Orville Wright had made the world's first powered, controlled and heavier-than-air flight only a few years before. The victim of the accident was one Charles Rolls, of the recently founded car and aero-engine manufacturer, Rolls-Royce. Just two years later, in 1912, came the first independent air accident investigation and subsequent report. The report foreshadowed a century of increasingly sophisticated and extensive safety investigations. In this case, errors made by the pilot were considered a primary cause, and the report admirably recommended design changes – to aircraft seat restraints, as it happens – to reduce the likelihood of similar events.

As the aviation industry has grown and evolved, so too has its infrastructure for learning from accidents and incidents. The foundation of this infrastructure is defined and formalised in international conventions. As the Second World War drew to a close, international arrangements were drawn up to govern international civil air travel, culminating in the establishment of the International Civil Aviation Organisation (ICAO), an agency of the United Nations. In 1951, ICAO published the first international standards and recommended practices on aircraft accident and incident investigation – quite appropriately as Annex 13 to the international convention on civil aviation. Annex 13 continues to be regularly updated, and specifies the responsibilities of states to investigate and improve aviation safety following air accidents and incidents.

As accident rates have fallen, the airline industry has expanded its search for safety improvement. The industry continues to investigate and learn from failures, but has turned increasingly to mining a deeper and less pure seam: close calls, near-misses, operational incidents and events that can often look like the ordinary fluctuations and variations in performance you might expect in complex and highly specialised organisations. Over the past several decades, the infrastructures and systems that support investigating and learning from failure have become particularly sophisticated. All major airlines maintain safety teams with experienced investigators who monitor flight safety and lead investigations into safety incidents. Safety incident reporting systems provide one of the core components of airline safety management systems, and investigating safety incidents is an ongoing and routine activity in most airlines. Tens or even hundreds of investigations can be active at any one time in a major airline, some of which are short, but many of which are lengthy and multidisciplinary, spanning several departments and many months. Aviation regulators oversee these activities and operate their own incident reporting programmes (e.g. CAA, 1996; NASA, 2013).

To understand how flight safety investigators monitor safety, interpret incidents, analyse risk and oversee improvement, it is first necessary to get a sense of the practical work this involves and the organisational setting this is conducted in. This chapter sets this organisational scene by describing the common structures, processes and practices that make up typical flight safety incident reporting programmes. There will always be differences in the specific structure of the committees and groups responsible for overseeing safety in organisations and the tools and information systems that are in use. But there is considerable commonality within the aviation industry – and indeed across other industries too – regarding the tasks, activities and work involved in analysing incidents, overseeing safety and managing risks. The descriptions presented here offer a composite image of the typical arrangements that are found in large international airlines. The broader purpose of these descriptions is to set the scene for understanding the interpretive work and cultural practices of the technical community of safety investigators who are responsible for analysing incidents within the airline industry.

This chapter aims to provide a picture of the typical organisational arrangements and practical work of analysing safety incidents to manage risk and improve safety in airlines. To retain a sense of the richness, complexity and practical challenges that flight safety investigators face, three vignettes of work in the field are presented first. These vignettes exemplify the common challenges and complications of understanding and investigating safety incidents, and making sense of the fleeting operational fluctuations and disruptions that incidents often represent. Next, to put these fieldwork vignettes into context, the organisation of airline flight safety oversight is examined. This focuses on the design and operation of airline flight safety incident reporting programmes and also considers the use of a common tool of risk analysis widely used in the airline industry and elsewhere. The final section of this chapter depicts the practical tasks that investigators routinely perform in their management of flight safety incident reports and safety investigations.

Vignettes of incidents in the field (and the air)

The work of airline flight safety investigators is varied and involves a range of activities and responsibilities. In the very worst and rarest of cases, it could involve travelling to the site of a major accident and working with state accident investigators, picking through the wreckage of one of their airline's aircraft. But such work would be exceedingly rare and extraordinary. The normal work of investigators focuses on managing safety through more routine activities and less dramatic events. A sense of the complexity and variety of this work can be gained through examining three short vignettes that describe investigators' practice and its organisational context. These vignettes present three significant and extended moments of safety investigation and management. The first presents the analytical work and shifts in understanding that result from a pilot pressing the wrong button. The second describes the investigative work done around a rejected take-off. And the third depicts the assessment and oversight of problems encountered while parking.

These vignettes retain a degree of the technical detail and analytical complications that are present in investigators' daily work, though they are considerably simplified accounts of the discussions and work that take place. The focus of this book is, after all, on the processes and practices of safety management, not on the intricacies of operating an airline. The vignettes also give a sense of the range of activities that investigators engage in, and the range of personnel they engage with, in their work managing safety. These activities span from reviewing technical incident data, to coordinating investigations with operational departments, to liaising with other organisations and agencies, to working with the various boards and committees that oversee safety across the airline. The vignettes each show the particular complexities and challenges of investigators' work, and a typical day might be made up of some combination of these activities, supplemented by a healthy serving of more routine and administrative activities. The latter are described later. Here, these three vignettes show some of the challenges of interpreting incidents, investigating risks and managing safety. They show the close calls that investigators must routinely make in their daily work, and how considerable attention and sensemaking efforts become organised around otherwise brief and transient fluctuations in operational activities.

Pressing the wrong button

It's 0800 hours and the operations centre is abuzz. Several hundred people work here, coordinating and supporting the front-line operations of the airline, and thousands pass through its doors each day. The building rarely sleeps. Cabin crew bustle through the atrium wheeling their luggage, pilots crowd the computer terminals checking the details of their upcoming routes, and staff congregate in the cafes and restaurants catching up as they pass through en route or before heading home. On the ground floor, taking up the central offices of the building, is the Safety department. Safety is subdivided into different divisions, and the desks of the flight safety investigators line the triple glazed floor-to-ceiling windows, looking directly out over the runway. Aircraft thunder silently past, their wings sucking plumes of moisture out of the damp November air as they lumber into the sky.

I'm sitting with Ben, the on-call investigator, going through the 'morning sweep' of safety incidents. As the on-call investigator this week, Ben carries the emergency phone 24 hours a day and is responsible for responding to any urgent safety incidents that are called in, at any time of day or night. It's rare that the phone rings. Most incidents are dealt with by crew filing an incident report in the airline's safety management system. The on-call investigator starts each day by reviewing every incident freshly logged in the system. There's usually a couple of hundred new incidents reported each week from flight crew, a similar number from engineers, and about half that amount in total from cabin crew and ground staff. Anything notable, unusual or unclear is marked down in a log of significant events and initially followed up with phone calls or a quick trip over to the department concerned. Ben talks me through each incident in turn, and passes quickly over one report that reads:

On handover, with the aircraft fully established on approach in landing configuration the copilot inadvertently pressed the autopilot switch.

Disconnected manually and the flight director recycled, approach continued manually to normal landing. Minimal deviation from glideslope.

Switch pressed accidentally, he explains—here we go: on this particular fleet of aircraft these switches are close together and in the opposite orientation to the design used on most other aircraft types. This seems to go in spates, he explains, they probably have new pilots just joined the fleet who aren't used to it yet. When this particular switch is pressed in this phase of flight it engages automated systems to provide full engine power, which might be needed if, for instance, the pilot decides to abort the landing and go-around. What seems to happen is that crew move on to this fleet from other aircraft types and are used to an auto-pilot disconnect switch being in that location instead. So when they go to disconnect the autopilot for final approach at around 1,000 feet, they sometimes inadvertently hit this activation switch instead and the engines briefly start spooling up to full power before the crew catch it. If the increase in power disrupts the approach then the crew follow the standard procedure and go-around: they abort the approach, circle and start again. This type of brief 'switch mis-selection' incident is a known event and one that flight safety investigators encounter relatively often. In this case, the error was caught quickly and corrected by the crew and it didn't disrupt the final approach.

Over the next couple of months two more switch mis-selection incidents of this type are reported. The first follows the common course of events: a brief mis-select and a quick correction by the crew maintains a stable approach. The second incident occurs much later in the approach, at 300 feet, and despite the unexpected and late addition of power the crew continue, resulting in a hard landing—the aircraft carries too much energy and lands with a thump. Any hard landing is detected by the airline's automated Flight Data Monitoring system, which continually scans hundreds of parameters from each flight and identifies any that exceed pre-determined limits of acceptable performance. The late error, the decision to continue and the hard landing all attract attention in both Safety and the Flight Operations department, or "Flight Ops". Investigations are begun by Flight Ops to debrief the crew and review the event in more detail just as the airline's quarterly Flight Safety Oversight Committee (FSOC) convenes. This committee brings together senior representatives from all the aircraft fleets and operational areas of the airline to oversee and review the safety management activities of Flight Ops, and to report to the main Safety Oversight

Committee of the airline's full board. A considerable amount of FSOC time is spent reviewing recent significant flight safety incidents. Flight safety investigators collate and provide these materials, set the agenda, and the Head of Safety and an investigator sit on the committee to provide input and challenge.

Switch mis-selection is high on the list at FSOC and is the cause of some frustration. The issue is long standing and viewed as partly rooted in the unusual design of this fleet of aircraft. The options open to address the issue are seen as limited, and the airline sees one of these incidents every two months or so. Pending further investigation of this latest incident, an interim consensus emerges: while the design of the aircraft is as it is, eradicating the error is not believed to be a realistic option. Instead, they need to keep 'cutting the grass': they need to stress to flight crew to go-around and follow the appropriate procedures if their approach is disrupted, ensure that all Training Captains regularly emphasise the possibility of this type of error, and continue to highlight it regularly in crew newsletters and other communications. In the complex environment of modern aircraft cockpits many different types of switch mis-selects can occur. A brief mis-select of this particular switch, resulting in a standard go-around manoeuvre, is believed to be a relatively safe set of circumstances. This view is revised over the next few days.

It's early on Friday morning and I'm sat with another investigator, Alistair, working through the morning sweep. One incident grabs his attention. It is two lines long: Go-around from 600 feet due to switch mis-selection. During the go-around autopilot re-engaged—speed dropped but stall warning did not activate. Alistair is concerned and considers this a significant event. He thinks in the confusion of pressing the wrong switch it looks like the crew forgot to reset the autothrottle. So this looks like it was an error on top of a switch mis-select, and the speed of the aircraft decayed a little before the crew noticed. As an aircraft loses speed it also loses lift. If the speed drops too low a stall warning system in the cockpit activates to alert crew to urgently address the situation. In this incident, the slight drop in speed was not enough to activate the stall warning system, but Alistair is worried that the speed began to drop at all. Alistair says that the fleet are good at investigating this sort of stuff, and decides to check in quickly with what's happening and then wait for an update. When Monday morning arrives Chris, the Head of Flight Safety, is back in the office after a few days flying. He sets up an impromptu early meeting and there's one key item on the agenda—switch mis-selects. Alistair updates him: this has got a lot of people talking. The investigators pull the relevant section of the manuals for that aircraft and the other types the airline flies and pour over the diagrams of the layout of the cockpit. With the different arrangement on this fleet they're surprised it's not a more common event. Matt, a former pilot turned safety investigator, asks, is this event monitored by the Flight Data Monitoring (FDM) system? I'd have thought most people don't report it and don't think it's worth raising a report, except the conscientious ones. They agree and Matt heads upstairs to the FDM team. He's back in a few minutes—from tomorrow it will be an FDM event and any switch mis-selection of this type will be automatically detected and logged for analysis.

At the next flight safety investigators' regular weekly meeting, the focus of conversation is the switch mis-select incident. They go over the data that's been collected and a draft briefing for FSOC that has already been prepared. Chris, the head of the team—and also an operational pilot—fills them in: 'I don't know how much detail you've all heard on this, but it was a bit of a mess'. In part he's not surprised. Go-around manoeuvres might be common across the whole airline, but an individual pilot in typical operations may only have to do one go-around a year, if that. They train for it: the crew go into the simulators every six months, but in that situation they are expecting to do a go-around. As Chris explains—you're expecting it and it's straightforward. It's just, call 'go-around, flaps 20, gear up.' But the thing is, when you're actually faced with it in real life you're not expecting it. It comes out of the blue. And with the switch mis-select events it's even worse as there's no reason to go-around—and suddenly the aircraft is just flying away! So you've initially lost the plot, unless you're quick, 'FMA disconnect, disconnect,' and you're stable in five seconds. But if you're not quick, at ten seconds in you're still wondering what's going on.

The current picture is complicated. Chris describes that it seems what happened was the co-pilot pressed what he thought was the autopilot disconnect, but the plane started rearing up and accelerating—so he pressed the switch again. A double press of this switch turns on a flight mode that provides maximum power, not modulated power, 'so now they're on full power like a home-sick angel'. The Captain quickly brought the power back, but the autopilot failed to acquire the target altitude and didn't level off but automatically maintained a nose-up pitch, and it was that pitch that contributed to a drop in speed. Ben chips in—right, it uses a complex logic that flies the planned trajectory, but the aircraft's quite passive in that mode, that could be a good scenario for the simulators to include in routine training. Later in the day one of the flight safety investigators working with Flight Ops gives everyone an update having reviewed the crew debrief and spoken with some of the technical specialists in the area. The investigation is continuing, but this, he emphasises, has fundamentally changed how this particularly type of switch mis-selection is viewed.

The investigation moves quickly under the oversight of the investigators, and within a week Flight Ops have a clear picture of what occurred in those brief moments on the flight deck, and the momentary confusions that arose. The crew became focused on addressing the rapid acceleration and vertical pitch. They weren't communicating effectively. While one pilot was pulling the nose up, the other was reducing the power to address the rapid acceleration, and each was so focused on the various issues that arise from suddenly and surprisingly hitting such rapid vertical acceleration they hadn't gone through the go-around procedures of bringing the flaps and gear up—which add drag to the aircraft and impacts its speed.

Over the next few weeks, the implications of this brief operational fluctuation are clarified and the recommendations and actions decided on. Bringing together all the materials and findings for the airline's full Board meeting, the investigators convene. The investigators' core concerns remain focused on the recovery from the initial error and the interactions and communication of the crew. Investigators have extremely high expectations regarding the quality of coordination and communication on the flight deck, and the ability to manage disruptions, and in this case their exacting standards and ideals were not met. Despite the brevity of the event and the marginal impact on the performance of the aircraft, their judgement was harshly framed. Ben sums it up: the crew seemed to lose it on all of it—gear down, flaps down, nose up, they had two different mental models of what they were doing. Alistair adds that's right, there were no plans in there, they were pulling things left and right. Ben continues—right, they were no longer working as a crew. While the investigators' judgement is tough, it is not directed at the specific crew in question. Investigators' concerns are instead focused on the unexpected gap that the incident has revealed, between the assumed and actual impacts of this type of switch mis-selection.

As a result of the investigation, a range of actions and improvements are undertaken. The approach procedure is closely reviewed, and it is still determined to be best practice to ensure that pilots take full control of the aircraft prior to landing. Without being able to make retrospective changes to the design of the flight deck a range of interventions focus on crew training, preparation, briefing and communication. The crew training teams revise how they train on disruptions to speed and altitude of all kinds, both in this phase of flight and more generally. Additional training is developed to improve how crew share mental models of what's going on in unexpected circumstances, and specifically with regard to activating this particular switch. And an issue with crew communication is highlighted for further investigation—it seems that some of the instructions passed between the Co-Pilot and Captain may not have been heard at the crucial moment. The simulator training provided for crew regarding go-arounds is revised and extended, introducing a range of different variations on go-around circumstances and unexpected interruptions. And a group begins examining how crews can include more detail in their approach briefing, conducted at the start of the approach to land, to cover different versions of go-around manoeuvres that might be encountered and to turn a broader range of unexpected errors into prepared events. A brief moment of organisational life and a relatively minor fluctuation in organisational performance has provoked wide ranging and considerable improvements to the design and organisation of airline practices.

A rejected take-off

A Boeing 747 begins its take-off roll heading towards the Indian Ocean and back home. All signs are looking normal as the aircraft approaches its "V1" speed – the decision point beyond which it is safer to continue the take-off than to attempt to stop, even if faced with a problem. Past V1, if there is problem the aircraft must become airborne before circling to jettison fuel and attempting to land. On this occasion, just as the aircraft reaches V1 engine number two fire warning goes off declaring a fire in the engine requiring immediate attention. The pilot in control takes an instant decision and elects to abort the take-off. Power is pulled back and brakes applied. The aircraft continues to accelerate for another 10 knots or so due to inertia and the downward-slopping runway, but finally lumbers to a stop just before the end of the tarmac. The aircraft is taxied back to stand and all passengers disembark safely. Aborting a take-off at such high speed carries additional risks and is a consequential decision. The V1 decision point is specified by the airframe manufacturer and reinforced by company policy. It is basic airmanship to always continue a take-off beyond V1, and these procedures and protocols are strongly enforced in airlines.

The first I hear of the event is arriving in the office of the airline's safety team on a Monday morning. The air safety investigators are in a huddle talking about it. The call came in over the weekend to the on-call investigator. An event like this is considered serious enough to contact investigators on the emergency phone in the middle of the night. One investigator who formerly flew these aircraft asks what speed this occurred at. It was relatively high, at 140 knots. There is shaking of heads and sucking of teeth all around – it is considered close to the limit. They spend the day making phone calls to the engineers out at the aircraft and to technical managers back at base. A team has been sent out there overnight to investigate. Quickly it is clear it wasn't a fire in the engine, but a spurious fire warning. The central safety team are happy that the Engineering investigation is underway as it should be, and wait for the Flight Ops department to debrief the flight crew and get their side of the story on record. All details of the investigation will be entered by each team into the investigation record on the Safety Management System, creating an evolving, detailed and auditable account of the investigation.

A week later, this story is taking shape. A safety officer from Flight Ops recounts that the story so far from engineering is that someone was doing maintenance and removed the wrong sensor unit. He is very experienced, widely trusted and had just moved to this role from previous work with a highly respected team on another fleet. At this point, it looks like he forgot to go back and tighten the bolts – 'And here's the interesting thing: the work was signed off but the card wasn't checked.' Engineering tasks are structured into 'cards' of specific sets of tasks. Each card is signed off by the engineer completing the task to demonstrate compliance and as a check of the work. The concern for the investigators is that this is 'a whole bunch of human factors issues, it's suggesting the system's not working properly'.

The event is a top priority item at this airline's Flight Safety Review Committee a month later, where all the strands of ongoing investigations are brought together for discussion by senior leaders. Flight Ops think the flight crew did well in this situation. It was a difficult decision, but entirely defensible and they were within limits when the decision was made. It takes a few seconds to retard the power which carried the aircraft through V1, and then inertia pushed them further before slowing. They've spoken with the crew and the fleet captains, they've 'pulled the traces' from the Flight Data Monitoring system, which automatically records, downloads and analyses hundreds of system parameters and control inputs from the flight deck on every flight. And they believe the decision making, crew communication and control of the aircraft were sound. This is such a critical and closely investigated topic because, as the flight operations director chillingly notes: high-speed rejected take-offs 'don't have a good history – they tend to go on fire and kill people'.

It is considered that the crew did well, and from a Flight Ops perspective they are comfortable with their performance. All of these investigations into staff actions in relation to safety events are governed by a clear statement, signed by the airline's Chief Executive, that investigations are to focus on learning and improving safety. No staff will be considered culpable, or will be punished, for errors or mistakes made within accepted professional conduct and that are appropriately reported and recorded; only actions that would be judged by peers to be grossly negligent, bring professional competence into doubt or are hidden on purpose would be subject to any disciplinary investigation. And the flight crew on this occasion are considered to have performed professionally and entirely appropriately.

The next week, this event is discussed at the airline's full Board Safety Group, which meets quarterly, includes all senior directors and is chaired by the Chief Executive. This is now six weeks after the event. Engineering have established a full account of the event and the circumstances leading up to it, and this highlights concerns regarding the work allocation 'card' system. It appears that when engineers take a card, one per task, 'in theory' they look up the details in the Aircraft Maintenance Manual – a huge volume of material that describes all the procedures necessary to maintain a fleet of aircraft. But in practice the engineers don't always do this for the most basic of tasks that they perform routinely. In this case, the engineer responsible for removing the plates holding the fire sensor didn't have any specific experience of this task on this aircraft type, so he followed the instructions referred to by the card and removed all the plugs. The more experienced engineers had found they could do the job more effectively without needing to remove all the plugs. So when the next engineer came along to do the next part of the job – replace the plugs – he only replaced the ones he would usually replace according to local practice, not the full set as specified on the card. That resulted in the sensor being left slightly loose, and by the time it had flown out to its destination, it ending up shaking free as the aircraft started its take-off roll for the journey back. So, as the senior investigator described, ironically and laughing – so he's the guilty bastard to shoot! He swiftly continues – 'No, of course not. The system fell down. But the problem we have as an oversight body is that if it says those tasks on the card, they should be doing those tasks. So we need to review customs and practices and make sure they are woven into the manual'. Ultimately no individual engineer is considered at fault, but the way engineers work and the systems they operate within becomes the subject of a broader review, to ensure that the full range of routine engineering practices remain effective, safe and are properly represented by formal procedures.

Problems parking

An investigator is scanning through the new incidents and reads the first four words out loud, 'Aircraft marshaled too far . . . now I bet I know where this is'. He's right. It's at a new terminal area just completed at a major international airport. He asks rhetorically and with frustration, 'And how did I know that? Because two weeks ago they did exactly the same thing and the engine hit a concrete pillar. So what does this tell us people have learnt? Absolutely nothing'. He turns to the other investigators and tells them it has happened again. This time, the marshals on the ground directed the aircraft so close to the stand that it nearly collided with a jetty. There is strident agreement amongst the investigators that it is seriously poor show that this happened again. The investigator sends out a request, through the safety management system, to the airline's ground representative at that station asking for an assessment of what happened and an update on the actions taken.

Later in the day more information is sent through noting a range of issues that seem to have been at play and that have been highlighted by the still ongoing investigation into the first event. The markings on the stand that designate where different types of aircraft should be parked appear to be worn, there seem to be issues with training as the marshals aren't always sure what type – and therefore length – of aircraft they are dealing with and there are no markings painted on the ground for the A320 at all. These issues are being investigated by the airline's Flight Technical Support team in collaboration with both the local contractor that provides the marshals and the airport itself. Flight Ops have also organised that aircraft dispatchers will provide crews flying to that airport with up-to-date information on where specifically these problems are occurring at the terminal. The coordinating investigator is comfortable with the investigation being conducted by the Flight Tech team and is cautiously happy with the work that is going on at the airport. He explains – we get these sorts of niggles all the time all over the place, and it looks like these guys are on top of it, but if it happens again we might take coordination of this investigation from here.

A month later, it happens again. This time another investigator, Tim, is sitting working through the day's new incidents and calls out, 'they've just tried to taxi another one into a pillar'. His colleague turns around: that's ridiculous, it's in the board papers this month. Tim explains it was on the same aircraft type again, and they missed the pillar by a metre. His colleague can't believe it: 'First they hit an engine, a few weeks later they nearly do it again and now another near-miss. Usually it goes the other way around doesn't it: near-miss, near-miss, then hit!' Tim joins in the wry joke – well, at least they're showing an improvement. All agree that something has got to be done on this. Tim gets up and heads to speak with the head of the team, who calls a meeting the next day with all the investigators. He's spoken to the senior managers in Flight Ops and this has been discussed at the airline's weekly operational review committee that convenes all the senior heads from each operational department. 'They're saying at the station, we've done everything and briefed the marshals – well they obviously haven't as it still keeps happening!' As an interim measure he's asked Flight Ops if they have briefed the crews on this and Flight Ops are putting together a new procedure for crew to divide their attention and position themselves to look out of side windows to watch the wing tips – duplicating, for now, the primary role of the marshals. But the main investigation and improvement actions are in the hands of other organisations – the marshals and the airport itself, with only limited input possible from the airline's local representatives on the ground. For now Flight Ops is putting in place its own compensating mechanisms and is increasingly challenging and chasing the operational units at the airport to complete the required actions.

A week later, Tim looks up from his computer while doing the morning sweep: 'you won't believe this. If I tell you the location, you guess the incident . . .' Everyone gets it right. The same airport. Another aircraft marshaled past the stand. Gary, the investigator now monitoring this issue, immediately follows this up by speaking with Flight Tech and the managers in Flight Ops. He says he put this in the weekly briefing for the Flight Ops managers that day and the patience is gone now. 'We're pulling rank and running the investigation from here'. He sends out a request for a full run-down of all documentation and data collected by all the local teams, and within a couple of days they receive an update, pulled together by an Operations manager on another floor of the building. Most of the incidents have been on a particular stand, C10. There was an unrelated incident nearby, on C8, the one that resulted in damage. The marshaler didn't recognise the aircraft – or its size – and he's been given additional training. But it turns out that stand C10 doesn't have any lines marked for the A320. It is quickly determined that stand will not be used by the airline until further notice and until the markings have been measured, painted and checked. The problems at the new terminal have only been encountered on these stands, which also happen to be the only ones the airline uses at that destination. It looks like all parties now understand the situation and have agreed on a specific plan of action, but Gary, the investigator overseeing this process, will be contacting the airport and the marshal contractor as well to 'make sure everyone's on the same page'. Tim explains that the underlying and deeper concern is damaging an aircraft on the ground and then putting it in the air. He explains – it's like at Abidjan a few years ago: an airline got ground damage to the angle of attack vane on one of the aircraft, but it wasn't noticed. It gave a stall warning as soon as they were in the air, and the crew followed the stall warning and pushed the nose down – all the way into the sea. Aircraft are fragile and need to be handled with immense care and respect, and even parking problems can potentially result in catastrophe.

Just two days later, two new incident reports from the same airport arrive. The first reports no stop markings on a different stand now, another reports a crew being cleared by traffic controllers onto one stand but the marshal directed them onto another. Gary reads through the reports – it now looks like the airport have removed the incorrect markings on all of the stands, but haven't yet painted any new ones! And the marshalling issues are clearly continuing, though 'we wouldn't normally bother too much about that particular mistake if it wasn't here, but they've damaged one before and they're going to try putting one in the air with damage soon, that's what's really worrying'. So these fleeting mistakes point to deeper problems at this location, and the potential for a more serious event is seen as lingering ominously in the background. Later that day a pilot stops by the desks of the investigators; he wants to talk about marshalling at the same airport. He says the marshalling's pretty terrible there, I'm not even sure they're following basic procedures, they just seem to put the marshals out there and leave them to it – but I don't know enough about it so I can't record that in an incident report. The investigators are interested in the feedback – and encourage 'keep the reports coming, every one we get is useful'.

As the investigation is completed, the immediate recommendations and actions are simple and basic: the correct markings need to be measured and painted on each stand for each aircraft type that uses the stand, and the marshals must be appropriately trained at recognising aircraft, communicating and signalling. These tasks are eventually completed to the satisfaction of investigators. But in coordinating the investigation from the Safety department, the investigators' attention turned to their own organisational processes too. Of considerable concern was why these issues were picked up one at a time through incidents; why weren't the new stands assessed, measured and checked by their own airline prior to them using them? Through the investigation, investigators had become concerned with a broader question: we have processes in place to assess new airfields and routes, but how do we assess new stands at an airport we've been flying into for decades? 'Do we just assume they are standard regulation stands and the airport is capable of operating them? We need to be proactive here. We need to know who does this in the organisation, who is going to be responsible for it'. A brief series of parking problems at an airport far away has been used to expose a small gap in how the airline monitors its own processes and assures itself of operational safety.

Organising airline flight safety

The preceding vignettes capture the complexities, complications and uncertainties in interpreting close calls and addressing risks. There is no typical incident as such, and no typical investigation, and these three vignettes depict some of the most significant and consequential investigations that investigators might routinely engage in. They also demonstrate some of the common elements that feature in the more intensive work of investigators. Information is hard to get hold of early on, the picture continually changes and evolves, understandings shift over time – occasionally quite dramatically, different people can move into and move out of the activities of a specific investigation, and action and improvement result from collaborating with and influencing a range of departments, personnel and other organisations. Airlines are complex places in which large numbers of specialists must coordinate to perform difficult tasks. The role of investigators is to both understand this sociotechnical complexity and to intervene in it to improve safety. The technical complexity of the airline industry is mirrored by its social complexity, and flight safety investigators must master both.

Investigators occupy a central and distinctive place in a much broader sociotechnical infrastructure of safety. This infrastructure spans from the international bodies that govern aviation and set standards for safety management and investigation, such as the International Civil Aviation Authority and the International Air Transport Association, to state and national agencies responsible for certifying new aircraft and investigating major air accidents such as the UK's Civil Aviation Authority and Air Accident Investigation Branch, and the US Federal Aviation Administration and the National Transportation Safety Board, all the way to the analytical and improvement work that is done by technical specialists in the hangars and offices of each individual airline, manufacturer and service provider. Airline flight safety investigators are just one piece of this complex infrastructure of safety. The work of investigators is focused on overseeing and improving the safety of front-line airline operations. These front-line operations involve technologies, equipment and organisational processes that have already been subject to intensive scrutiny, risk analysis, certification and safety testing. The incidents and close calls that safety investigators are presented with are therefore likely to be defects and irregularities that were not foreseen or anticipated in these predictive, anticipatory processes of design and certification. Investigators occupy the sharp-end of risk management and are responsible for understanding the unusual, unexpected or irregular events that crop up when work and technologies are actually put into practice.

Aviation is an industry in which the range of ultimate harmful outcomes is well known. There are only so many ways to crash or damage an aeroplane, and history has provided ample time for them to have been extensively experienced, investigated, categorised, documented and analysed. There is an air accident shorthand: loss of control (LOC); controlled flight into terrain (CFIT); runway incursion; runway excursion; fire, fumes and smoke; mid-air collision; structural or mechanical failure. And several more. At this level of generalisation, the list of possible accidents is short and comprehensive. What remains incomplete, and perennially so, is the knowledge of the specific circumstances, permutations and contributing factors that might bring about one of these accidents. While there are only so many ways to crash a plane, there are infinitely varied routes to achieve that outcome. The work of flight safety investigators is largely oriented to spotting and addressing the antecedents of accidents, well before the airline comes close to having one – and often long before it is entirely clear how such an accident might precisely unfold.

Safety investigators work continually to prevent things that almost never happen. To understand the context of this work, and investigators' place within the organisational infrastructure of safety, the remainder of this chapter considers the typical structure of airline operations and safety oversight, the processes and systems of incident reporting and analysis, and the routine activities that occupy much of investigators' time. This presents a fuller picture of the work of investigators, and also provides a descriptive backdrop for the more detailed analysis of the work of interpreting, analysing and learning from incidents and close calls that is the focus of the remainder of this book.

Airline operations and flight safety oversight

The operational or 'line' departments in airlines are typically divided into four main areas: Flight Operations, Engineering, Cabin Service and Ground Operations. Each line department is responsible for a different aspect of the operation. And each, to a greater or lesser degree, contributes to – and impacts on – flight safety. Flight Operations, invariably termed 'Flight Ops' in most airlines, operate the aircraft. Flight Ops deploy the flight crew: the pilots who fly the planes. Larger airlines can employ several thousand flight crew, all of whom undergo extensive and ongoing training and work in a heavily proceduralised environment. Pilots are supported in Flight Ops by 'flight technical', or 'flight tech', personnel. Flight tech organise the technical aspects of operating the aircraft. Their tasks include, for instance, managing the provision of onboard navigation charts and airfield plates, ensuring that destination airports have suitable facilities to operate into and making sure the flight briefings and notices supplied to crews prior to departure are comprehensive and up to date.

Engineering perform the technical servicing, maintenance and repair of an airline's fleet of aircraft. It is responsible for keeping aircraft in an airworthy condition. In larger airlines, these number several hundred aircraft, maintained by 7,000–8,000 or more engineering staff. These staff range from young apprentice mechanics to higher-degree educated engineers certified by regulators to redesign or modify specific aircraft components. The basic tasks of working on the aircraft are specified in the manufacturer's 'Aircraft Maintenance Manual'. And any work conducted on an aircraft, on any one of its millions of parts – down to pulling a single circuit breaker – is recorded in that aircraft's individual electronic technical log. 'Ground Ops' deal with operations on the ground at airports. Ground crews direct aircraft on to the stand and, using tugs, push them back off it. They refuel the planes, provide de-icing, plug in electrical power and provide other ground-based services. And Cabin Service provide the flight attendants or cabin crew for each flight, responsible for serving and directing the travelling passengers. Moreover, airline operations are dependent on a large range of other organisations. These include airports, air traffic control services, regulators and, of course, the manufacturers of equipment – such as the airframes, powerplant and aircraft systems. Airlines operate within a complex ecosystem of organisations that produce the global aviation system, and work closely with a range of different organisations.

Flight safety oversight in airlines is primarily provided by safety investigators based in independent, and relatively small, safety units. These units monitor, investigate and report on flight safety in the organisation, and answer directly to chief executive, director or board-level executives. As is common with many risk management organisational structures, safety units do not have any authority or executive capacity. They do not have direct control over or responsibility for line operations. As such, these units cannot enforce or mandate action: responsibility for flight safety ultimately lies with those in the operational departments. The separation of safety oversight from operational and executive duties is designed to render the oversight of safety relatively independent and isolated from commercial or operational pressures and to clearly distinguish safety concerns from disciplinary matters. The independence of safety oversight is highly prized, both within individual airlines and in the broader aviation industry, where state agencies responsible for air accident investigation are purposefully separated from and independent to the national regulatory, policy and commercial structures. Safety investigators derive their legitimacy and authority from their expertise, their independence and their ability to report on and hold others accountable.

Where do safety investigators come from? They typically have lengthy operational experience and their career path often sees them moving into flight safety positions from technical or operational roles on the line. For instance, previous roles of the investigators I worked with include commercial pilots, flight engineers, 'spanners and scratched knuckles' mechanics, higher-degree educated engineering specialists, flight training personnel, former military pilots, former rotary-wing pilots, state accident investigators and chief pilots on their airline's most prestigious aircraft fleets. Operational experience is considered a valuable prerequisite for the job. In many cases investigators are either seconded- or management-pilots, retaining part-time flying duties in their airline. Safety investigators conduct a range of oversight work within airlines. They sit on various policy and review groups to monitor the decision making there and to offer their input. They conduct rolling programmes of safety audits and safety culture reviews. They provide ad hoc safety analysis, work on joint safety projects with other organisations and agencies, and respond to requests for safety information and advice from within their own organisation.

Investigators have access to an enormous amount of safety-relevant data that are captured within the airline, along with a large amount of information that is circulated within the broader industry. Within their own airline, this includes each aircraft's electronic technical log, which records in detail the technical history of the aircraft. Investigators can request tapes of radio communication between pilots and air traffic controllers from air traffic service providers, for example, along with computer simulations of the movement of aircraft during an event. They can ask for in-depth technical analysis of faulty components from manufacturers. And, of key importance, they can request analysis of flight information from their airline's Flight Data Monitoring programme. These programmes record and monitor hundreds of flight parameters – such as air speed and control inputs – on every flight that an airline flies. Flight data are automatically monitored and alerts are triggered when predetermined performance standards are exceeded – for instance, a very hard landing or excessive bank angle. Simulations of a specific flight can then be created to review a safety event. The technology is impressive and investigators find it a hugely valuable tool. An aircraft's flight can be recreated on screen, with a simulation of the flight deck, instruments and inputs recreated for any phase of any flight. This approach to continually monitoring flight safety was pioneered in the UK almost thirty years ago and has more recently become an international requirement (e.g. Wright and Lyons, 2001; Savage, 2004; Reason, 1997). In addition to all these data, a huge amount of information on air safety is widely available and shared within the industry. Much of this is largely derived from the analysis of other operators' past accidents and serious events and from analyses of specific safety issues by state and non-governmental organisations. Accident investigation reports, in-depth risk analyses and annual reviews of safety programmes are widely and routinely circulated. Despite being immersed in this data-rich environment, investigators nonetheless see safety incident reporting programmes as one of the core elements of their safety oversight systems and one that is deeply connected to and supportive of their safety oversight work.

Safety incidents, and reports thereof

At core, safety incident reporting aims to make use of the knowledge and experience of front-line personnel to identify and address emerging safety issues. While these programmes are commonly referred to as 'incident reporting systems', this is barely a fraction of the story. The real value and purpose of incident reporting lies in the resulting investigations, analyses and improvement actions. A better and more appropriate term for these systems might be 'incident reporting, investigation and improvement systems' – and several airlines and regulators even refer to their programmes with the appropriately urgent acronym 'ASAP', or Aviation Safety Action Programme. Of particular importance, these programmes function as safety oversight, reporting and investigation systems – not as operational or executive systems. Safety incident reporting is primarily part of an oversight process and separate from the local operational processes in place for addressing problems and managing safety. Operational departments remain responsible for managing safety and addressing risks, and safety management is a core component of those operational activities. Incident reporting is not a mechanism to request 'fixes' for problems, and operational departments do not sit on their hands and do nothing until they hear back from the safety department. So, for instance, engineers don't just report to investigators that they have found signs of electrical arcing and then wait. They conduct their own investigation and fault finding and take action to understand and address the problem within their own organisational unit. That is their job. Likewise, flight crew report problems they have encountered – and usually also how they have dealt with them. Managing and improving safety is an operational issue and continues regardless of whether investigators decide to get involved or not.

The activities that unfold around safety incident reporting programmes provide additional layers of oversight, support and constructive challenge to the safety management process. They support the meta-management of safety, allowing safety investigators to monitor and review problematic issues, intervene and coordinate cross-department investigations, integrate and distribute transferable lessons, and ensure that safety management activities are functioning as they should. The substantive, day-to-day work of safety management remains the responsibility of operational departments. As such, airlines do not use safety incident as merely an operational system to log and solve operational problems; they instead use safety incident reporting as an oversight system that allows investigators to monitor the ongoing management of safety by operational departments, and to coordinate more detailed investigations where necessary.

Airlines operate incident reporting systems for flight crew, ground crew, cabin crew and engineers. Operational personnel are required to submit or 'raise' reports to notify investigators of any operational mishap or safety event, according to set reporting criteria. A number of specific types of reportable occurrence are typically defined. These are in line with the requirements of the national regulator, any additional requirements determined by the airline – along with a request for anything else that may be useful if reported. For example, for flight crew in one major airline these criteria are based on thirty-four specific types of events, including warnings of smoke or fire, go-arounds, exceeding prescribed aircraft performance limits and encountering deficiencies in operating procedures or manuals. Two additional criteria specify any other events "where safety standards are significantly reduced" and that "may provide useful information for the enhancement of safety" (Si1-D). If an event is particularly serious, personnel are also required to notify investigators immediately by telephone, and at least one investigator is always on call twenty-four hours a day, seven days a week in airlines.

Incidents are reported by front-line operational personnel: pilots, engineers, flight attendants, ground crew. As such, the events reported concern the immediate work of operating and maintaining the aircraft – the 'sharp-end' of operations. And reports from flight crew are considered to be from the sharpest-end of all, as they often involve problems encountered in flight. The incidents reported to investigators are a broad range of operational mishaps and upsets, practical problems, minor failures, close calls, errors and organisational inadequacies. For instance, flight crew might report when a cockpit computer fails, when they mishear an instruction from Air Traffic Control (ATC) or when they receive an indication of a loss of tyre pressure prior to landing. Pilots also report situations that might cause problems or provide the opportunity for error, as in this case of a report highlighting the similarity in radio call-signs of three flights:

> Company flights 'A2490', 'A2940' and 'A2840' all operate from [the same station] at the same or similar departure times, which causes call-sign confusion for ATC and flight crew. (Si4-D)

Incidents directly relevant to flight safety are predominantly reported by flight crew and engineers, as they are the people primarily responsible for maintaining and operating the aircraft. But reports from all operational areas can have implications for flight safety. Issues of 'flight safety' do not only emerge while the aircraft is in flight. For example, cabin crew might report how they had noticed and alerted the pilots to snow building up on the wing prior to take-off, ground crew might report when they have caused a small amount of damage to an aircraft fairing or engineers might report that they have discovered signs of electrical arcing on one of the dense wire looms running throughout the airframe. The incidents reported by personnel therefore span a vastly broad range of operational problems. While quantitative Flight Data Monitoring systems commonly monitor around a hundred or so predefined types of event, qualitative incident reporting deals with literally any event that personnel encounter and decide is relevant to report.

Reports themselves are typically brief. The reporting forms are laid out on a single page – traditionally on paper but now on electronic screens of one sort or another. Reports require essential details of the flight, such as destination, aircraft type and weight, technical log references and the like. They also ask for a short description of the event: its immediate cause, the actions taken and their results, and any other relevant information, including suggestions for preventative action. At most, descriptions of an event run to a hundred words; the most succinct, five or six. Usually they amount to a fifty-word paragraph. These descriptions provide a highly technical, jargon-ridden and abridged account of an event. To demonstrate with a relatively lengthy and verbose example, the following report was raised regarding an error made by the flight crew while entering their departure plan data into a flight computer. It describes this:

> During pre-flight checks, the wrong SID was entered into MCDU. Copied to secondary flight plan in MCDU. Error in primary noticed and changed to correct SID (mid 6T); secondary held CMK 6T and performance figures for full length 31R departure. This was not 'over-written'. Full length used when secondary flight plan was activated. CMK 6T SID was not noticed and this 'incorrect' SID was initially flown. ATC intervened when aircraft turned left on departure and tracked towards 'CMK' VOR, an instruction to "Turn to 'CLN' VOR" given and correct SID re-inserted and flown. (Si4-D)

Ignoring the acronyms and technical terminology, this report describes how a data input error was noticed and corrected on the primary computer, but not on the backup – and the information in the backup was subsequently used for the departure, leading to an incorrect turn to the left after take-off. The air traffic controller queried this manoeuvre, the error was noticed by the crew and the appropriate heading was entered into the computer and followed.

The information provided by incident reports therefore gives investigators a relatively superficial and truncated account of what happened. The reports themselves do not explain the incident; they only describe it, often in the barest terms possible. It is up to investigators to interpret what the event might mean in terms of operational safety and what organisational problems or risks it might point to. Incidents are typically equivocal in their immediate impact on flight safety, as is the case above. By definition, incidents are relatively minor events with little – and usually no – actual adverse outcome for the passengers or the aircraft. Reports often report how events were responded to and addressed, not only that something had gone wrong. They describe some operational irregularity or anomaly where things weren't quite as they should have been – but were dealt with, caught, corrected or compensated for.

In most airlines incident reports are raised by personnel in large numbers. One of the large airlines that provides the focus for this study deals with between 9,000 and 10,000 reports a year from flight crew alone, and the same from engineers. Cabin crew and ground staff report in fewer numbers. This typically provides an ongoing stream of around 400 to 500 incident reports a week to be reviewed by the investigators. Incident reports are stored, and investigations and actions are managed, within a dedicated safety management and information system. These systems bring together all safety-relevant data within an airline, they include tools for safety analysis, and they provide the technological platform through which incidents, analyses, investigations and improvement are organised.

Within these safety information systems, each incident is categorised according to a taxonomy of event types and key features – 'keywords' or 'descriptors' – that describe and classify the incident such as 'Flight Crew Illness' or 'Auxiliary Power Unit fuel leak'. The precise taxonomies vary depending on the software in use and the requirements of the organisation. This categorisation allows for detailed trend analysis and retrieval of past reports, in what is usually a large incident database. At the time this study was conducted, for example, the largest airline involved had over 120,000 reports in its current database, collected over the past fifteen years. The safety information system software usually allows reports to be given a short title to aid recognition and retrieval. And there is also some means of assigning a risk or priority level to events, usually in the form of a risk matrix – a tool which safety investigators often find problematic, some of the reasons for which are discussed shortly.

The information system is also used to coordinate and manage investigations. It is accessible to a range of designated personnel throughout the organisation. If further investigation is required, investigative tasks or 'actions' are assigned to suitable personnel by way of the system. These personnel then record their findings and any actions that have been taken to address the problems identified, as a growing conversation around an incident and additional material and information is appended to the original incident report. At one extreme, an investigation can involve a single specialist briefly providing a technical opinion. At the other, it can require a cross-departmental team to conduct a lengthy and in-depth investigation of the circumstances and processes surrounding a range of events, involving other organisations such as Air Traffic Service providers and airframe manufacturers, and on occasion state agencies such as regulators or accident investigators. Given the sparse and sometime cryptic information provided by any initial incident report, these investigations often involve going back to the original reporter of the event to get a more detailed account of what has happened. The information system is therefore primarily a tool to mediate and coordinate these investigative activities and record their outcomes.

A note on risk assessment

One of the most fundamental challenges that faces investigators when dealing with large quantities of relatively minor incidents is how to identify and assess the risk of what is reported, and so properly focus attention, prioritise action and allocate resources within the organisation. In practice, the primary tool provided for this purpose in most safety information systems is a risk profile matrix, risk table or risk map. These are simplistic tables

		Low	Medium	High
	High	C	B	A
Probability of occurrence	Medium	D	C	B
	Low	E	D	C
		Low	Medium	High

Risk key
A - Extreme
B - High
C - Medium
D - Low
E - Negligible

Severity of outcome

Figure 2.1   Generalised example of a simple risk-profile matrix

that allow an ordinal level of risk to be allocated to incidents according to the assessed severity and likelihood of harmful outcomes (e.g. Figure 2.1). These risk assessment matrix tools are based on current normative models of risk management (e.g. Breakwell, 2007; Institute of Risk Management, 2002; Cabinet Office, 2002; Health and Safety Executive, 2001) and are used widely in safety incident reporting programmes and in risk management systems more broadly (e.g. McIntyre, 2002; Reason, 1997; Cooke, 1991; National Patient Safety Agency, 2001).

However, while investigators routinely use these tools to apply risk grades to incidents, the tools do not closely fit investigators' expert understandings of risk and their analytical practices. Using the risk matrix does not provide investigators with new insights about the importance of an incident. Nor does it reveal risks that investigators otherwise could have missed. As the primary instrument of risk assessment, the role of the risk matrix in overseeing and assessing flight safety is decidedly limited. As such, while risk matrix tools are appropriated by investigators for the purpose of indicating priority and allocating resources, the use of these tools is problematic. As will become apparent throughout the remainder of this book, these tools offer a particularly narrow, limited and flawed representation of risk that does not closely fit the analytical practices of risk assessment that investigators engage in. When speaking bluntly, investigators suggest that the risk matrix provides little more than a "Noddy's guide" (Si5-14) to risk assessment. The assessment and analysis of risk is an ongoing process throughout incident reviews and safety investigations and is conducted in relation to an evolving understanding of safety in a particular area of operational activity; it is not tied solely to the brief activity of "putting the letter in the box" (Si2-6) of the risk matrix, one incident report at a time. In practice, the assessment and interpretation of risk is a broad and integral aspect of investigators' work, and depends on a complex and sophisticated practical theory of safety.

The work of flight safety investigators

The practical work done by flight safety investigators to interpret and analyse safety incidents and organise investigations and improvements centres on a number of core activities. These are reviewing and analysing incidents as they are reported, investigating incidents and their implications for safety, and communicating risks and reporting on significant incidents to various audiences. These activities are often performed by individual investigators, but their work remains inherently social.

Investigators routinely and regularly communicate with each other and with personnel from around the organisation in order to understand and investigate incidents – either in person or mediated through the safety information system or other communicative vehicles such as briefing materials, reports and other documents. Each of these aspects of investigators' work – reviewing, investigating, communicating and discussing – is described in turn.

Reviewing incidents

Once incident reports are raised by personnel and entered into the safety information system, investigators review and analyse them. Typically, each day the new reports are briefly looked over by all investigators to see what sorts of things have been happening. In particular, the investigator who is 'on-call' that week, and responsible for dealing with any urgent safety events at any time of day or night, conducts a detailed daily review of all new incidents. Any incidents of special significance are recorded in a large log book or electronic file that is kept close to hand and frequently referred back to, for instance, when fielding enquiries from other departments or to look back over recent significant events to spot potential connections or patterns. Each incident report is individually reviewed by an investigator. This typically requires the investigator to take 'ownership' of a report within the safety information system, taking responsibility for administering it through the system. Investigators read through the flight information and event description in the report. Given the brevity of reports, this usually takes little more than a few seconds. Investigators often conduct quick searches of the database to verify whether similar events have occurred previously or to remind themselves of the details of similar events that they remember.

In many cases, with around half the reports, the event is considered to be simple to understand and something that has been encountered before and is well understood and under control. For instance, this includes events such as "smoke seen from landing gear, no indication on flight deck, found to be de-icing fluid" (Si4-D). This was deemed "no worry" (Si4-1) as it is well known that the aircraft's brakes are often still hot as the aircraft are de-iced, and fluid can drip onto them and harmlessly boil off. In cases such as this, a brief reading of the details of the report is usually enough to satisfy the investigator that the incident pointed to nothing untoward. These reports have a low-level risk assigned to them, as described in the next section, and are then 'closed' – that is, they require no further action and are filed in the system for future reference and trend analysis. Likewise, other reports may be closed after the investigator makes only a few enquiries into them – perhaps a quick phone call to a specialist in the area concerned, or making reference to a technical manual or database – without requiring any further action or investigation. A case in point concerned a report by flight crew of lightning being seen to strike the aircraft nose. Lightning strikes occur often and are relatively routine events. Aircraft are designed to withstand them, dissipating the charge through small pylons called 'static wicks' that line the trailing edge of the wings. Investigators see similar reports "a hell of a lot" (Si4-4). In this case, the investigator took the reference number from the report and logged on to the aircraft's technical log. He found that an engineer had inspected the aircraft and found slight damage to the nose cone, but this was within allowable limits. Satisfied with this, the investigator pasted the details of the engineering check into the incident report, assigned a low-level risk and closed the report.

In the remaining cases, investigators want to find out more about an event. Incidents lead them to question the safety of a particular aspect of the operation, which they want to examine more closely. Sometimes, the preliminary enquiries made by investigators – checking the technical log, say, or telephoning a colleague in Engineering – reveal more of a potential problem than they originally suspected, and which they want to find out more about. And often, reports simply don't contain the information they need to fully understand the event and its implications. In all these cases, investigators seek out more information and coordinate further investigation.

Investigating issues

Where investigators consider that an incident requires further investigation or action, they initiate this by contacting the relevant personnel in the operational departments, typically through the safety information system. They determine the appropriate managers or specialists who need to be involved – usually from memory, sometimes by asking their colleagues and occasionally by consulting the relevant documents listing the personnel with safety responsibilities in each operational area. Specific actions, in the form of questions and queries, are then assigned to those people. Investigators routinely ask for the operational processes around an event to be reviewed and assessed and for the findings of this review to be reported back to them. A relatively simple instance concerned an incident in which the required en route diversion charts were found missing by a flight crew. The investigator wasn't sure and didn't have access to a list of which charts were meant to be carried on that particular flight, so he decided to "give this to the library guys to review and to make sure we haven't missed anything" (Si4-4). A request was put, via the safety information system, to a fleet library manager – based in the same open-plan office as the investigator – to both review this specific incident and assess their procedures for keeping on-board charts up to date.

Other investigations might require the involvement of more people who are spread around the organisation. A reported 'early rotation' incident – where the pilot pulled the nose of the aircraft up at too low a speed during take-off – was sent to the fleet manager to debrief the crew and find out in more detail what had happened. It was also sent to the Flight Data Monitoring team to "pull off the trace" (Si4-6) to see precisely what the aircraft did and when. In extreme cases, rotating at too low a speed can cause the tail of the aircraft to strike the runway, as the aircraft fails to take off, and the investigator wanted to pull together a more detailed picture of what had happened. Other reports, such as repeated instances of ground damage while aircraft are being parked, might require the involvement of Flight Tech managers and their counterparts in Ground Ops to determine if there is a problem with specified clearance margins between aircraft and other obstacles, along with input from personnel from the relevant airport and firms that provide other ground-based services.

In particularly serious events, investigators can be called out to supervise more major investigations on the ground. This was the case when an aircraft made an emergency landing with the crew believing – erroneously as it turned out – that both engines were surging and losing power. The on-call investigator travelled to the station where the aircraft had diverted to and supported and coordinated the Flight Operations and Engineering teams in their investigation. For other long-standing investigations, investigators also, for example, sit in on the debriefing of flight crew or other investigation meetings, to garner as much information as possible. In their investigative work, investigators work with personnel based in the operational departments. They oversee and organise investigative actions to ensure incidents are properly investigated and learnt from. But they do not conduct each and every specific task in an investigation. Rather, they 'take coordination' of investigations: they coordinate, organise and integrate the action of others.

Once a set of requested actions are complete, these are reviewed by investigators. If required, further actions are then requested and assigned to the same people or to other people from areas or organisations that might now appear relevant. For particularly problematic issues, this process can lead to lengthy exchanges and meetings between specialists and investigators that are spread over weeks, or even months, with the various actions and subsequent responses documented in the safety information system in an emerging story of the various investigative and improvement actions.

When investigators and all other parties are satisfied that the incident and any underlying risks have been properly understood and appropriate improvement recommendations have been defined and actions taken, the incident is closed. For instance, the actions for the early rotation incident mentioned above were completed and reported back in just a few days. The fleet managers explained that the co-pilot called for rotation ten knots early, due to a mis-set 'speed bug' – a mark placed on the air speed indicator that highlights the speed at which the call for rotation should be made. In this case, the investigator wanted to know how far the bug had been placed from the correct speed readings, and why – questions he again put to the fleet manager. Within a week the manager reported back that the crew had been interrupted during a pre-departure checklist by a radio call and, unusually on that aircraft type, the bugs are set manually rather than being generated by the computer, so the only confirmation of whether and where they are set is from the crew – and on this occasion they had erred. It was confirmed that ways to avoid interruptions upsetting crew cross-checks had been discussed with this particular crew, and that the issue was going to be highlighted to the crew trainers at their next meeting, and so would find its way into simulator training, briefing materials and the route checks of pilots that are conducted by training captains during pilots' normal flight schedules. The investigator believed that, for this incident at least, the actions were sufficient and he closed the report. But he also determined that this related to a bigger safety issue of missed checklist items that they were currently worried about, and decided that the information needed to be fed into higher level groups in the company for further consideration of the general issue.

Communicating risks

A key role of investigators is reporting on safety and communicating risks, and particularly highlighting the occurrence of significant safety incidents to different organisational audiences. Investigators report on safety both to high-level safety boards and senior managers within the organisation, and back to front-line operational departments. Investigators typically produce a range of reports that publicise incidents and communicate risks. They provide regular briefings for senior management and operational personnel. In one of the largest airlines studied here, for instance, two weekly briefs are produced that review the past week's most significant flight safety incidents and are distributed to slightly different audiences. One briefing is distributed to managers and directors across the whole airline. The other is circulated amongst senior managers in Flight Operations. Both briefings are between two and three pages long, containing a list of incidents along with a brief description of each event. Sent out on Monday mornings, they both importantly have a dedicated organisational forum in which the brief is reviewed by senior managers – a weekly Flight Ops senior management meeting and a weekly cross-departmental operational performance meeting. Investigators also report back on incidents and related risks directly to front-line operational personnel. For instance, summaries of significant flight safety events are typically distributed to flight crew, by way of dedicated safety bulletins or articles that are included in monthly crew newsletters. The weekly significant incident briefings are displayed prominently in crew areas within the operations centre. And the Safety department produces quarterly magazines focusing on practical safety issues and recent events. Investigators also report on safety events to board level within their organisations. A significant amount of directors' time at safety board meetings is spent reviewing past events. Investigators are instrumental in selecting which incidents are included in the board papers, which risks and issues are highlighted and examined in-depth, and what quantitative data and trend analysis are presented. This provides investigators with an important mechanism to both set the agenda and influence the discussions that are had at the very pinnacle of their organisation.

Discussing safety

Investigators regularly and routinely discuss incidents in their day-to-day conversation and in more structured meetings. These discussions are integral to their work of assessing and managing incidents. Assessing and managing reports within the safety information system are tasks for individual investigators, but these tasks are situated in a social context. Investigators talk to each other about incidents and to their colleagues and acquaintances who work elsewhere – both in their own organisation and in others. Incidents are one of the principal topics of conversation for investigators. They talk about reports that worry them, and they often discuss incidents that they are currently reviewing or working on to their colleagues. They raise operational problems they have noticed and they ask each other for advice and whether they know anything more. They talk about the recent accidents and major events of other operators in the industry, and discuss what other people have heard and said in the various meetings, boards and committees that they attend. And the big aviation safety issues of the day are discussed at length. Such conversation is a regular feature of their daily work.

Preparing publications, papers and briefs is a particularly important activity around which investigators come together to discuss events. Weekly briefs provide a regular opportunity for investigators to review and discuss the past week's events as a team, as well as to publicise those events to others. Investigators hold weekly meetings to discuss the past week and plan for the next. Safety incidents, and what has and should be done about them, are the main topic of conversation. Moreover, putting together papers for board meetings requires considerable work, and every three months investigators meet regularly for several hours at a time to finalise which incidents merit going to which oversight committee or board. In these meetings all the incidents that are considered to be of most importance from the past few months are reviewed, along with the current state of the investigation – what is known, what has been done, what is still to do. This provides investigators with a natural rhythm to review and take stock of the current state of play in safety investigation and to account for it to a challenging audience. And, while this is a process that takes place once every three months, it presents investigators with a continually open question the rest of the time: what would be suitable to go to the next board meeting? What is really important? What matters? As such, what will be presented to board-level directors – and what will be fed back to different operational departments – is a frequent topic of discussion and debate.

3
Understanding and Interpreting Safety

"The most important part of the safety enterprise is thinking about how to think (and, therefore, how to act) about risk" (Wildavsky, 1988, p. 2). So, how do investigators understand safety? And how do they think about risk? The answers to these questions are fundamental to explaining how risk is analysed and safety is managed in practice. Traditionally, risk is viewed in terms of future harm: the likelihood and severity of future adverse outcomes. Safety is commonly defined as a double negative – the absence of harm or the avoidance of risk – captured pithily by the granite sign standing outside the offices of the UK's aviation regulator that reads 'Safety is no accident'. But flight safety investigators do not entirely agree. The absence of harm or the avoidance of adverse outcomes can at times be helpful indicators, but they do not tell the whole story. Investigators work in a context where errors and incidents are profligate, where the potential consequences of accidents are catastrophic, but where actual harmful events are extraordinarily rare. As such, investigators draw on a shared practical theory of safety that is both more nuanced and more pragmatic than traditional ideas that focus on the prediction or absence of harmful outcomes. Understanding the nature and substance of this practical theory of safety is essential if we are to understand how safety investigators work to analyse risk and improve safety.

Investigators' working theory of safety structures how they interpret incidents, understand risks and manage improvement. This working theory is typically left implicit and unarticulated. It is not neatly documented or carefully defined, but is revealed through investigators' daily practice and in the way they analyse and communicate about safety incidents and risks. This practical theory of safety provides an interpretive framework, or interpretive schema, within which investigators make sense of organisational events and determine what they mean for organisational safety. This is based on a shared set of assumptions, collectively held beliefs and a common set of concepts and ideas that investigators find useful. The structure of this shared practical theory of safety is important and deeply consequential. It frames what investigators notice and how they make sense. It provides ideas and concepts that determine which features of organisational activities investigators attend to and consider important and which they take for granted and ignore. It provides the categories and logic that investigators apply to incidents to understand them and explain what they mean and whether – and why – they are considered important or not for flight safety. In short, investigators' underlying practical theory of safety represents the cultural wisdom and collective knowledge of this professional community, and distills this into a shared way of seeing, thinking and acting about risks. There is, after all, nothing so practical as good theory (Lewin, 1951).

This chapter is concerned with the substance and structure of this interpretive framework. It explains the core assumptions, beliefs and ideas upon which safety management is built. Investigators act as both a key repository and a primary source of safety expertise in their organisations, and are influential in both setting the general tone and defining the specific features of what effective safety management should look like – and what counts as a worrisome risk. This practical theory of safety provides the underlying interpretive framework within which risks are understood and analysed. In practice, investigators' understanding of risk and safety are inextricably entwined. Both risk and safety are interpreted in organisational terms as properties that emerge from organisational activities and processes – rather than in terms of the presence or absence of adverse consequences and future outcomes. At base, one of investigators' most fundamental and consequential assumptions is that the operations of airlines always hold the potential for catastrophic accidents. They also regard all aspects of sociotechnical organisation to be inherently imperfect and fallible – and therefore believe that the potential for organisational catastrophe cannot be eradicated but must be continually guarded and protected against.

A key idea used by investigators to understand this protection, and one ubiquitous in the field of safety management, is that of organisational safety defences. Such defences are understood by investigators as taking the form of practical, social and technical activities that are intended to catch and correct failures. These defences are not seen as passive 'things', but as active practices that are carried out by personnel in interaction with others and with operational technologies in every area of the organisation. Investigators view these practical defensive capabilities as providing resilience to operational mishaps, allowing the organisation to accommodate failures and bounce back from errors that occur. To assure safety, networks of organisational defences must not only provide the active capacity to catch failures when they actually occur, but they must provide the latent capacity to protect against the potential for failures developing into catastrophic organisational breakdowns. That is, to investigators, safety not only means the ability to catch and bounce back from failures that occur, it also means maintaining adequate and systematic defensive capabilities to deal with the risk of possible failures occurring, as well as the risk of those failures then enlarging further.

As such, investigators conceive of safety as more than simply resilience to failures. In this safety-critical context, 'safety' means the capacity for *resilience to risk*. Investigators conceptualise safety as *risk resilience*: the organisational capacity to protect operations from the potential of operational mishaps and fluctuations developing into catastrophic and disabling organisational breakdowns. They use incidents to diagnose weaknesses in the organisational capacity to accomplish safety, rather than to predict the future outcomes of individual events. In this sense, investigators assess risk relatively, as the degrading of this organisational capacity for safety. When investigators assess the risk of incidents, their focus is on understanding the adequacy of the underlying practices that produce safety in a particular area of the organisation—it is not focused on attempts to predict future outcomes.

The attributes that these assessments of organisational safety are based on are considered in detail in the next chapter. In this chapter, the basic assumptions that underpin investigators' practical theory of safety are first explained. Then, the nuanced and sophisticated way in which investigators understand safety defences is examined, explaining how this key construct is employed to understand risk and safety. Next, the chapter considers how situations of risk and safety are interpreted and understood by investigators, and what these terms mean in the practical work of analysing risk and managing safety in airline flight operations.

Safety-critical assumptions

Some of the most basic assumptions that shape investigators' practice concern the safety-critical nature of airline operations. Investigators assume airline accidents to be catastrophic. And they see failure and error as inevitable features of organisational activity. Taken together, these assumptions underpin a core belief that airline operations hold an inherent potential for catastrophe and that while these risks are largely manageable they are ultimately ineradicable. In practice, this set of assumptions and beliefs are deeply consequential. They represent some of the most fundamental premises that shape investigators' perspective on safety and their practices of risk management.

Accidents and catastrophic outcomes

One of the most basic and fundamental assumptions that guides the work of investigators is that the consequences of air accidents are typically catastrophic. This assumption is neither as simple nor as trivial as it may seem – and neither is it an assumption that necessarily flows from historical data. Historical accident data show that the vast majority of passengers unfortunate enough to be involved in an airline accident survive (NTSB, 2001). Of all recorded commercial jet airline accidents between 2002 and 2011, around 80 percent were non-fatal (Boeing, 2012). Planes crash, but lives are not always lost. These finer points of survivability are largely unimportant to investigators. There is a deep and pervasive assumption that the consequences of major air accidents are always extreme. The statistics might provide some comfort, but not to investigators. For them, aircraft fly in an environment of unforgiving extremes – of temperature, pressure, speed and altitude – and in such an environment accidents can have equally extreme consequences. Lives are always at stake, and this responsibility is keenly felt: "Within this industry the consequences of our errors at altitude are not very good . . . If you have an accident [and] are a service provider like us, then you will kill and injure people" (Si3-7).

The severe social consequences of accidents are not a constant feature of investigators' talk, but they are referred to with some regularity. This is particularly the case when discussing the big safety issues of the day. Investigators will unambiguously refer to these as being "the ones that can kill people" (Si2-6) or as "one of the biggest killers at the moment" (Si2-3) and that, bluntly, accidents leave "bereaved families" (Si3-3). The potential social costs of accidents are keenly felt. In many ways this is unsurprising. Air safety investigation is a profession that, over the long course of its existence, has routinely encountered catastrophe. The small core of its practitioners that work for national air accident investigation organisations routinely work on accident sites, picking apart pieces of wreckage and the remains of victims. That broad collective experience of catastrophe pervades how this professional community understands itself, its work and the risks that must be managed.

This catastrophic thinking is also applied to their own organisations and airlines. There is a pervasive assumption that an air accident will damage or destroy the airline just as much as the airliner involved. Investigators have seen this before:

It's things like how close to a smoking crater are you? Like the Manchester 'Airtours' fire, all people saw after that was a smoking hull with 'Airtours' on the side, and that was the end for them. (Si5-6)

You would say, holy shit we nearly repeated someone else's accident – and that's the end of the airline. It would do so much damage to the airline, forgetting about the death and destruction on the day. (Si2-1)

To investigators, operating an airline is a deeply unforgiving business. Accidents are considered likely to bring the airline as a whole to a disastrous end. Reason's (1997, p. 240) call to remember that "it only takes one organisational accident to put an end to all worries about the [financial] bottom line" represents an unassailable truth for investigators, a truth that shapes their most fundamental assumptions about the risks facing the organisation. Managing flight safety is seen as integral to the survival of the organisation, not merely an operational issue. History does, of course, provide occasional examples to the contrary – of airlines crashing planes, sometimes quite often, and continuing to do good business. But the idea that an air accident is something that the company would simply shrug off does not easily fit within investigators' view of the world. These catastrophic assumptions both reflect and reinforce investigators' view of their own responsibility and role: for safety investigators, an accident constitutes a total and unmitigated failure.

These assumptions are consequential for practice. One of the most immediate consequences is that investigators are less concerned with predicting the severity of outcomes than established risk models would assume. Accidents of any form are expected to be catastrophic and represent the outcome that investigators work continually to avoid. Investigators' primary concern is therefore not predicting and reducing the severity of harm caused by an accident – it is preventing the accident in the first place. The work and worldview of investigators is strongly oriented to prevention. As a result, investigators believe themselves to be less "hard nosed" (Si1-4) than risk analysts in other industries: they do not work with calculations of the price of a life or the expected numbers of fatalities from particular accident scenarios. Their catastrophic assumptions underpin an approach to safety management that is heavily focused on the prevention and avoidance of catastrophic outcomes.

Inherent failure and normal error

A related assumption that pervades and structures the work of investigators is a deep belief in the imperfection of organisations, technologies and people. Technical failure and human error are expected as an inherent and, to a large degree, unremarkable feature of organisational life. Failures are not viewed as abnormal or extraneous events that occur outside the range of routine operations, rather the opposite. Errors and failures are entirely normal. It is assumed that no organisational process is perfect, nor will everything work correctly all of the time. Every aspect of the organisation is "fallible and frangible" (Si3-5): people will make mistakes as part of their daily activity, and components will fail as part of their natural lifecycle. One investigator describes it thus:

> In an ideal world it [error] would be close to zero, but because of reality we have humans involved that think in different ways and act differently . . . if you put different people in different situations [errors] are inevitable. (Si3-9)

Error is an inherent feature of the "real world" (Si1-2) for investigators. It can be managed, with its causes addressed and its occurrence driven down. But there is presumed to be a lower limit to how far errors can practically be reduced: error can never be eliminated entirely. Technical equipment is viewed the same way. Faults and failures are understood as a natural part of operating large, complex technologies. Equipment can never be entirely failure 'free'. One clear illustration is the Minimum Equipment List (MEL) for an aircraft. These lists specify the technical faults that it is considered safe for an aircraft to fly with, in different circumstances and with various caveats – an organisational manifestation of this deep presumption of normal failure:

> It's like the concept of a MEL. A perfect aircraft has everything working all of the time, but there is no such thing. So you have a list saying if this doesn't work then you can go if you do this, this and this. (Si3-1)

Machines are not perfect entities. Any aircraft at any given time will have a number of defects on it, waiting to be fixed. For investigators, this is a normal part of organisational life. Organisational activities are designed to accommodate and account for normal error and routine failure. This assumed normality of error has important consequences for risk analysis. One implication is that individual faults or failures are not interpreted as simple and direct indications that a system needs redesigning. Neither is every error viewed as an aberration suggestive of some troubling and deep-seated organisational problem. Airlines are littered with errors and failures. They are ubiquitous, but only some are a valuable resource for learning and improvement. Indeed, the normality of error is one of the premises that safety incident reporting is based on: to allow personnel to report the failures and mishaps that occur in their day-to-day work (van der Schaaf, Lucas and Hale, 1991). The large quantity of incident reports that investigators deal with provides an ever accumulating mass of evidence that reinforces their view that error and failure are an inherent feature of organisational life.

Investigators live in a world of routine failure and normal error. The normality of error dramatically complicates the task of interpreting incidents, assessing risk and sorting signal from noise. This complication shapes many of the subsequent strategies of risk management and models of safety that are employed by investigators. Considerable work must be done to determine whether a failure should be considered normal or whether it represents something more troubling and problematic. Much of investigators' work is concerned with determining which errors matter, which don't and how to tell the difference. Errors, failures, defects and incidents in themselves are not used as a signal of risk. As is elaborated throughout the remainder of this book, difficult analytical and interpretive work has to be done to determine an event's meaning for organisational safety.

Catastrophic potential

Taken in combination, these basic assumptions of investigators underpin one of the core beliefs that shapes their work: that airline operations contain the inherent potential for catastrophic consequences. A core belief of investigators is that major accidents result from a unique combination of otherwise banal and seemingly trivial failures – the sort that can, and do, occur everyday. Investigators view their work as a continual struggle for safety: the potential for a catastrophic accident can never be completely eliminated and forever lies dormant in the routine activities of the organisation. Investigators immerse themselves in analyses of past accidents, the findings of which invariably present stories of unimaginably complex and unexpected disasters emerging from cascades of seemingly humdrum and trivial events. Common images used by investigators are the 'accident pyramid' or 'incident mountain', where the small peak of a major accident is built on a large base of minor events (e.g. Heinrich, 1931) or of small failures and mishaps 'linking' or 'chaining together' to cause a more serious accident. In both images, the understanding is that a range of minor failures, unremarkable in themselves, can combine together to produce a catastrophic breakdown in the organisation. One immediate implication of this is that investigators are deeply respectful and attentive to the data contained in incident databases. They presume that the organisation's next major problem or potential accident is "in there somewhere" (Si3-8) but in the form of apparently unrelated and seemingly minor operational events. Many safety incidents are therefore perceived to be normal, ordinary and expected – and also potentially carrying the first signs of an extraordinary and surprising catastrophe. This deep ambiguity in the status and meaning of incidents is a persistent concern of investigators that animates their conversations and analyses. Past accidents in the industry often provide stark illustrations of this for investigators, with one recalling the loss of a Concorde supersonic airliner in July 2000 as a definitive case of how small moments of failure can rapidly combine to cause disaster. In that accident, a small strip of metal fell off another aircraft onto the runway, the departing Concorde then ran over the debris, which caused a tyre to burst, which lead to fragments of rubber hitting the wing, which sent a shock wave through the fuel tank in the wing—which ruptured and started a fire:

> The classic one is . . . the causes of the Paris Concorde accident. And it's fascinating, the number of factors that led to that accident, fascinating. And any one of them would have stopped that accident, and yet they happen every single day – every one of them. You just have them sitting in your database day after day, after day, after day. (Si6-5)

Seemingly trivial failures and events, of the type that are reported to them everyday, can come together to produce hugely disproportionate effects and catastrophic accidents. Any minor event therefore has the potential, in some complex way, to produce an accident – given the liberal involvement of, in investigators' terms, 'Murphy' and his law that what can go wrong invariably will. (As it happens, Murphy's law was born in aviation and is originally attributed to Edward Murphy, an aeronautical engineer working at Wright Field Aircraft Lab in the 1940s.)

In practice, this deeply held view that any minor incident contains the potential for catastrophe consequences is in tension with common risk management guidelines and tools. A number of complications flow from this. Typical risk assessment models define risk in part on the predicted severity of future adverse outcomes. But investigators are professional pessimists. In their view, if they factored in all possible failures to accommodate the 'worst case' outcome – as some risk assessment guidelines recommend – then "every incident would be a catastrophe" (Si5-12). Conversely, when faced with risk management guidance that suggests only considering the failures that might reasonably be expected to occur, investigators feel it overly constrains their naturally dark imaginations, and conflicts with their view that accidents typically emerge from the most unreasonably complex and surprising combinations of events.

This conflict points to one of the key challenges in understanding the risk of safety incidents. If risk is assessed based on the predicted outcomes of an incident, the potential 'worst case' could, for investigators, always be catastrophic – any incident could conceivably progress unchecked and combine in some dire way with countless other failures to cause disaster, even if the likelihood of this occurring might be remote. In contrast, if risk is assessed based on the actual outcomes of an incident, in terms of the adverse consequences that actually result, then these are almost always trivial or non-existent: these are, by definition, merely safety incidents and not accidents. As such, neither worst-case predictions nor assessments of actual outcomes offer particularly sensitive frameworks for investigators to understand and differentiate risk. This disjunction between formal definitions of risk assessment and the deep assumptions and beliefs of investigators shifts their approach to risk analysis away from a predictive calculation of adverse outcome towards a more pragmatic and practical approach based on organisational capacities for accomplishing safety and control.

Controlling the ineradicable

The belief that seemingly trivial and ubiquitous failures have the potential to combine catastrophically is a key logic underpinning the work of investigators. Investigators view their work as an ongoing effort to continually manage the risk of potential catastrophe, tempered by a deep awareness that the risk inherent to many organisational activities can never be eliminated. As such, risk management is the art of controlling the ineradicable: airlines are in the business of flying aircraft, but flying aircraft always entails risk:

> The problem with safety management in aviation is that if you want to keep everything free from risk, you don't fly the aeroplanes. That's as safe as you can get. So you have to accept within the aviation

environment – and all of the transport industries – that you cannot make it free of risk. That defies human capability. (Si3-5)

This sentiment is often echoed: "The safest thing to do is to leave the aircraft on the ground. As soon as you take-off or spool up the engines, you are taking a risk". (Si3-7) And, "We're in the risk management business – the safest place for these planes is on the ground with no passengers on board" (Si3-9). The airline could be completely free from risk only by stopping what it does. Threats and dangers are ever present in organisational activity. The risk of accidents can be managed and reduced. But in this safety-critical context, as investigators see it, even a small level of residual risk can hold the potential for catastrophe. This creates a further consequential tension between their working assumptions and normative models of probabilistic risk assessment. Estimates of the likelihood of an accident occurring are of interest to investigators, but in many ways are viewed as being of limited practical use. A probabilistic risk assessment may measure the risk of an accident to be low: on balance, there may only be a remote chance it might happen. But for investigators, the potential for catastrophe nonetheless remains very real in the day-to-day operations that they oversee, even with extremely 'low' levels of assessed risk. This is illustrated with the vanishingly small probability ascribed to an 'uncontained' – and catastrophic – engine failure:

> We know that there is a 10^{-12} likelihood of failure of a full [fan] disk leaving an engine. It is improbable, but we know it is catastrophic, simple as that. We know aeroplanes can't be designed to withstand that; they can take a third of a disk. (Si3-2)

A remote statistical probability may offer some degree of comfort in the abstract, but in managing safety in day-to-day operations, "if it is 10^{-9} then that is great. But it still might happen tomorrow" (Si3-2). Low predicted rates of adverse outcomes, in themselves, do not confer any sort of active protection or assurance of safety. They are viewed as merely a prediction of a certain type of future outcome that is based on assumptions about the risk controls in place and the scenarios expected in a particular calculation: they are predictions based on expectations based on assumptions.

For investigators, even if a catastrophic accident is calculated to be a remote probability, it is still a permanent possibility. A vivid illustration of the strength of this belief is provided by Extended Twin Engine Operations, ETOPS, where twin engine aircraft such as Boeing 777 are certified to fly long distances over wilderness or ocean and therefore several hours from an emergency diversion airfield. These operations are stringently certified and managed, based on predictions of extremely low rates of in-flight engine shutdown and the subsequent ability of aircraft to conduct a lengthy diversion on one engine. But investigators almost relish highlighting that there is still a chance of losing power on both engines, that one investigator here calls '*x*':

> *x* is not zero, and the industry has to accept that the risk is there. And when you count the number of hours that commercial aviation racks up then you have to say that *x* is out there waiting for someone who is flying a twin across the Atlantic. At some stage they will have both engines failing. (Si3-5)

As if to prove his point – that the potential for catastrophe is lurking ever present – this investigator followed up by pointing out that, "interestingly enough" one carrier had an ETOPS aircraft divert into the Azores with both engines out only recently. This, presumably, was made all the more interesting to this particular investigator as he flew ETOPS twinjets across the Atlantic for a living.

Investigators live in the permanent shadow of potential catastrophe, and this deeply influences their understandings of risk and their practices of safety management. More bluntly, and in dark humour, the ETOPS acronym is on occasion recounted as meaning "Engines Turning or Passengers Swimming" (Si4-3). A constant feature of investigators' interpretive framework is a deep acknowledgement of the inherent potential for catastrophic consequences, the ubiquity of error and failure and the continual struggle for safety and control that this therefore necessitates. These core assumptions and beliefs shape the way investigators understand safety and the way they work to assess and manage risk in fundamental and far-reaching ways.

Concepts of organisational safety

Even superficially simple safety incidents, such as pressing the wrong button on a flight deck, represent a complex web of interactions between different people, contexts and technologies, and emerge from and are contingent on a convoluted organisational history. To organise and make sense of this complexity, investigators deploy a range of conceptual tools and practical ideas. These concepts are the fundamental categories through which investigators think about organisational safety and understand risk. They are the basic building blocks of the practical theory that frames how investigators think about risk and interpret organisational events. These concepts provide the vocabulary and interpretive framework through which incidents – and therefore organisational safety and risk – are analysed and managed. More fundamentally, these practical concepts are the lens through which investigators see the world, make sense of it and seek to manage and act on it; these categories and concepts are deeply consequential.

Defences: Resilience to operational failures

One of the core concepts at the centre of investigators' interpretive framework is a deceptively simple concept: that of the safety defence. 'Defences', 'barriers' or 'controls' are key concepts routinely employed by investigators. At first blush this is unsurprising. These terms have a clear and well-established history in the analytical and theoretical models – and metaphors – that are widespread throughout this industry and others (e.g. Reason, 1997; Hollnagel, 2004; Svenson, 1991; Flight International, 2004; Maurino et al., 1997; Australian Transport Safety Bureau, 2004; Vincent et al., 2000; Vincent, 2010). What is surprising, however, is the nuanced, subtle and complex way that the concept of a safety defence is applied and put into practice by investigators – and what this reveals about how safety is understood.

Investigators use the idea of a 'safety defence' to refer to any feature of organisational activity that is intended to identify, counteract, correct or contain operational disruptions in some way. 'Defences' and 'barriers' are ubiquitous terms that are applied to any and all of these organisational features, including routines of cross-checking, automated monitoring and alerting systems, standard operating procedures, checklists, training programmes and standardised work routines, to name a few. A simple example of how an investigator considers that "the system works, the defences work" (Si5-2) is the case of a communication error being caught and corrected through the standard read-back procedure that pilots use to confirm to air traffic controllers their departure details after take-off:

> An aircraft reports back they're heading to 17,000 feet, the controller says no, only 4,000. The pilot normally says apologies, confirm to 4,000 feet. And that is why the departure report includes [altitude] levels – so they can be confirmed and challenged. (Si5-2)

This routine of flight crew reporting back their departure details to Air Traffic Control to allow for confirmation or challenge is just one of a huge variety of practices that produce opportunities for errors to be noticed and corrected – and that are labelled by investigators as a 'defence'. Similar activities include the routines of flight crew cross-checking one-another's actions on the flight deck or the work systems in which engineers check off maintenance tasks on specific cards – cards that can then themselves be reviewed and checked by supervisors before an aircraft is released for service. These organisational arrangements are designed with the intention of ensuring that errors are caught and corrected. Likewise, on-board systems that monitor engine function and warn of irregularities, or provide an aircraft with multiple back-up hydraulic systems, are designed to allow failures to be identified and accommodated. Investigators view all of these, and more, as safety defences. In this usage, a 'defence' produces resilience to failures in day-to-day operations: it provides some capacity to catch, contain and correct the mishaps, disruptions and fluctuations that are inherent to all organisational activity. That is, defences provide resilience to operational failures and disruptions.

While defences and barriers are the pervasive and underlying categories, the vocabulary deployed by investigators is nonetheless rich and varied. Other common terms include "procedural nets" (Si2-4), "robust processes" (Si4-1), "checks and balances" (Si5-15), being "covered by systems" (Si3-3), "safety cushions" (Si4-4), "system redundancies", (Si2-7) "error tolerance" (Si3-1), "process controls" (Si6-4), "multiple back-ups" (Si3-9), "fail-safe design" (Si4-4), "excess reserves" (Si4-3) and "layers of protection" (Si4-6). These terms may not be synonyms, but they point to a common underlying idea. They are used constantly and liberally: they are the common currency of analytical talk.

Sociotechnical defensive activity

The prevalence of these terms should not hide the subtlety that lies behind them and their use. The ideas that underly the simple language of 'defences' is complex and nuanced. First, defences are understood as inherently practical. A defence is not seen as a static and independent entity or 'thing' but as an emergent property of practical work and ongoing activity within the organisation. Second, defences are sociotechnical. Safety is produced, by necessity, through the interaction and interrelationship of people and technology that, in combination, produce capabilities to deal with failure. And third, defences are distributed. The capability to deal with any specific failure is a product of the coordinated effort of a broad network of professionals and practices that are spread across the organisation and throughout the industry. Taken in combination, defences are therefore viewed as distributed sociotechnical practices: practical interactions between people and technology that take place around the organisation – and beyond – to produce the capability to handle operational disruptions.

When thinking about the underlying mechanics of organisational safety, investigators think in terms of practices and practical work. This is striking, given the highly systematised, standardised and technological nature of airline operations. Particular emphasis is put on the social and practical elements of airline operations, "because of the operational complexity in an airline . . . we rely an awful lot on training and procedures and supervision and those kinds of elements" (Si3-7). These social elements are always viewed with reference to the technology: operating and managing an airline is a technical business. But a premium is placed on the competence and ability of the people who do this operating and managing. Other investigators put it more bluntly: even the most advanced technologies are "deaf, dumb, stupid and blind" (Si4-1), and so the capability for ensuring safe operations hinges on the personnel who are designing, managing, maintaining and making use of those technologies. On the flight deck this is particularly the case. "Alert, switched on crew are important because a lot of the other stuff can lead you up the garden path or fail – at the worst possible time" (Si3-1).

Operations are rarely – if ever – considered to be effectively protected by technology alone. Technologies need to be used, monitored and maintained by competent personnel. This social grounding of safety is largely founded on a strong belief in the need for human control and understanding to assure safety. Consider the view of this investigator who had previous experience as an air traffic controller:

> I think of breakdowns in [aircraft] separation as 'controlled' and 'uncontrolled', which might sound strange, but if the controller was aware, and was actually managing, but the judgement just wasn't there on that occasion and they passed four and a half miles apart rather than five, was that really a breakdown? There was no surprise, they knew what was happening. But if the controller was not aware and they pass that close, you think, how did they get into that situation? (Si5-2)

The production of safety – and the substance of a safety defence – is viewed as an in-the-moment performance that depends on competence, cognisance and capability in undertaking the task in hand.

Despite investigators' emphasis on human control and understanding, a neat line is not drawn between the human and the technical aspects of organisational practice. The practices that produce defences are viewed as inherently sociotechnical. These deep interactions between people and technology are illustrated by one investigator's explanation of the automated traffic warning system 'TCAS', the Traffic Alert and Collision Avoidance System. TCAS is an onboard system that alerts pilots when other aircraft traffic is on a course that is conflicting with their own and likely to bring them into close proximity with one another – it is another 'defence' designed to maintain safe aircraft separation:

> You want to see the crew saying, we are likely to get a [traffic] warning out of this, and you want ATC to pick it up too. So that is a system getting close to the edge but the monitoring is good, so when the RA [traffic warning] does go off, the crew is ready for it. So that's a system that even though a defence operated, it didn't operate as the final, 'holy shit what was that?' So that is what counts, multiple systems and the crew at least having some knowledge of what is going on. (Si3-1)

Automated warnings need to be expected, prepared for, responded to and integrated into the repertoire of ongoing practical activity. Defensive capabilities are seen as interactions between social and technical aspects of practical work: resilience is founded on sociotechnical interactivity. The practices that produce a defence are considered to be sociotechnical – even though, for communicative ease and economy, a 'defence' is typically referred to as a single and static 'thing': the 'TCAS defence', the 'ATC defence'.

The idea that social and technical activities are deeply enmeshed in the production of resilience is represented by investigators' view of the Ground Proximity Warning System, the 'GPWS'. The GPWS is an automated warning system on the flight deck that warns the flight crew of terrain hazards. The system either notifies the crew that they are approaching terrain ('soft' warnings) or directs them to take avoiding action ('hard' warnings). Investigators often refer to the GPWS as simply 'a defence' or just 'GPWS', implying that it is a single thing that is either there and working correctly, or is not. But what investigators are referring to, as revealed through their detailed discussions and analysis of GPWS-related incidents, is actually a set of interrelated sociotechnical practices, rather than an automated warning system that is either in place or not. Investigators routinely point out that, on its own, the warning system itself simply provides an alert. Crews have to know how and when to act on that warning appropriately, they have to be prepared and capable of doing so and they have to notice the warning and react competently when required, integrating the required manoeuvre into the flow of their ongoing work of flying, navigating and communicating through airspace. Equally, the GPWS technology must be designed, built and maintained effectively, with the technology functioning as intended on the flight deck, continuously monitoring traffic and issuing valid alerts and minimising the number of false alerts that are issued. As such, the 'defence' of the GPWS terrain warning system is understood and analysed as an admixture of social and technical practices that work in mutual interaction. Social and technical activities each support, shape and contribute to the activity of the other. What is labelled simply a 'defence' is, in practice, less determinate and singular than often assumed.

Distributed defensive activity

The sociotechnical practices involved in producing and reproducing a 'defence' are viewed as widely distributed, taking place across the organisation and often beyond. Even an apparently simple defence is understood to be produced through a networked constellation of practices. To function as an effective 'defence', the GPWS depends in part on the appropriate practices of flight crew in relation to the GPWS hardware and the warnings that it produces. These practices, in turn, are shaped by training and performed with reference to relevant rules, procedures and prior experience. The delivery of training and the development of procedures are equally seen by investigators as organisational practices that are essential to maintaining and reproducing the GPWS 'defence'. Likewise, maintenance and testing practices by engineers in the airline's hangars, and the work of manufacturers in designing and producing the system and software updates, all fall within the purview of the distributed constellation of practices that produce this 'defence'.

As a result, investigators can become deeply concerned by, and involved in, how effectively the related crew training is being conducted and managed or how associated procedures are being reviewed and updated. Training depends on the practices of training personnel, and the details of these activities invite as much scrutiny – and are as relevant to investigators – as any other activity within the organisation. The same can be said of the development and maintenance of the standard operating procedures that govern how crews should respond to GPWS warnings. The work of updating an airline's GPWS procedures by an operations policy group within the airline was closely monitored and overseen by investigators. Investigators were keen to ensure that the new procedures being produced were practical, accepted and followed by crew. As one investigator recalled, "there was a lot of effort making sure flight crew saw the GPWS procedures as sensible, otherwise you're wasting your time" (Si2-1). Modifying and developing procedures is itself a practical activity, requiring ability and effort to undertake effectively, and is seen as integral to maintaining the effectiveness of the 'GPWS defence'.

Investigators hold a nuanced view of the basic mechanics of organisational safety. Safety defences are interpreted as constellations of distributed sociotechnical practices. Interconnected networks of practice produce the capability to deal with the disruptions and errors that are an inherent part of organisational life: resilience is produced through distributed defensive practices. A 'defence' is therefore not something that stands apart from organisational practices, protecting them from externally derived threats and hazards. Rather, safety defences are viewed as emergent and inherent properties of practice itself: they are the self-regulating, self-monitoring and self-correcting features of organisational practice that provide the capability for those same practices to compensate, correct, adjust and adapt to the variations and disruptions inevitably produced and encountered in operational activity. Defences are the features of organisational activity that, in simple terms, provide resilience to failure and allow operations to respond to errors and bounce back from momentary disruptions.

This view of safety defences as constellations of distributed sociotechnical practice strongly shapes how investigators analyse safety and assess risk. A consequence of this view is that similar ideas and explanations tend to be used to understand the activities and the mistakes of personnel doing the 'hands-on' work – flying and maintaining the aircraft – and of everyone else around the organisation, such as personnel in support roles and 'further up the food chain': supervisors, technical managers and directors. Because of this, investigators are at times sceptical of any safety analysis methods and classification systems that do not do justice to the complexity of organisational practices away from the 'sharp-end' of operations. When thinking about safety, relatively abstract or general categories such as 'supervision' or 'communication' or 'training' might be used by investigators to initially label a problem or to aid communication, but these do not provide much practical insight:

One of the problems is, when we do our analysis on practically everything that we do on the aeroplane, eighty percent of the things we look at, the defence is 'training'. And training is a very big word to say, well, what training, where and how? (Si6-6)

Understanding safety defences requires detailed knowledge of the practical specifics – the 'what, where and how' of organisational practices and how these interrelate with and support each other. General categories of defensive activity are used by investigators, but like the simple term 'defence', these categories are a simplifying shorthand: they provide economies of communication and convenient labels that serve to highlight and bracket certain aspects of organisational events within an otherwise complex, dynamic and ongoing flow of activity. Rather than seeking to classify different types of safety defence or general categories of failure, investigators are more concerned with the inherent qualities and characteristics of the organisational practices that produce and support defensive capabilities. The practical framework and pragmatic concepts that investigators draw on when analysing safety and assessing risk is examined in detail in the next chapter. First, there is a more fundamental issue to consider: what does organisational safety look like? What does it mean to be safe in a world of ubiquitous error, complex defences and the inherent potential for catastrophe? What is the working theory of safety that shapes investigators' interpretations of risk and their practices of safety management?

Practical theories of safety and risk

What does it mean to be safe in inherently complex, hazardous and error-prone organisations? Investigators understand the basic mechanics of safety in terms of defensive practices that provide resilience to operational disruptions. But a more nuanced and fundamental set of ideas underpins how investigators think about how organisations produce and accomplish safety. This set of ideas forms their practical theory of safety and therefore underpins how they understand, interpret and manage risk. For investigators, the meaning of safety is thoroughly bound up with the meaning of risk. The two ideas are inextricable. To assess risk, investigators draw on their implicit theory of safety: a theory which provides a normative ideal against which actual organisational activities are compared – and typically found wanting. Safety is understood to be more than mere resilience to operational failure. The ability to catch and correct mishaps forms the basis of organisational safety, but is not the whole story. Neither is safety understood simply in terms of the avoidance or absence of adverse outcomes. The avoidance of accidents is too blunt a definition of safety to be of any practical use to safety investigators. Instead, investigators understand safety in thoroughly organisational terms, as an organisational capacity that is produced by networks of defensive practices that protect organisational activity against the potential for catastrophic breakdowns. That is, organisational safety is defined and understood not as resilience to failure, but as resilience to risk: the organisational capacity to protect against the potential for operational disruptions developing into disabling breakdowns in organisational activity. As such, 'risk' is understood and assessed in somewhat relative terms, as the degradation of the organisational capacity to assure safety. Organisational risks are viewed as systemic deficiencies or weaknesses in safety defences which leave organisational activities relatively unprotected, uncontrolled and exposed to potentially catastrophic breakdowns. In practice, assessing risk is therefore both a more subtle and a more tangible process than attempting to predict the future likelihood and expected scale of some imagined adverse outcome.

Risk resilience: Ideals of safety

The practical theory of organisational safety that underpins the work of investigators is complex and nuanced. For investigators, safety is *the organisational capacity to protect operations from the potential of mishaps and disruptions developing into catastrophic and disabling organisational breakdowns.* This view of safety is not focused on how organisations handle failure and error as such but on how organisations handle risk: the potential for brief moments of disruption to develop into catastrophic breakdowns of organisational activity. The immediate role of defences is to deal with failures and errors – to catch and correct them if and when they occur. But failure and error, in themselves, are not the key concern of investigators. Their overriding and focal concern is the need to protect operations against the potential for catastrophe. And safety is understood as the organisational capacity to actively protect operations against potential catastrophe. When thinking about safety incidents, investigators are literally interested in "What are the things that stop this being a catastrophe?" (Si3-2).

In this view, safety is not predicated on defences merely catching failures when they occur and providing resilience against actual disruptions. Rather, safety is predicated on there being sufficient defensive capacity remaining in any situation to protect against the risk of failures 'developing further' or 'getting worse' – to stop a minor disruption developing into a major breakdown. This is a subtle but deeply consequential shift in thinking. It represents a broadening of attention to encompass the positive characteristics, organisational practices and latent capacities that provide resilience to the risk of operational disruptions enlarging and aggregating into something worse. This practical theory of organisational safety can therefore be best captured by the term *risk resilience*. Many of the details of this practical theory of safety become most apparent when they are being tested against organisational reality, and when that reality falls down: where organisational safety is determined to be weak or degraded in some way. Much of the work of investigators, and of safety management in general, is concerned with finding deficiencies in safety and then working to address those gaps. Investigators' practical theory of safety as risk resilience provides the broad benchmark and normative ideal, against which actual organisational events are compared – and typically found wanting.

How investigators understand safety determines how they understand and assess risk. Investigators understand risk in terms of safety – and its relative absence. Their ideals and working 'model' of organisational safety provides the notional counterpoint against which actual operations are compared. The degree of danger, threat or risk in any situation is primarily equated to the degree of deficiency or weakness in the organisational capacity for safety; operational risks are assessed as the degree to which safety is degraded. For investigators, degraded risk resilience leaves organisational activities relatively unprotected from and exposed to the potential for catastrophic breakdown. This notion of risk is frequently and simply explained by weaknesses in safety defences that open up the potential for catastrophe:

> I think it [risk] depends how many defences are in place. Have you lost one out of ten or one out of one? How well is it covered by other systems and procedures? That is partly it. Also, had you lost the next defence, was it going to be really terrible? Something that has the potential to cause harm is serious. (Si3-3)

Organisational risk therefore relates to the extent to which the organisational capacity for safety has degraded, and how 'close' a specific situation has come to exposing the potential for a further collapse in operational activities. In this view, the reference point for the meaning of risk has shifted. Investigators do not attempt to predict the likelihood or severity of a future accident, but instead assess the degree to which organisational activities are capable of protecting themselves against breakdowns when encountering operational disruptions. In practice, these ideas of risk, safety, defences and the potential for accidents are deeply interlinked. The connections that exist between these ideas represent investigators' practical theory of safety and support their practical approach to assessing risk. Assessing risk is viewed as akin to identifying where safety defences have been 'eroded' or appear to be weak: "looking at the defences is very much like looking at the risk" (Si6-1). Or as another investigator described it, "What we want to get at is the erosion of defences, defences being whittled away, the system not working – say, by robbing Peter to pay Paul" (Si5-3). Weaknesses in safety defences are considered a useful and practical way of understanding and thinking about risk. This is not simply to do with what defences failed or how far an incident progressed before it was caught. Investigators are equally concerned by what defences remained in place, what alternative means existed to contain or correct the situation and what additional capacity there was to maintain safe operations in light of the disruptions that occurred. In short, risk is indexed to an understanding of what could stop an event getting worse and how effective those remaining safety measures appear to be.

Investigators' practical theory of organisational safety has numerous dimensions and, as a practical theory, it is rarely articulated or made explicit. It is organised around two complementary and related principles which structure investigators' thinking and provide a foundation for their risk management practice. First, safety, in the view of investigators, is thoroughly organisational. That is, it is based on systematic, persistent and reliable features of organisational activity: things that can be counted on and assured. Safety is a product of organised and systematic activities, which is to say it is not the product of fortuitous skill, improvisation, happenstance or good fortune. As one investigator puts it:

> When it is down to a single piece of kit or just the crew, experience has proven that it is not a good defence at all in a lot of cases. It might be sometimes, but not across the board. (Si2-1)

Safety, for investigators, is systematic and assured. It rests on organised processes and dependable routines that can be counted on and exist 'across the board'. Isolated actions or fortuitous judgements might save the day, but they are not considered the basis of organisational safety. Safety depends on organisational practices that can be designed, trialled and tested, that are performed routinely and that can be relied upon – a view that is somewhat at odds with more recent ideas on the role of heroism (Reason, 2008) and improvisation (van Eeten, Boin and de Bruin, 2010) as sources of resilience and safety. Rather, organisational safety is understood as depending on the existence of persistent defensive capacities that are maintained and lie latent and dormant within the organisation, remaining in place and available to be activated as needed if and when disruptions occur. The GPWS, again, provides a clear illustration of this, with investigators expecting that this system will always be available, that crews will remain alert to ground proximity warnings and that GPWS alerts will always be followed, even if the crew are convinced there is no apparent danger:

> If you are below your safe altitude and you have a warning then you have to treat it as genuine, as every person that has crashed into a hill has got a warning and ignored it. They would say no, I know exactly where I am. Smash . . . Using your judgement when you're seconds away from hitting the ground isn't the right time to do it. (Si2-3)

Organisational safety requires having systems and work routines in place that are able to respond to failures – and making sure that those systems stay in place at all times and are activated when they may be needed. For investigators, their ideal of safety depends on ensuring there is a persistent capacity to respond to disruptions and to call on latent systems and work routines that are lying dormant, ready to be activated if needed.

Second, safety is viewed as depending on numerous and varied means to respond to disruptions and catch failures available in any operational situation. Operational safety, for investigators, is based on having a variety and an excess of defensive processes in place. For example, a troublesome issue referred to as 'sleeping receiver' problems was subject to active investigation in one airline, in which a technical glitch resulted in crews briefly losing radio communications. This is deeply problematic and concerning, and can leave crews out of contact with Air Traffic Control and other aircraft. Yet the overall operational situation is still one in which there are a diversity of protections:

> Taking the loss of comms event – the potential is a mid-air [collision] but . . . you've still got ATC radar, they've got alerts, you've got TCAS [traffic warning system], you're looking out the window, you've got HF [radio], you lose your HF you can come back. (Si6-5)

In any situation, organisational safety depends on multiple and diverse capabilities to deal with unintended and unexpected disruptions: social and technical redundancy. Safety also depends on maintaining excess defences and capacity in reserve, beyond what is actually called upon to catch a failure. Investigators are interested to see how well a particular failure has been dealt with and whether it was effectively caught. But they are equally concerned with what defences remain beyond that point: what further capacity is there to capture and contain an emerging problem; what variety of defensive opportunities are available? The ability to simply catch errors is necessary but not sufficient for safety. Organisational safety depends on there being excess capacity available in any situation to both catch a disruption when it occurs and to have the excess defensive capacity to ensure that the disruption could not get worse. Often this is put simply: "What stopped it progressing, what defences were left?" (Si5-1). This idea is clearly akin to the technical notion of 'layers of protection' or images of 'defences-in-depth' (Reason, 1997) – having excess defences in place beyond those which are immediately called upon. In any situation, organisational safety depends on multiple and diverse capabilities to deal with unintended and unexpected disruptions. A single defence does not assure safety.

In this view, organisational safety is represented by there being both a variety and an excess of defensive capacity, that is persistently present and systematically assured, to create 'distance' between current organisational activities and potential catastrophic breakdowns. In this view, safety is a capacity that is oriented not solely towards protecting operations against actual failures and disruptions in and of themselves, but rather is an organisational capacity oriented to protecting against the *risks* of those failures and disruptions enlarging, combining and leading to a serious collapse or breakdown in organisational activity. As such, there need be no adverse outcome or accident for safety to be deemed entirely absent. Safety represents a positive capacity for control: the ability for organisational activities to protect themselves against breakdown, not merely the absence of 'negative' adverse outcomes. While these are investigators' ideas of safety, they are also their ideals. Investigators want to see them represented in actual operations—though they are often disappointed.

Degrading safety: Undefended operations and exposed potential

Investigators understand and assess risk as a relative absence of safety. They do this by considering, in any given circumstance, what defences failed, what remained and the effectiveness and strength of the remaining defences that were in place. It is this latter point that is emphasised by investigators as being central to understanding risk, rather than merely analysing failure. This is because analysing the barriers that actually failed in any incident "shows how far it got – but not if it'd go further. Looking at the other side does, like if you have an altimeter problem it can take you through lots of barriers" (Si2-2). At the heart of investigators' understanding of risk is the potential for an incident to 'go further' – to get worse and lead to a state in which operations are poorly protected and therefore exposed to potentially catastrophic breakdown. The level of risk in any situation is equivalent to the extent to which activities are judged to be poorly defended, or entirely unprotected, from the potential to unravel catastrophically. Investigators' practical theory of safety therefore underpins their work of assessing risk.

In practice, investigators analyse the capacity for organisational safety in any given situation, in order to determine the relative risk that operations are exposed to. These assessments are focused more on processes than outcomes. Judgements often concern the efficacy of defensive practices that remained in place – 'what else there was' or 'what was left' to assure safety:

> I think the idea of looking at breached defences is a good, valid way of looking at [risk]. I think that is what we are doing in our heads – thinking of what was left. (Si3-1)

> You're making an assessment based on what is left, and the barriers are a good way of thinking about it. (Si3-2)

Weaknesses in organisational safety are typically interpreted as inadequacies in the practices intended to protect operations from the potential for uncontained organisational breakdown. Incidents are often described as indicating that a "process was slipping" (Si4-3), indicating a degradation in the control of organisational activity, rather than indicating that the actual consequences or outcomes of an event were of any particular concern. Critically, what is considered to be 'at risk' is the ability of organisational activities to control and protect themselves from the potential impacts of disruptions. In this view, the main reference point for assessing risk is therefore not a harmful accident or adverse outcome; rather the reference point is that safety itself is at risk: the organisational capacity for assuring safety is itself weakened or breaking down.

This orientation, that equates risk to indications of degrading safety, has an immediate practical consequence. It leads to the amplification and enlargement of concerns around what might otherwise appear relatively insignificant events that have negligible actual impact. Take, for example, an incident in which a take-off was rejected at low speed due to an 'engine exceedance warning' – a warning that indicates that fan blades in one stage of the engine have begun to spin too quickly, reducing thrust. The crew pulled off the runway and reported this back to engineering, but the required checks on the engine were not carried out by engineering because, as can often happen, the warning cleared itself and engine performance returned to normal. Complex machines do sometimes experience intermittent fluctuations and variations in their performance, and engine exceedance warnings are relatively common across a large fleet of aircraft. The aircraft was therefore allowed to depart, and the flight proceeded without incident. But as the reviewing investigator explained, it appeared that the appropriate protocol was not followed: "this wasn't checked when it should have been, so this is to do with the process of the event, although the actual event wasn't that serious" (Si4-2). In this situation, there was no adverse outcome to concern themselves with. And it would have been far fetched indeed to predict any serious future adverse outcome either, based on this relatively minor performance fluctuation in a single engine. But investigators were nonetheless concerned. The incident suggested that required checks might not be routinely conducted, and therefore the organisational practices around this aspect of operations may be providing less protection – and therefore be less safe – than expected. Organisational activities may be creeping closer towards unprotected territory, where operations are more exposed to the potential for small disruptions escalating unchecked into more serious ones.

The potential for a catastrophic outcome – a major air accident – is the persistent touchstone and overriding concern for investigators. But it does not provide the immediate reference point for their assessments of risk. The reference point is more tangible and concrete, focusing on the practices that support safety: to what extent do defensive practices provide the organisational capacity to catch disruptions and provide protection against any failures escalating out of hand? If engine warnings are not being routinely checked then, for investigators, this moves operations a step closer to an unprotected, uncontrolled zone of organisational activity. Increasing risk is represented by organisational activities moving towards the point at which there is limited or no systematic mechanisms to catch, control or counteract operational disruptions.

Investigators' view of air proximity events also provides an illustration of how much emphasis is placed on all organisational activities remaining within a safe and controlled zone of operations. Air Traffic Control processes that aim to maintain five-miles clearance between aircraft can be found lacking by investigators – even without any actual infringement of the five mile separation requirement. Even though aircraft separation itself did not breakdown or 'fail', weaknesses in the practices of "separation assurance" (Si5-2) can nonetheless suggest activities have moved out of an effectively protected zone and are beginning to expose the potential for severe breakdowns:

> Say, two aircraft pass six miles apart, so they have to be five miles [apart], but there but for the grace of God – it is good luck but not good management that they did [maintain separation], so we would be putting those down on potential. (Si5-2)

It is in these 'process' weaknesses that investigators look to uncover the degrading of operational safety and the potential for uncontrolled breakdowns. Without effective organisational controls, investigators view safety as being at serious risk – even when aircraft pass, in this case, even further apart than normal and without any adverse outcome resulting. Investigators take the view that in such circumstances of degraded safety, nothing materially 'bad' may happen and no adverse operational 'outcome' may result. It's just that it could. Safety is no longer being positively assured, and operations are becoming more exposed to the whims of 'Murphy' or the laws of chance. The organisational capacity for assuring safety is reduced, and risk is therefore increased.

This principle is further illustrated by one 'rather nasty' incident that caused a great deal of interest and concern amongst investigators for just this reason. An airline's aircraft had to reject a take-off, albeit at a low speed, having seen a 'Fokker' type aircraft crossing the runway in front of them, without permission from the control tower:

First investigator: The guy came across the runway, didn't respond to any instructions to stop. What else do you need? If the guy hadn't looked up, or there'd been some distraction at that point you would have had Fokker all over your windscreen.

Second investigator: Yup, that's Tenerife all over again.

First investigator: Add in some fog, him not looking up and you're there.

Second investigator: The potential's there. (Si4-1/2)

The reference to 'Tenerife' relates to an infamous runway collision that occurred there on 27 March 1977. Two Boeing 747s collided on the ground after one erroneously began its take-off roll while another was taxiing down the runway (e.g. Weick, 1993b), resulting in the largest loss of life ever recorded in an air accident. Here, it was the potential for a similarly catastrophic accident, resulting from the Fokker's runway incursion, that had the investigators concerned. They made no concomitant predictions of the precise likelihood or the exact extent of the damage and destruction that could ensue. Understanding the severity, scale or likelihood of the ultimate outcome was not their primary concern. What concerned them was the apparently clear weaknesses in the safety defences in this area of operations. To their minds, a small slip of attention or different weather conditions at that moment could have proved catastrophic. There appeared to be very little capacity to protect operational disruptions developing into disasters.

Of particular note is the fear and concern that is still generated by reference to a catastrophic accident several decades ago. These live on in the collective memory of investigators and continue to powerfully shape their practice. A similar, if hypothetical, example was provided by another investigator:

> If you [ask ATC for permission] to turn onto a runway and are cleared on it, start and then abort because there was equipment on it and it was a closed runway – like in Taipei – and we stopped without any damage at all and didn't even overheat the brakes, but if we hadn't stopped we'd have died, then that's an 'A' risk. The potential is so huge, it puts it straight up there, even though you have to say, well, it's only happened once in ten years, that's low [likelihood]. (Si2-1)

Again, as is common, a connection is made between a past accident – here the runway accident at Taipei, 31 October 2000 – and their own airline's current operations being exposed to the potential for a similar catastrophe. The purpose and use of past accidents as retrospective referents are examined further in later chapters. What is important here is the common linkage between the perceived potential for an uncontrolled catastrophe, the weakened defences in a specific area of operations and the level of risk therefore attributed to these organisational activities. This linkage is characteristic of how investigators interpret incidents and make sense of safety. Indeed, the 'worst case' scenarios alluded to by investigators are often strikingly cases where no actual harm results. They are instead where operations are entirely exposed to 'potential' – where operations are dependent solely on 'luck', 'chance' or 'the odds' falling in their favour: "Once you are down to luck, well, the risk doesn't get much higher than that" (Si3-1). Being down to 'luck', with nothing to systematically assure safety or provide resilience to risk, in what is considered an incredibly unforgiving, safety-critical environment, is considered "as bad as it gets" (Si2-1). In such a situation, operations have become utterly exposed to the potential for disaster: safety is lost. It seems, to investigators, that catastrophe is averted in such circumstances only through the sheer inattention of 'Murphy'. That, perhaps, provides the most succinct indication of investigators' theory of risk: the total loss of safety assurance and organisational control, leaving operations entirely undefended and exposed to the potential of brief disruptions developing into catastrophic breakdowns.

Organisational risk: Systemically degraded safety

Risk is interpreted by investigators as a fundamentally organisational phenomenon. Investigators assess and understand risks in terms of deficiencies and weaknesses in organisational practices and activities. Risk is not assessed as a prediction of the harmful outcomes of an incident. Rather, incidents may suggest operations are poorly defended and point to underlying and persistent inadequacies in the safety of organisational activities. As such, in contrast to standard tools of risk assessment, risk is not a property directly associated with or attributed to an individual incident or error. Rather, risks are viewed as organisational deficiencies: they are weaknesses in certain patterns of organisational activity and in the quality of networks of defensive practices related to an area of operations. Investigators assess risks organisationally, using incidents as fleeting symptoms of underlying, persistent organisational weaknesses. Reason (1997) terms these the 'latent conditions' present in the organisation, and investigators' view of risks closely approximates that idea. Risks are organisational in the sense that they are literally viewed as properties or attributes of current organisational arrangements: they are systemic deficiencies in safety. A risk represents the underlying and persistent inadequacy that exists 'in' the organisation and its current work systems – rather than the fluctuations, variations and transient hiccups that are routinely reported as incidents.

The practical consequences of this thinking are that, in day-to-day practice, investigators use incidents to diagnose where organisational weaknesses are emerging and where safety might no longer be assured. An often used example of this 'classic worst case' loss of safety is a hypothetical incident in which flight crew receive a 'hard' warning from the GPWS, to urgently pull up away from terrain – a situation where there is very little keeping the aircraft from disaster. But getting into such a tight situation in the first place necessarily means that lots of things in the organisation have already failed:

> The GPWS is the classic really, that's a worst-case, if you get a real one you've lost it really, it's one circuit breaker left to protect you. You are down to tight stuff. So there have been some major failings before the aircraft got too low on approach. The training has fallen over for a start. (Si2-1)

In such situations, the 'major failings' are interpreted by investigators to have already existed before the actual event – and presumably still exist after it. The risk, as investigators see it, is posed by these systemic organisational deficiencies and not by the individual incidents themselves. Reported incidents bring deficiencies in safety to light – but do not in themselves pose a 'risk', in large part because they are in the past: they have already happened and have been dealt with. The risk, rather, is a function of the associated organisational weaknesses that underlie this incident and presumably persist in the organisation. As such, organisational risks are interpreted as distinct from the actual consequences of safety incidents. Investigators consider the degree of risk to be relatively independent of the actual consequences and outcomes of specific incidents:

> Of course, a near-miss is the same as a head-on [collision], that is the whole principle, it is just the outcome that is less significant. (Si5-6)

> Some say, this is unlikely to happen so it doesn't matter – but funnily enough it matters when there is an accident. That is the mentality that I struggle with. The end result shouldn't matter. (Si3-1)

The 'outcomes' or 'results' of events are taken to be of limited use in assessing the safety of operations (e.g. Reason, 2000). Investigators hold the consequences of events in relative disregard – analytically speaking, at least. This is not to say that potential consequences and outcomes are irrelevant: far from it. Their perspective on safety is, after all, fundamentally shaped by their sense of the inherent potential for catastrophe and a keen understanding of what those catastrophes can look like. But predictions of the outcomes, or likely consequences, of incidents are not at the heart of investigators' practices of risk assessment. At the heart of how investigators make sense of risk are their efforts to uncover and assess the scale and severity of underlying systemic organisational weaknesses.

Consider the case of a straightforward engineering incident. An engineer had found that a torque tube for the flaps drive – which is an aluminium rod that rotates to move a control surface on the wing – had become 'badly worn' by running against an incorrectly routed electrical conduit. In reviewing this incident report, it was judged by investigators that the torque tube failing and the flaps becoming inoperable would be 'nasty' if it occurred in the final landing manoeuvre, the 'flare' before touch-down. As the investigator described, "We don't want that tube going, that'd be nasty in the flare, I don't know what would happen but it wouldn't be pretty" (Si4-1). The potential consequences of this event, and all others, are considered in only the broadest terms – that it would probably be 'nasty', not 'pretty'. The main focus is instead on the organisational practices that were implicated by the incident. How had the conduit come to be fitted incorrectly in the first place? Why hadn't the problem been noticed sooner? Was this an isolated case or is the failure common, with potential issues across the entire fleet and beyond? It is these organisational concerns that drive the assessment of risk – and not a prediction of how 'nasty' or 'pretty' the ultimate outcomes might be.

There are two key facets to organisational risks that investigators consider in their analyses of safety. First is whether these organisational features are permanently posing a threat to safety, and the threat is persistent: whether it is likely to manifest as a potential stream of future incidents that would eventually take their toll.

First investigator:	If you get this many events they will manifest themselves at some point, they will be one of the links in the [accident] chain because there are so damn many of them, that's why they become important.
Second investigator:	It's just the number of hits on a defence isn't it, and eventually it's going to chip its way through. (Si6-1/5)

Second is whether such systemic failures suggest, in themselves, further organisational failings – that the underlying problems have not been noticed or effectively addressed. Persistent failures are seen as 'organisational' in large part because they are allowed to persist. They suggest that the organisational activities that should deal with and resolve problems are themselves struggling, or inadequate, or absent. For investigators, this can include failures of their own monitoring, analysis and oversight work – issues which are explored in detail in Chapters 5 and 6 that follow.

Evidence of a persistent issue can indicate as much about the organisation's ability to manage and assure safety as it does about the specific factors implicated: "If you have lots of incidents, then it suggests systemically bad safety management. It shows poor management of the operation . . . Therefore sooner or later catastrophe will arise" (Si1-4). 'Risk' is therefore a category that is attributed to a particular set of features of organisational activity, rather than a specific incident or a predicted outcome. Investigators often emphasise this, describing the assessment process as one of considering the 'bigger picture' or 'bigger issues' that the incidents are part of. "It's not the risk of each incident report but the general risk level that's important" (Si4-2), and "it's in the bigger risk to the airline . . . rather than the actual events themselves" (Si3-3). Investigators look beyond individual events to get a view on the underlying organisational capacity for safety, and this is a defining feature of investigators' analytical work. Risks are seen as 'general' problems – the organisational conditions – that lie behind and generate incidents. As such, organisational risks are understood to be systemic in the literal sense of the word: they are problems that "hang around" (Si4-3), are persistent and so literally are systemic properties of organisational systems and activities. Assessments of risk are used to designate and bracket a currently problematic aspect of organisational activity – rather than being used to measure some predicted future harmful outcome. In this sense, risk is an interpretive rather than a calculative category. It is used to do work: to direct attention and focus further analytical work onto specific elements of organisational activity.

It is important to note that while risks are assessed as organisational conditions, their status as 'general' problems or 'bigger issues' does not preclude them from being tangible and concrete. Systemic does not mean abstract. And being systemic in nature does not imply they are unmanageable and hidden deep within the system. On the contrary, these 'systemic' risks can – and often do – concern highly local, practical and specific problems. The organisational problems that a risk represents are inevitably deeply practical issues to do with work practices, technologies and routines. One example is the use of circuit breakers during maintenance work. Circuit breakers, or 'CBs', on the flight deck are 'tripped' to isolate electrical equipment on the aircraft. This allows systems to be worked on safely by engineers, or it allows faulty or inoperable equipment to be deactivated while it awaits repair. Over the course of a few weeks a couple of incidents were reported that related to CBs having been miss-set. On the first occasion, the CBs for some cabin heaters were found by the flight crew to have been left tripped and 'collared' – to prevent them being reset – when they shouldn't have been. On the second, an engineering check revealed that the wrong CB had been tripped prior to releasing the aircraft back to the line: the CB adjacent to the one intended had been selected. This meant that: "this is a double whammy, something that should be deactivated isn't, and something that shouldn't be is. This isn't something to be sloppy over" (Si4-1). For the investigator concerned, these incidents pointed to a small yet seemingly systemic and general issue: "that's management of CBs there" (Si4-1). These incidents allowed investigators to identify and assess an organisational risk: an apparent deficiency in the organisational practices surrounding the management, selection and checking of CBs during aircraft maintenance.

Other cases can relate to more significant and prolonged issues, such as an issue relating to flight crew miss-setting flaps and, more broadly, missing items on checklists; and another to do with the maintenance processes surrounding the servicing of engines immediately after landing. These were all considered to be 'broader issues' and systemic problems in how organisational activity is conducted. But equally, they are all viewed as highly practical and specific problems that can be investigated and acted on. As one investigator put it, "These are our risk areas, it is part of the world, we've got to get into it, a specific thing in a part of the world. And then this is what you've got to do about it . . ." (Si6-1). For investigators, a risk is a tangible, practical feature of organisational activity that can be analysed, explored, managed and improved. Risks are systemic safety deficiencies in organisational activity. Risks are interpreted by investigators as inherently organisational in nature – and organisational activities are seen as necessarily practical. These assumptions, beliefs and ideas combine to produce investigators' practical theory of safety. This practical theory shapes the work of investigators and provides the interpretive framework within which they think about risk, make sense of incidents and manage safety. It provides investigators with a set of ideas, concepts, principles and ideals against which actual events are tested in the process of analysing safety and assessing risk. How investigators do this in practice, and the organisational characteristics and qualities that they pay attention to when they assess and analyse risk, is the focus of the next chapter.

4
Analysing and Assessing Risk

How do investigators analyse safety and assess risk? The way investigators understand safety – their practical theory – shapes how they think about and analyse risk. This, in turn, structures how risks are responded to and acted on. Investigators' practical theory of safety determines which features of organisational activity are attended to, which are considered problematic and which are viewed as acceptably safe, and provides a framework to distinguish between these. The previous chapter explained the fundamental assumptions, concepts and beliefs that constitute investigators' practical theory of safety. One of the central principles of this practical theory is that safety is an organisational property that is actively produced and accomplished through networks of defensive practices that are distributed widely around an organisation. These defensive practices provide resilience against the risk of mishaps and fluctuations developing into major organisational breakdowns. This chapter examines the specific attributes and characteristics of organisational safety that investigators routinely attend to and that feature prominently in their analyses of risk. It also examines how investigators assess risk and distinguish between acceptable safety and relative risk.

Investigators assess risk by analysing the quality of organisational practices that underpin safety in an area of operations. They work to discern where and how those practices might be weak and in what ways they need improving. The defensive practices that are implicated by an incident can be complex and hugely varied. To interpret and make sense of this complexity, investigators commonly focus on a relatively small set of organisational characteristics that allow them to determine the quality of defensive practices that support safety in any particular operational situation. These organisational characteristics and attributes are key elements of the interpretive framework that shapes investigators' analytical work. They provide a frame of reference that organises investigators' attention and structures how investigators identify, extract and embellish specific information and particular cues from incidents. What is striking is that these organisational attributes and characteristics of safety are not formally represented in the risk assessment tools or safety information systems that investigators routinely use to assess and manage risk. They are a culturally defined and collectively held model of organisational safety, but one that receives little practical support or reinforcement from organisational and analytical technologies.

The attributes of defensive practice attended to by investigators are also somewhat unusual in that they are applied to networks of practices in any area of organisational activity. They are applied to the front-line activities of piloting the aircraft and repairing engines as much as they are to the broad network of practices involved in developing new operating procedures, designing maintenance tasks, ensuring the safety of new airport stands or keeping aircraft documentation accurate and up to date. That is, these are attributes of the sociotechnical practices that take place throughout an organisation in support of safety, and encompass interactions between technology, people and organisational context. They represent the key organisational qualities of resilient practice that are routinely attended to, discussed, considered and challenged in investigators' analysis and assessment of risk. Each of these key characteristics of safe practice is examined in turn, before turning to how investigators assess and distinguish different levels of risk.

Qualities of resilient practice

Investigators routinely attend to and consider six key characteristics of organisational safety when analysing risk. Taken together, these attributes represent the qualities of sociotechnical practice that investigators believe are essential to accomplishing safety. These six organisational characteristics are:

- Ability: the capability that exists in any organisational situation to comprehend, prepare for, perform and control the required work tasks.
- Awareness: the degree of understanding in any organisational situation and the extent to which this is actively created, supported and maintained.
- Communication: the quality of the processes that share and integrate relevant information and build collective understanding.

- Verification: the effectiveness of practices that seek to confirm and establish that organisational activities are progressing as expected.
- Specification: the goodness of fit between organisational activities and how they are defined, designed and planned—and how those specifications are produced.
- Margin: the degree to which there are excess reserves and capacity in organisational activities, and how those reserves are managed and maintained.

Each of these represents a key organisational attribute of safety that is analysed and judged by investigators to be either effective or lacking in some way. As such, these six organisational attributes are key markers of the quality of the defensive practices and organisational arrangements that produce and support safety. Investigators expect all organisational activities to exhibit these six qualities of resilient practice. Deficiencies in these characteristics are interpreted by investigators as signs of weakness and potential concern – and it is not unlikely for several to be implicated by a single event. These attributes are not exclusive or comprehensive and in many ways are interactive and related properties of safety. For instance, if some aspect of communicative activity is viewed to be weak, this is likely to be reflected in a reduced awareness of organisational circumstances amongst those concerned and a concomitant reduction in the organisation's ability to effectively perform certain work tasks. Each of these attributes of resilient practice is explored and characterised in turn. After that, the ways in which analyses of these attributes leads to assessments of risk are examined in more detail.

Ability

Investigators routinely judge the quality of organisational practices on the basis of the underlying ability for a task or activity to be supported and properly performed in a given situation. Judgements of ability consider such things as whether conditions for a task are conducive to it; whether appropriate equipment is available and operable; and whether the personnel possess the requisite skills, knowledge and competence. At its most simple, investigators can become concerned because a supporting technology or piece of kit doesn't appear up to standard, as in the case of an aircraft tug at a new destination airport that simply "wasn't man enough for the job" (Si4-4): it was having difficulty controlling and stopping even an empty aircraft. But more complex judgements are common. A range of factors are perceived to potentially impact on the ability to perform in a situation. Unnecessary pressures or distractions feature high on this list. In the case of incidents of unusual fumes being detected on the flight deck, the ability of flight crew to perform effectively was seen as being significantly tested by these events. In some cases crews had donned oxygen masks as a precaution, which is an unusual situation, and with the masks on "they loose peripheral vision I'm told, and it's extra pressure" (Si4-4). As another investigator explained:

> It won't be the smoke that does it but the crew error. We had one where they had smoke in the cockpit and so went on oxygen, then they had an engine that felt as though it were failing, although it was reporting fine – and then the cabin crew came in to say there were electrical smells in the cabin, so they almost lost it in that sense. You have to look at the bigger picture, you can't keep subjecting the crew to that and expecting them to perform. (Si4-1)

Additional pressures and complications in such situations are regarded as eroding the ability for effective performance. In these circumstances, crews are not expected to consistently perform well. The overall ability of the work system, including crew, technology and their social interactions, is challenged.

Other sources of concern include error 'traps' present in the design of systems or technologies that can catch out crews and impact organisational ability. In one case, the ability to ensure the aircraft was properly set up for take-off was viewed as adversely impacted by a 'trap' arising from the introduction of a new automated system. The new system automatically calculated the aircraft configuration settings for take-off – settings that used to be calculated manually – such as the flap selection required and the various take-off reference speeds at which critical actions are completed, such as rotation. Historically, take-off had always been with 'Flap 15' set, but the new system could provide a range of more specific settings to optimise fuel burn and reduce noise. In one incident reported to investigators, a crew had used reference speeds provided by the new automated system, but reverted to the old standard flap setting of '15' out of habit, and only noticed once they were airborne. Selecting the wrong flap setting for take-off may seem a simple error to make, but it is also a potentially consequential one and brought ability in this area of operations into question. "The issue is that these are new procedures, and they followed the new procedure for the speeds, but did what they always did with the flaps. So this is a trap that they've obviously fallen into . . . they let experience override it" (Si4-6).

The introduction of a new automated system had created a performance trap that presented a challenge – albeit temporary and small – to setting up the aircraft properly. The ability of flight crew and the overall work system had been impacted by activities elsewhere in the organisation of implementing a new automated system and associated procedures. Organisational ability was therefore questioned in both these areas of activity. This is a common and repeated pattern in the analytical work of investigators.

Other scenarios that investigators interpreted as impacting organisational ability included occasions where the scheduling of maintenance tasks introduced what was seen as an unnecessary trap and distraction for flight crew, impacting their ability to perform. A minor technical defect on an aircraft had been raised as an 'ADD' – an Acceptable Deferred Defect that it is admissible to fly with for a time until repairs can be scheduled. However, this particular defect required the flight crew to manually operate an otherwise automatic system that moved the slats on the wing, which left two investigators unhappy. As they saw it:

First investigator:	This is just one more thing to be accommodated by the flight crew.
Second investigator:	Exactly, this is an avoidable man-made trap. (Si4-7/9)

In itself, the defect was minor. But by providing an extra and unusual task for crews during a busy phase of flight it had created an unnecessary 'trap' for the crew, added to their workload and potentially impinged on their ability to perform the task in hand. At the same time, it led investigators to question the ability of the engineering teams to 'action' ADDs – the Acceptable Deferred Defects that must be fixed within certain time limits. This particular defect was still within its prescribed time limits for repair, but investigators felt it could and should have been fixed sooner. Both the ability of flight crews and the ability of engineering were therefore brought into question, and became a concern for investigators. The ability of organisational systems to support and deliver effective performance is a key attribute of safe practice, and investigators seek to understand where this ability is being infringed across the organisation – whether that relates to the ability of flight crew to interact with operational systems and fly the aircraft or an entire department's ability to solve a particular problem or design and implement a new set of procedures.

Awareness

Considerable emphasis is placed on awareness, monitoring and cognisance as core qualities of safe practice. Investigators see it as essential that personnel, and the systems they work within, are properly aware and informed of the operational situation that they are working in or on – and specifically of the presence and nature of any problems. This awareness might be created and supported by technical systems, such as weather radar or TCAS, the Traffic Alert and Collision Avoidance System. It might be seated in the capacity of managers to build a picture or 'mental model' of the operational environment in order to manage or redesign an activity. Or it might be the situational awareness of personnel monitoring and supervising operational processes themselves. The latter includes, for instance, crews monitoring the autopilot and autothrottle – automated systems that ease physical workload for flight crew, but then require active monitoring to ensure the systems are tracking course and speed as expected. Investigators have high expectations of crews' awareness of these sorts of automated systems, as made clear by one investigator's blunt summary of a 'distraction type' event, where the autothrottle failed to maintain the required speed: "if the autothrottle didn't manage the speed then someone should be watching it" (Si4-1).

In contrast, investigators are comforted to see instances where crew are demonstrably alert and monitoring a situation effectively. In one case a display unit on the flight deck failed, swiftly followed by an electrical overheating smell and shortly after that the failure light for the unit showed. The investigator explained:

> This one seems fair enough . . . they knew what it was, the display lights came on and they noticed them. It's the unknown smells that you don't know where they're coming from and they sneak up on you that we don't like. (Si4-1)

The crew noticed the signs, understood what was causing the smell and were aware what was happening and why. This compares to more insidious situations that can "creep up" (Si4-1), with the crew not knowing what's causing them or being aware of the situation: "it is really as the defences slip by unnoticed, that is the problem" (Si2-1).

Being aware of operational problems and properly understanding them is an important attribute of safe practice and is important all over the organisation – not only on the flight deck. It is, for instance, a crucial aspect of technical fault finding by engineers, an activity central to maintaining the reliability of aircraft. One incident that illustrates this involved electrical smells in the passenger cabin during cruise. The smell dissipated when the In-Flight Entertainment (IFE) equipment was isolated. Later, on the ground, engineers examined the wiring and concluded the cause was debris around the wires. This debris was cleared and the IFE was reinstated for the return flight. More detailed investigation back at base revealed that unrelated screws had actually been driven through the IFE wiring. "They convinced themselves into thinking it was just the debris, so it wasn't investigated properly down route, a cock-up. Then later they found the real problem" (Si4-6). This fault finding and resolution activity was found wanting in terms of the production of awareness. The investigation was not thorough enough for the engineers to find the problem – particularly when there was an easier explanation to hand, leading them to miss the 'real problem' and therefore allowing it to persist. Indications of degraded awareness such as this are routinely identified and focused on in reported incidents. These are often referred to by investigators as cases of people simply having the wrong 'mental model' (e.g. Weick, 1989).

One noteworthy case from some years earlier was recounted by an investigator in which flight crew hesitated to respond to a terrain warning because, in the crew's minds, it just couldn't be true. As far as the crew were aware, the standard departure route that they were following took them straight out over the sea with no land for hundreds of miles. But, this was wrong:

> For me it was a classic wrong mental model, where they thought they couldn't get a GPWS [terrain warning], and spent their time convincing themselves they were somewhere else: 'Hey, what are those mountain goats doing up here, in cloud, over the sea?' (Si4-1)

The mental models that people work with, referred to here, represent the awareness and understanding that people have of a situation. These models are built on the basis of information provided by a variety of different organisational sources, technologies and practices. In this case, while the crew were cognisant of the departure plan, that plan had been incorrectly drawn up. Their shared mental model was in line with the standard departure plan, but the departure plan that had been provided to the flight crew had itself been produced incorrectly. The organisational systems designed to produce and ensure cognisance and awareness in this situation had failed. The attention of investigators is routinely focused on how a wide variety of practices around the organisation – and in other organisations – contributes to collective awareness, understanding and cognisance of specific operational activities. Indications that these practices are deficient can cause considerable concern.

Communication

The quality of communication between different parties is a key attribute of practice that investigators routinely attend to. Simply, this can mean the 'loss of comms' events that result from the 'sleeping' radio receivers, mentioned previously. But effective communication is not seen as simply passing appropriate information between relevant parties, but is viewed as a set of practices that build collective awareness and intersubjective understanding as the basis for coordinated action. Relevant information must be shared. But equally important is that this information is comprehended, and that it supports coordinated activity. It is relatively unsurprising that the quality of communication is a key concern for investigators. Communication problems are regularly found to be key contributors to adverse events and accidents (e.g. Reason, 1997; Sutcliffe, 2003). And, as Weick (1993b, p. 186) has argued, communicative practices are central to organising: "organisations are built, maintained and activated through the medium of communication. If that communication is misunderstood, the existence of the organisation itself becomes more tenuous". In front-line operations, meaningful communication is often referred to as the active sharing of mental models and effective coordination – communicating and interacting to build a collective and intersubjective understanding of the situation being faced, the activities being performed and the objectives being targeted. Deficiencies in communication on the flight deck, for example, are often noted as a crew not sharing their understanding of the situation, or working with different mental models – and therefore literally "they aren't working together as a crew" (Si4-3). Communication is at core viewed as a coordinative activity.

Investigators are similarly attuned to potential imbalances of communication, where junior personnel might not voice concerns to those in a more senior position, where "they were all being too polite" (Si4-4). Investigators are particularly attentive to signs that may be indicative of crew training and communicative norms that are not supportive of appropriately open and challenging styles of communication. The incident just discussed involving the incorrect departure plan and terrain warning was, in part, explained in this way. Ineffective communication resulted in an early opportunity to resolve the problem being missed:

First investigator: The heavy [off-duty] First Officer didn't say anything, and the working First Officer had stayed in another hotel – there was no social communication, in fact it was icy on the flight deck, like the Boeing 73[7] into Kegworth. The crew wasn't talking . . . It always amazes me how it's good people that get into these situations. The heavy First Officer said to me, 'I thought it was odd, but these are top people on the fleet'.

Second investigator: Mm, so you can die with the best of 'em. (Si4-1/8)

Investigators seek out and focus on signs that effective communication might be stifled or stilted or might simply not be as effective as it ought to be. This is as much the case away from the flight deck as it is on it, for other activities such as aircraft maintenance and repair work. Due to the collective way that maintenance activity is organised, with numerous engineers working in stages on the same job, proper explanation between engineers handing over a job to the new shift is crucial – as described in the rejected take-off vignette presented in Chapter 2.

Investigators are equally concerned with understanding the quality of communication across departments or between different organisations, and routinely consider the quality of those interactions and interrelationships. One area where a set of investigators began to doubt the quality of communicative processes was in relation to a technical advisory unit within their airline that passes real-time operational information between engineers, flight crew and those in charge of dispatching the aircraft. Following a few incidents where important flight information didn't appear to make it to the dispatchers, two investigators were quick to follow this up and harsh in their judgement, as advising and distributing information was seen as that unit's main role:

First investigator: It looks like they're not communicating with dispatch.

Second investigator: Along with all the others they're not communicating with. (Si4-4/6)

Communication is considered central to the coordination of operational activities and a key attribute of safe practice. Signs of weak communicative practices are a key focus for investigators. Effective communication is seen as essential to co-ordinating and binding organisational activity together, and is one of the core qualities of practice that investigators attend to.

Verification

Investigators routinely consider the extent and efficacy of practices of verification throughout operational activities. Seemingly all aspects of airline operations include means to check and substantiate that things are as they should be, usually several times over. These checks provide an important way to identify errors and failures in practice. For flight crew, checks and cross-checks of, say, the data input to the flight computers are basic and fundamental routines. Incidents are often interpreted by investigators as indications of problems associated with these verification practices. The practice of flight crew cross-checking each others' actions is a useful case in point – particularly regarding the setting of 'speed bugs' that mark the take-off reference speeds on the Air Speed Indicator (ASI). There was a known general issue on one aircraft type, where bugs that were incorrectly set on the Captain's ASI weren't often caught by the other pilot, as they were awkward to check:

> It's hard to cross-check from the right hand seat due to the angle of the dials, so this is a general problem and we're going to do something about it. They may be changed to all digital screens. (Si4-4)

The design of the flight deck here reduced the ease and efficacy of cross-check practices in this particular task. Investigators expect equipment to support practices of verification, and this deficiency was a concern. Practices of verification are likewise enacted throughout the organisation, and feature in a huge variety of operational activities, not only those that take place on the flight deck. Investigators are just as interested in these. One example concerns the minor defects listed as outstanding on aircraft, the 'ADDs' previously mentioned. These sometimes need to be recorded on to the flight plan as 'performance penalties' that may require additional fuel to be carried as a precaution. These defects and the associated penalties recorded in the flight plan are checked by dispatch personnel and then checked again by the flight crew, to make sure they match up. On a couple of occasions, flight crew reported incidents where they had found that a penalty was not reflected in the flight plan. For investigators, this indicated that the earlier verification practices had failed in some way, and needed attention.

Investigators pay similar attention to signs of deficiencies in practices of verification with maintenance checks and routine inspections. For example, one incident reported that during an aircraft's approach to landing, the speed brakes – flaps on top of the wing that are raised to reduce lift and slow the aircraft – were deployed, but one failed to extend. This caused the aircraft to begin to roll, which the pilot had to counteract. In itself this was deemed "a bit iffy" (Si4-3). Investigation revealed that the control cable for the failed speed brake was broken at the pulley and, as the investigator reviewing the event made clear, "this isn't very good. They should be inspected before they break, we don't expect failures on those" (Si4-3). As far as investigators are concerned, maintenance inspections should check for wear on control cables to make sure they aren't going to break – and replace them before they do. The apparent failure of this verification activity was of considerable concern. Investigators expect to see effective checking and verification across all aspects of operations. Indeed, verification and cross-checking is so deeply embedded in the way that aviation is organised that even flight computer systems are set up to check each other. Big jets carry three Air Data Computers for calculating air speed and such like, and the three are set up in a polling system to compare the calculations of each for reliability. The paradoxical question of who checks the checker does of course emerge here, and investigators understand that there are natural – and technical – limits to multiple checks. Practices of verification can only go so far:

> Duplicate inspection is more and more a thing of the past. That's how you used to tell that it is right: someone else came along to have a look. But it only works for superficial things – literally. If someone has taken a gearbox to pieces and puts it back together again, the only duplicate inspection is taking it back to pieces and putting it together again. All you do is wear the parts out. (Si3-8)

Nonetheless, practices of checking and verifying are seen as a key facet of organisational safety, and the qualities of these practice are routinely attended to and checked (of course) by investigators.

Specification

Investigators pay close attention to how well specified organisational practices and activities are and how closely those specifications represent and support actual practices. Specification most obviously takes the form of the established standard operating procedures of an airline or the plans prepared and followed by personnel during the course of their work. But specification also exists in numerous other ways. These include the precise operational envelopes that are set for equipment, the work routines and 'customs' established for countless manual repair tasks, the profusion of checklists that flight crew work through, the 'memory drills' pilots learn by rote for certain situations and company policy on, say, the reporting of safety incidents or the safety assessment of new destination airports. Airline operations are highly specified and standardised environments. In their analysis of safety, investigators habitually consider whether the appropriate procedures, limits, conventions or plans had been put in place, whether these are fit and suitable for the job in hand and whether they are practical and are actually followed. The attention that is paid to making procedures practical and accepted by personnel, as in the case of modifying GPWS procedures, has, for example, already been discussed.

Investigators commonly and frequently attend to issues of specification in organisational activities. Procedures and checklists specify nearly all of the routine activity of flight crew – and much of the non-routine stuff too. Crews' compliance with procedures is considered essential. In terms of the practices of flight crew, the first question is usually put the same way: "Did the crew action the checklist and follow procedures properly?" (Si4-4). The completion of checklists, in particular, is a common area of focus. For instance, one incident that was reported simply stated that the landing checklist hadn't been completed: the electronic checklist icon, that clears once the electronic checklist is fully worked through, was noted to remain on the display after landing. This was of immediate concern to the investigator concerned:

> This is a classic really. They didn't do the checklist, the captain seems to have done it off the top of his head. We're finding that they are not actually pulling the checklist out and reading it, which is bad as the checklist stuff is stuff that can kill you. (Si4-4)

Investigators become particularly worried by signs that crews might not be completing checklists thoroughly, as the actions specified in checklists are critical – "stuff that can kill you" – which is the reason the items are in the list. Instances of missed checklist items suggest to investigators that the specified control of organisational practices is being lost; it begins to suggest "things are not under control here" (Si4-2).

Investigators also regularly consider whether specified processes are properly constituted and designed – that is, whether they actually work as intended. Typically the answer is yes, but sometimes it can be no. The Quick Reference Handbook, or QRH, is a detailed document carried on the flight deck that specifies in rather abrupt language the actions that flight crew should take in out-of-normal or emergency situations, such as indications of engine malfunction or warnings of possible equipment failures. In the majority of cases the specified QRH actions deal with the problem, and after investigation it is commonly concluded that, "the QRH worked very well, that's well thought out, this isn't something to worry about" (Si4-1). But occasionally flaws can be found. Faced with electrical or other smells in the cockpit, one of the key instructions in the QRH is to isolate the air conditioning packs that draw pressurised air from the engines, in case that is the source of cabin air contamination. Even the order that these packs should be shut down is specified – and it was precisely this order that caught the attention of one investigator following just such an incident:

> In the [incident report] it shows that the crew actioned the QRH as far as shutting off the right hand engine [pack], so I looked into it and [the QRH] does say that, but that's no use as the cockpit draws off the left [air conditioning pack]. (Si4-3)

After further enquiry, it was decided that shutting off the left pack first was more suitable – a seemingly small point, but precisely the misspecification that investigators continually search for and aim to address. Such issues of specification are equally found away from the flight deck. Maintenance tasks are heavily proceduralised and laid out in the Aircraft Maintenance Manual, the AMM. For the most routine jobs, however, engineers rarely need to consult the manuals and sometimes develop collective practices on the hangar floor that are considered to be more efficient or straightforward than those specified in the manual. The rejected take-off incident, recounted in Chapter 2, demonstrates how the gap between these practical 'customs' and the actions specified in formal manuals can harbour a mismatch from which problems can emerge. These gaps can be exposed by, for instance, a new team member who does his part of the job 'by the book', unaware that the local customs specify different actions – as was the case when a few loose bolts caused a spurious fire warning during that take-off roll:

> Apparently it was a new person off [another aircraft fleet], he got the manuals out to do the job, and they say to remove all the bolts, but the customs and practices bit – you don't. So the guy that then came along to refit it only put the bolts back in that you would for the customs and practices. (Si4-3)

A common concern for investigators, here and in other cases, is not that the local 'customs' are necessarily wrong compared to the manual – but that the two should be in line with each other. Practices and specifications of practice should be consistent. "The problem we have with it here is that if it says all those things on the card then they should do them all. So the customs should be reviewed and woven into the AMM" (Si4-5).

Investigators routinely consider how well organisational practice are specified, not only in terms of the procedures and specifications themselves, but also in terms of assessing the match, or mismatch, between what happens in practice and what is specified on paper.

Margin

Investigators judge the degree to which organisational practices inherently create and maintain a suitable 'margin for error', or provide appropriate space for alternative options to be turned to, or produce and maintain reserves or 'slack' in activities (e.g. Schulman, 1993; Woods, 2005). Investigators are concerned with whether activities are organised with some form of 'excess' beyond the bare minimum required – whether of time, space, fuel, altitude, attention or any of the other sociotechnical resources involved in operating aircraft. This is commonly described as a 'buffer' or 'cushion'. Examples include the redundancy and multiple back-ups that investigators want to see in technical systems. Even the heavily standardised form of aviation English that flight crew use for radio communication – "victor bravo" instead of the letters "VB", for instance – adds redundant and excess syllables as a means of accommodating and reducing the impact of communicative disruptions. The number of wheels or engines are a simple case, where operations would not be unduly affected by the failure of one of them. For instance, one investigator's response to a report of possible engine surges on a jumbo jet's number four engine is typical: "If the engine is surging we should know about it, but this is one out of four so there's not too much wrong" (Si4-3). Similar reasoning is applied to other engineered features, such as aircraft tyres: "This example's very coarse, but say a tyre blew and you had eight, then it matters less to you; that is what you're doing [when assessing safety]" (Si2-2).

This deeply embedded notion is also reflected in jokes that are common in the industry. Investigators ideally want to be in a situation where the flight engineer can tell the captain that engine number *eight* is out . . . and the captain has to ask, on which wing? Another well-worn joke tells of an old pilot who will only fly aircraft with four engines – 'because they don't make them with five'. (Appropriately countering that, of course, another common observation amongst pilots and investigators is that when moving from a single engine aircraft to a twin engine, all you can be sure of doing is doubling your chances of an engine failure.) But margins are not solely about the technology. Investigators are wary of situations where, operationally, there is little tolerance of imperfection. Where, metaphorically, "you're trapped and you have got to get it right" (Si4-2). Investigators are interested in the extent to which organisational activities inherently provide a degree of latitude, or 'give', or 'flex'.

One simple case encountered relatively often relates to the length of the runway used. Investigators don't like to see aircraft having to use all of the runway to take off or land. And they are concerned by mishaps that are accommodated by a long runway – but may not be on a short one. Such incidents can include erroneously taking off with the provisional rather than final confirmed loadsheet figures. These figures give the weight of the aircraft and are therefore used to calculate the length of the take-off roll. "This was a small aircraft on a big runway, but if it they had been flying a big aircraft off a small runway then they could have had problems" (Si4-4). Likewise, a late landing – further down the runway than intended – due to a sudden squall is considered the same way: "this was on a long runway and you can almost do what you like, but on a different day somewhere else this may hurt them" (Si4-6). The safety margin provided by a long runway cannot be counted on everywhere, so investigators are worried when they see this margin being eaten up by minor errors, because such a large margin for error might not always be available.

Importantly, margins are expected to be actively produced and created by people – by personnel looking ahead, ensuring that foreseeable problems can be accommodated, and by making alternative plans to deal with problems if they are encountered. 'Alternate' destination airports are always planned for flights, and it is not unusual for aircraft to divert to them: "shit happens and that's why we have alternates" (Si4-6). What concerns investigators is when these alternates or escape routes have not been planned effectively – for instance, if the air conditioning systems failed and there is not the possibility of rapidly descending 'into oxygen', for instance, while over-flying a high mountain range on a particular flight plan. Equally, investigators pay special attention to whether the practices of flight crew planning ahead for contingencies are effective. One basic element of this involves maintaining fuel reserves, both as a 'safety cushion' in case of delay and to keep options open for diverting to another airfield if unexpected problems are encountered. To maintain this margin, crews "should be taking the decision early" (Si4-1) whether or not to divert, before fuel levels run too low. Here, as in other areas, investigators literally want to see people acting early to preserve and maintain their back-ups and reserves, rather than having to use them – or even worse, relying on them. This was clearly illustrated by an instance where a crew landed with less than the specified reserve fuel on board as it had been used waiting for a snow storm to pass:

> They had forty minutes of hold fuel . . . the hold turned out to be forty two minutes, then a heavy snow storm came out of nowhere – well they just don't come out of the blue! To me that's poor management and planning, it's all going to plan but they're not looking far enough ahead. (Si4-1)

Personnel should be actively producing margins and enacting 'slack' into their work (Weick, 1987). Likewise, investigators do not like to see engineers waiting until the last few days of the time period allowed on an ADD – an Acceptable Deferred Defect – to fix it. That is a sign, to them, of a department failing to maintain effective slack and margin in its activities, with the direct consequence of allowing defects to persist for a longer period in the organisation than is necessary. Investigators consider it important to see practices that actively maintain and preserve safety margins, as much as there being effective margins in place to start with, and they pay a great deal of attention to signs that these margins may be eroding.

Assessing organisational risk resilience

Investigators assess the quality of organisational safety – and the level of underlying organisational risk – along a broad spectrum. Investigators themselves typically describe incidents as representative of one of three 'types' or categories of risk. At one end are those where the underlying risk currently appears to be minor and is considered fairly insignificant in terms of maintaining organisational safety. At the other end is where an incident suggests there is a serious organisational problem or major issue to be dealt with: "the big ones" (Si4-3). Both of these categories are often viewed as relatively 'easy' to assess by investigators. In the middle are those that are more tricky: those in the 'mid-range' that suggest that operations are not as well defended or controlled as they could or should be – but, while performance does not appear to be up to appropriate standards, it is equally not entirely out of range or massively deficient:

> The middle category is one where something goes wrong, and they tend to be a little bit unique. They're all ones that say that something has gone wrong that shouldn't really go wrong. We have looked at this kind of thing before, and we built the aircraft this way, and we did this thing this way, and hmm, I am a bit irked that this has gone wrong. (Si3-7)

The state of safety in different areas of the organisation is therefore assessed, in light of the various attributes previously described, as exhibiting some degree – or absence – of risk resilience. Judgements are spread out across a wide range, but tend to fall into these three distinguishable categories, each of which is broadly linked to levels of action and response required within an organisation. The first category is where defensive practices are judged to be adequate and currently acceptable. Second is where risk resilience is considered to be reduced and exists in a somewhat deteriorated state. And third, where risk resilience is entirely degraded, deficient or absent. These categories are not merely analytical, but carry with them strong value judgements and implications and imperatives for action – assessment is not applied dispassionately. Adequate risk resilience is considered acceptable; the assessments that fall in the latter two groups are not, to varying extents.

This tripartite categorisation is in part a simplification, but it provides the broad structure within which risks are assessed and described by investigators. Assessments of organisational safety are complex. They draw together a range of subtle judgements on the various qualities of risk resilience, the degree to which any apparent deficiencies are potentially widespread or localised, and the extent to which these problems are systematic or haphazard. But they are, nonetheless, roughly partitioned into these three categories, where risk resilience is deemed acceptable, reduced or degraded. Or, as investigators would have it: the good, the bad and the ugly.

Acceptable risk resilience

Acceptable risk resilience is, for investigators, a close approximation of their ideal of safety. It broadly represents the 'normal' and unproblematic condition of operations being effectively and adequately protected against the potential for disruptions escalating. Many incidents are interpreted as indicating that – for the moment, at least, and in some specific area of operations – organisational practices appear to be effective and robust. These incidents are commonly referred to as being little more than minor 'inconveniences' that are effectively dealt with, rather than being any sort of 'real' problem. It is debatable whether these sorts of incidents are even seen as safety incidents at all or are simply "all part of normal operations" (Si4-4) – the normal operations that can adequately catch, compensate for and correct the anomalies and disruptions commonly encountered. Incidents that are interpreted as suggesting acceptable risk resilience are those that are expected and accepted features of normal airline operations. Indeed, some events can be viewed in a wholeheartedly positive light. Aborted landings, 'go-arounds', are a good example. Investigators are often pleased to see well-executed and appropriate go-arounds being performed and reported. This is especially so if the incident appears to demonstrate alert, able and well-communicating crew, who are planning ahead and acting with proper caution – such as calling the go-around early when there is a chance they wouldn't be stable for landing by the final 'gate' check at 500 feet. One incident was commented on as being an example of good airmanship. It reported a crew calling a precautionary go-around at only 100 feet, after they encountered unexpected turbulence: "They're always exciting, but that's good flying. The wise crew goes around" (Si4-1). Acceptable risk resilience is evinced by incidents that suggest that little is untoward in the organisational practices involved. However, this assessment is not proof of safety. Rather, it is a judgement that there appears to be, for now, relatively little evidence that causes concern: the organisational activities associated with an incident appear acceptably risk resilient – for the time being.

Some incidents can occasionally bring with them expensive consequences, such as ground damage to an aircraft. But the organisational processes concerned might still be interpreted as adequate and bear few implications for safety. As one investigator explained:

> Five weeks ago they towed an [Airbus] A330 into the back of a [Boeing] 777. Tremendous amount of damage. $3 million and an aircraft on the ground for a month. We were just getting over that one when they did it again, but this time they towed a [747] 400 under the tail of a 737. . . These are very expensive ones that get the attention of the leadership team and they say, got to do something about it, of course. But in fact, in the big picture, they are literally 'accidents' – the processes are good, the procedure is good, the training is good. It's just that on that day, something conspired against them. (Si3-8)

In these two cases – that were by chance expensive – the organisational activities concerned were not deemed to be suffering from any systematic deficiency. Occasional ground-handling problems on busy and congested airport stands are, to a degree, expected. Despite the unusually expensive outcomes, the incidents were largely viewed as the sorts of normal fluctuations and mishaps that characterise ordinary ground-handling work. The events did not provoke concerns that the related organisational activities were deeply flawed. But this is not to say that all aspects of ground-handling activities were therefore seen as 'safe'. This view did not prevent other aspects of ground handling or other processes of producing ground damage, from being interpreted differently – such as the parking problems recounted in the vignette in Chapter 2. It was just that the specific processes implicated in this incident were, for the time being, considered to be adequate despite the unfortunate confluence of events 'on that day' that resulted in a costly outcome.

Other instances in which incidents are commonly interpreted as representing no deficiency in risk resilience, but rather that operations are acceptably defended, are the occurrence of some types of aircraft 'configuration warnings'. These 'config' warnings sound a horn whenever the aircraft systems sense that they are not configured appropriately for the current phase of flight. In some cases, as discussed shortly, these warnings can be the last line of defence – and their occurrence very bad news indeed. But, in different circumstances, config warnings could represent next to no threat at all and have no negative implications for safety. For instance, in busy airspace the flight crew are often requested by Air Traffic Control (ATC) to slow the aircraft quickly and so select full landing flaps to help them lose speed, before they have lowered the landing gear. So the system "sounds an alarm to say hang on, you have landing flaps but no gear" (Si4-3). But the crews expect the alarm, know why they've got it – and have actually caused it by their rapid and adaptive response to an ATC request – so to investigators this doesn't reflect badly on the practices involved. It is part of normal, well-controlled operations. Equally, config warnings sound if the gear aren't all pointing straight ahead when take-off power is applied. If this is due to crew inattention, general sloppiness or an inappropriately small turning circle being available at the end of the runway, and the crew were just about to take off heading sideways off the runway, then that would be deeply problematic to investigators. But such config warning events may equally suggest that risk resilience remains acceptable:

> This is a standard event, a gear config warning. Often you find they apply power just to get through the turn [onto the runway] when

the body wheels aren't straight, and they get the warning. Here it's slightly different as they powered up the engines for a de-icing run while the gear weren't straight. But the risk is zilch, the warning system is there to tell them the gear are not straight, and that's what it did . . . It's when it's not there that we worry. (Si4-4)

Here, the crew remained in control, the warning wasn't a sign that operations were down to their last defence, and nor did the event indicate there was any systemic problem in the way crews were setting up aircraft for take-off. Context, intention and awareness are important: such events are not interpreted by investigators as meaning that organisational safety has deteriorated. Many incidents, in the view of investigators, are therefore "non-events" (Si5-1). A minor slip or fluctuation in performance is adequately caught and is acceptably protected against. Organisational activity is considered, for the time being and under these specific circumstances, to be appropriately defended and under control.

Reduced risk resilience

Reduced risk resilience is a broad and varied category that captures investigators' judgements that certain defensive practices, in specific areas of operations, appear to be performing at a reduced level. Practices underpinning organisational safety are interpreted as being less robust and effective than they should be – risk resilience is reduced in some way. These assessments are made by investigators with respect to events that point to some underlying and consistent organisational flaw or inadequacy. These flaws are systemic properties of organisational practices that are judged to negatively impact on the safety of operations, but they do not represent a dramatic or extreme loss of safety assurance. Operations remain protected but less so than investigators would want or expect. Reduced risk resilience signifies those judgements made by investigators that organisational practices appear to deviate from, or fail to satisfy, investigators' ideal of organisational safety: where safety is less than optimal.

Judgements of this kind do not indicate an outright breakdown of safety. One case in point involved drinks cans and empty water bottles – apparently innocuous objects that can become serious hazards on the flight deck. A number of incidents had occurred where empty drinks cans and bottles were found on the floor of the flight deck, wedged behind the rudder pedals. On reviewing these incidents, the most immediate concern of investigators was that these cans could cause an obstruction and prevent full use of the rudder:

> This could catch you out on landing with a cross wind, they might not get full rudder pedal. This is piss poor, it's basic cleanliness, it's obviously got there from a prior crew. (Si4-1)

This relatively simple lapse could have a disproportionate and dramatic effect on the crew's ability to simply control the aircraft. To investigators, this represented extremely poor practices surrounding this area of operational activity. Moreover, it seemed to be a persistent problem. In one event, the can had been picked up by security, not the flight crew on their check, "so it's obviously been there a while" (Si4-1). This problem had been encountered before the previous summer, so this incident was "a repeater" (Si4-6), or rather it was "a repeat of a spate" (Si4-4) of identical incidents that investigators thought had been solved by putting in place an extra check by the crew and raising crew awareness by putting out "a load of comms" (Si4-4) on it, such as in the crew newsletters and through the fleet captains. But investigators concluded that, clearly, practices were still not up to scratch in this area. As two investigators commented, on different occasions, "the processes aren't robust enough here", (Si4-4) and "we need more robust processes to catch this" (Si4-1). Investigators accept the practicalities of life: flight crew need to drink, and drinks containers may sometimes get dropped. Their focus was on getting more effective and more routine checks in place to ensure that these errors were identified, and that rudder pedals were kept free from obstruction. In this case, just as in many others, organisational practices in a specific area of operations were judged to be less than adequate – even if not completely defective – by investigators.

Occasions of reduced risk resilience can be complex, problematic and long-lived. A more complex case concerned activities surrounding the monitoring and servicing of engine oil levels, which were, for a time, suspected of causing intermittent smells of oil fumes in the cockpit – an issue that had emerged across the industry. This had become an ongoing and complicated issue that "was rattling around for a long time, and not being solved to too great an effect" (Si3-3). It first arose as a few instances when brief oil smells were detected by crew on the flight deck. Over time similar events accumulated, and extensive investigation by several airlines, manufacturers and safety agencies failed to pin down the underlying cause. This therefore had become "quite an issue" (Si3-3) that was causing considerable consternation – both within the airline and the broader industry. Operationally it was of particular concern as it occasionally resulted in flight crew being required to don oxygen masks, which put extra pressure on them. There are also, of course, health concerns related to breathing contaminated air.

From a flight safety perspective, some investigators' main concerns around this issue focused on the deficiencies in the organisational activities from which the problem appeared to have emerged in the first place, and the ongoing difficulties experienced in resolving it. A prime focus for investigators was a change in engineering policy away from individual engineers meeting each aircraft on arrival. They suspected that this may have affected aspects of the subsequent servicing activities, some of which needed to be completed within a fifty-minute window – between ten minutes and one hour after engine shutdown. After that, gradual oil seepage in the system may, they suspected, produce invalid readings of oil levels and lead to difficulties in servicing the engines. To add an extra layer of complexity, the electronic gauges and indicators on the flight deck only read up to '20', which was 'full', and not beyond. So neither engineers nor crew could easily tell if an engine was 'over serviced' and over-filled with oil. This may or may not have been the primary cause of the intermittent incidents, but investigators nonetheless judged that a range of organisational practices were less than effective and needed improving in this area. These ranged from whether flight crew knew the appropriate levels at which they should request servicing prior to a flight, to whether the level at which the system was 'full' was specified appropriately, to the change management processes surrounding the change in engineering policy along with the incident investigation processes in the departments concerned. So to investigators, the capacity for risk resilience was judged to be reduced, based on a range of organisational activities that appeared to be sub-optimal in this area of operations. Here, and in a wide range of other areas, risk resilience can be judged to be reduced and at varying levels of deterioration.

Degraded risk resilience

An assessment that organisational risk resilience is seriously degraded is the most serious that an investigator can make. There is a distinct and clear division between these judgements and those that fall into the other categories. This situation is, as far as investigators are concerned, 'as bad as it gets'. A judgement of this kind represented a belief that defensive activities in an area are systematically deficient, and provide only few or weak protections against minor disruptions and failures escalating into major ones. In such cases, investigators consider that relative safety in an area of operations has essentially been lost. This is as close an approximation of pure 'danger' – or risk – that exists for investigators. It is a judgement that the defensive practices intended to stop failures progressing are clearly degraded or unreliable. Put another way, it is where operations appear to be getting worryingly close to a situation in which there is very little to separate current operations and the whims of 'Murphy'. In such circumstances, "there is no next step" (Si4-2), no stage to move on to – aside from being completely exposed to potential catastrophe. This situation is like 'having one circuit breaker left to protect you', as one investigator recounted in relation to getting a final warning from the Ground Proximity Warning System.

Yet making an assessment that safety is totally degraded does not mean that catastrophe is bound to arise, or that there has been any adverse outcome. Far from it. Investigators believe that the organisation could carry on (and perhaps has been carrying on) in such a degraded condition for some length of time, without operations actually suffering a disastrous break down or harmful event. But safety is no longer assured: safety assurance is judged to have completely broken down. These judgements, as with all others, depend on a detailed understanding of the nature and status of organisational activities that surround a particular aspect of operations. Such a serious degradation of safety could, for instance, be flagged by a configuration warning event – that under different conditions can just as easily indicate acceptable safety. For instance, receiving a valid and unexpected configuration warning immediately prior to take-off is, "just one system that is keeping you away from disaster, as if the flaps aren't set it will be a smoking heap at the end of the runway" (Si3-3).

Investigators are seriously concerned when they identify an area of operations that appears to exhibit degraded risk resilience – and some worried that activities around pre-flight checks was one area that may just be starting to show the first signs of this. There are multiple defences to ensure that flaps are set before take-off, because without them the aircraft is unlikely to fly. Investigators noted with concern that there appeared to be specific problems emerging around crew completing pre-flight checklists – which constitute several of the key checks and procedures to ensure that flaps are set. All items on a checklist are considered important, and investigators worry if any are missed. As they said, these items are on the lists because they're not things that can be trusted to memory and many of them are there from hard-won experience: "lots of these items we've seen before in previous accidents, so it's worrying" (Si4-6). But on several occasions, investigators encountered incidents where crew were reporting that the flaps, in particular, had not been set at the appropriate time. These situations had been noticed and corrected by crews, usually sooner but sometimes later, and always before getting a configuration warning. A few incidents reported that crews had begun to taxi without the flaps set, but then the next (double check) checklist picked up the omission. Others reported that the crew did not appear to be communicating well while other things were going on – distractions such as radio calls:

> This is poor communication and a misselect, this is not doing the checklist properly then inadvertently pressing buttons . . . A lot of them are inadvertent and corrected immediately, as a result not a lot happens. The problem is if they do it and don't realise, and then get a warning. But in this case, he misheard the Captain and it was corrected immediately. (Si4-4)

In most of these incidents, the crew caught their error either immediately or in the next check. So, as this investigator pointed out, not much happens. There is still at least one defensive layer remaining – the config warning – as well as the monitoring and attention of the crew. But neither, on their own, are things that investigators believe could be counted on in isolation to assure safety. Investigators become worried about operations getting close to their 'worst case' situation – where the final config warning is activated and therefore where they are down to the 'last defence'. Further, with an accumulating – though still small – number of incidents related to this issue, investigators were beginning to suspect that this problem may be growing across that aspect of operations. These early signs of degraded risk resilience were interpreted as a systemic and deep-rooted problem, and such concerns can provoke a strong response from investigators:

Investigator: Here's another taxi without flaps. We're getting too many of them.
Researcher: Has there been a lot?
Investigator: There's been about a hundred. They're getting good at it. It's a checklist item and they're not finishing it, they get distracted or move onto another thing and then don't come back to it, then go to take-off and go 'oh'.

Researcher: Would they get another warning with that?
Investigator: Yeah, when you go to apply take-off power, but that's the last defence, so if that's not working then the aircraft ain't flying. Or it'll fly for a bit but then not fly. They're saying here ATC [Air Traffic Control] asked them to change runway. Bullshit, they're meant to be working through the checklist items and they clearly haven't. We need to get to the bottom of it. (Si4-6)

For investigators, it is not the specific crews or the individual incidents that needed to be 'got to the bottom of'. It is the issues surrounding why these organisational practices appeared to be becoming fragile and weakened, why there were signs that safety was no longer being assured in this area, and why risk resilience was perceived as degrading. Emotions can run high and feelings can be strong around such issues. Investigators feel a keen imperative to deal with these problems, and worry deeply about the emergence of a gap in risk resilience. This situation, for them, represents an extremely close call: where operations appear to be close to approaching a situation where defensive practices are breaking down and exposing the potential for catastrophe.

5
Overseeing and Monitoring Safety

How do investigators oversee safety and monitor risks? Monitoring the state of safety, and identifying where organisational safety is potentially degrading, is a primary objective of risk management and is one of the most fundamental aims of flight safety investigators. Monitoring and overseeing safety requires investigators to maintain a clear picture of the current state of safety across organisational activities and to notice and pick up on any early signs of emerging risks. This is challenging interpretive work that itself presents a range of risks and threats. If the early signs of risks are missed or misunderstood by investigators at this stage, then those risks are likely to remain hidden within organisational activities for some time – until they are realised in more serious, surprising and possibly harmful ways. Explaining the practical work of safety oversight therefore requires understanding how investigators view and address the interpretive challenges that they face, how they maintain up-to-date knowledge of organisational activities and risks, as well as how those risks come to be known about and identified in the first place. The previous chapters have examined how investigators understand organisational safety and analyse risk. This chapter takes a different angle and explores how investigators understand the risks and the challenges inherent to their own work of safety oversight and risk analysis.

The perspective that investigators bring to their own oversight and monitoring work is the focus here. This perspective consists of their basic assumptions about the purpose of their safety oversight and risk analysis work, and the challenges that face them in these activities. At base, both are about knowledge. Investigators see the role of safety oversight as one of maintaining effective knowledge of organisational risks. Oversight is about them being certain and sure – or assured – of safety: their work is an ongoing process of safety assurance. And crucially, it is also about knowing where safety is not acceptable and needs improving. Monitoring safety and identifying risks likewise depends on investigators' collective knowledge of operational and organisational activities. Investigators interpret incidents by drawing on their knowledge to determine what incidents might mean for safety. This knowledge is deeply practical, and is largely garnered through their own operational experience that is, in turn, developed through the analysis and investigation of large volumes of incidents and the study of past accidents and safety issues.

One of the most basic assumptions that investigators hold is that their knowledge of risk is always partial, limited and incomplete in some way. Some set of unknown or latent risks will always exist, and changes in the organisation, in operational design and in the broader industry will continually create new risks. As such, investigators consider their work to be an ongoing and relentless process of seeking out and identifying new or previously unknown risks. In one sense, safety oversight is a process of knowledge creation. The focus of investigators' attention and scrutiny continually shifts to newly problematic and troublesome areas. The fundamental aim of investigators, then, is to avoid being left ignorant of risks. For them, being caught out or surprised is to have already failed. This distinct perspective that investigators bring to the work of safety oversight can be characterised as *interpretive vigilance*. This perspective underpins a common approach to making sense of safety incidents and interpreting and identifying the early signs of potential risks. The interpretive practices that underpin this approach are examined in more detail in the next chapter. In this chapter, the focus is on the fundamental assumptions, underlying beliefs and shared perspective that defines how investigators understand the challenges and risks of their own work of safety oversight and risk management. First, investigators' perspectives on the inherently interpretive nature of safety oversight and risk analysis are examined. Next, investigators' beliefs about their own ability to know – and equally to be ignorant – about risks are explored. That is, this chapter seeks to explain how investigators understand the interpretive challenges, and the analytical risks of risk analysis, that they continually confront.

The work of safety oversight

The work of safety oversight and incident analysis is centrally about knowledge. For investigators, effectively overseeing safety means knowing about the current state of safety within the airline, along with any problems associated with it. Investigators analyse incidents by drawing on broad and practical knowledge of the organisation, of socio-technical practice and of risks, to interpret what events might mean for safety. This is a collective, social activity. Knowledge of operational risk is shared amongst investigators through the incidents they discuss and the stories they tell. These conversations and the activities of review-ing and analysing incidents are interpretive work that is directed at understanding safety. This interpretive work recursively draws on, and develops, a shared knowledge of risk.

Knowing risks: An integrated view of safety

Investigators understand their role of safety oversight as one of know-ing risks: of overseeing and being sure of safety. In their view, in an ideal world this would require them to maintain an up-to-date and comprehensive knowledge of operational safety. In particular, oversee-ing safety depends on them knowing about and being aware of the safety problems and risks that currently exist. This knowledge is for a purpose. They need first to know about risks in order to assess and manage them. Knowledge of risks is seen as the basis of safety assur-ance, and is one of their foremost aims. Through their oversight activ-ity, investigators want to be sure that the organisation is safe – and to know where it isn't. One of the key metaphors that investigators use when discussing their work is that of vision and sight. They are, after all, engaged in oversight and supervision. A common aspiration voiced by investigators is wanting a good 'picture' or 'view' of operational safety. They are involved in "building a picture" (Si4-3) of risks – and not just a static picture, but an evolving story. Oversight is literally about seeing risks, or as Reason (1997, p. 37) puts it, making risks visible.

For investigators, the fundamental aspiration that guides their oversight work is knowing and being sure of what is 'going on' in the organisation. For many of the events that are reported to them, "there's nothing intrinsically unsafe, we just want to know" (Si3-8). The emphasis, for investigators, is on knowing what is happening and integrating this into a coherent view of safety. Investigators want their view of risk to be broad. They aim to see across – and literally, over – all operational areas and departments, "as we want the big picture" (Si5-6). And they aim to "keep the big picture, so you can consider all the ele-ments" (Si5-14). Failing to maintain a broad and integrated view across the organisation is seen as a considerable threat, and investigators attribute several high-profile accidents in other industries to failures of integrated safety oversight:

> They don't have any overall picture and everything is done in little teams, and sporadically. Reporting is in pockets with nothing over the top of it. That's not good. Everybody can be having the same problems and not knowing it, which would mean a nice global fix. So the overview is important. (Si3-1)

The fundamental purpose of safety oversight, as investigators see it, is knowing about operational safety and putting an 'overall picture' together – so that problems are visible and connections between different elements of the organisation can be understood. The ongoing stream of reported incidents is prized by investigators as key to this because it allows investigators to 'keep in touch' with operational realities and 'the real world' of operations (e.g. Weick and Sutcliffe, 2001). Incident reports provide investigators with a detailed, practical and specific stream of information from the front-line. Varying their metaphor slightly, staff reporting incidents are considered "the eyes and ears" (Si5-6) of safety oversight. Investigators are unequivocal on this point: "without reporting, we are blind" (Si1-4).

It is through reports of disruptions and failures that investigators begin to build an image of organisational risks. Incident reports are valuable because they come directly from the "frontline" (Si4-9) of operations. It is here – on the flight deck or the hangar floor – that safety deficiencies throughout the organisation become manifest and are revealed: "it's where everything meets and feeds into. If there's a failing there it's because there have been failings elsewhere that lead into it" (Si4-9). So for investigators, incidents tell things as they are. They provide direct feedback on how operations are actually being carried out and the sorts of issues actually arising on the front-line. Investigators value incident reports because they provide a way of keeping in touch with operations more directly and in richer detail than other methods, such as audits or one-off reviews. Incidents are reported in near-real time, they are from the perspective of those actually doing the work and they report specific, concrete events that have actually happened.

For instance, incident reports provided investigators with a clear indication that problems around the intermittent detection of fumes in the cockpit persisted, despite the ongoing efforts to solve them. One investigator described how an issue might be addressed at all the relevant board meetings and committees, "but then we would see that there is no change in the [incident] trends. So they are talking a good story, but the proof isn't there in the pudding" (Si3-1). The continued occurrence of incidents can show unambiguously that there is still a problem to be addressed and that safety is still degraded, quite simply "because we keep having events" (Si4-3). So, put straightforwardly, "incidents show us what's going on out there" (Si5-9). More specifically, incidents help investigators see not just what is going on, but what is going wrong. Incident reporting provides a focused stream of information that allows investigators to keep in touch with the current operational safety situation through its failures and moments of weakness. The aim of oversight is to remain attentive to the front-line and see, and be sure of, organisational safety. Incident analysis supports this by continually updating investigators of operational failures and allowing them to develop an evolving picture of current and emerging risks.

Interpreting incidents: Contextualising events

Incident reports are brief. They refer to highly specific, local and usually minor occurrences. A core objective in analysing these reports is understanding what they mean for organisational safety. For investigators, what a particular incident means is dependent on seeing it in its organisational context. Interpreting incidents is a process of contextualisation, in order to understand them and get a view on their importance and their implications. What is acceptably safe or potentially problematic is not self-evident in incident reports but must be actively determined by investigators. This involves active interpretation and a continual struggle to make sense of the masses of incidents being reported to investigators – a struggle that investigators see emerging in other industries as incident reporting programmes become more widespread:

> I think the [airline] industry as a whole is a victim of data paralysis. Thanks to modern technology it's easy for technology to give us a huge amount of data in a rather mindless way, but it's getting our heads around it, and how to effectively use it. And I think the other industries are going to struggle, they'll suffer the exact same problem, they'll get the data coming out of their ears – but it's actually using it in a meaningful way. (Si6-4)

Getting incident data is only the first step. The key – and the key challenge – is then to make sense of it, to understand it and to interpret its meaning for organisational safety. To do this, investigators work to contextualise incidents, drawing on their own knowledge and experience. Interpreting incidents depends on knowledge of things beyond what is specifically mentioned in a report. It involves understanding the broader operational processes surrounding the event, knowing about the organisational policy and procedures pertaining to those operations, being aware of any similar problems experienced elsewhere in the industry and knowing the operational history of the implicated processes – such as when and why they had been developed.

Interpreting incidents is a process of making reported information meaningful to organisational safety by connecting broader and contextual knowledge with the specific information in the report. As such, investigators believe that incidents can only be properly understood and assessed by those with a good grasp of the operational processes and context. The importance of an incident – what it means for organisational safety and what risk it implies – is interpreted in light of knowledge of "things outside the report" (Si3-9). As one investigator explained, it "is based on knowledge of what else goes on in the world, not necessarily in the incident. It has to be a knowledge of what else is going on" (Si2-2). Knowing what else is 'going on' in the organisation and in the broader industry is key to understanding incidents and assessing risk. Investigators' knowledge is based on lengthy, practical experience, both of airline operations and of managing safety. Experience is considered essential for the task of interpreting incidents: the process is "very experience driven" (Si5-1). "Risk [assessing] anything is a feel or a sense, you need experience of the systems, and of flying, before you can make a value judgement. And you need experience of doing it [the analysis]" (Si2-7). The experience required is both practical operational experience – knowing about the work that's done 'on the line' – as well as practical experience of safety management and incident analysis. Investigators consider this invaluable and essential to them understanding the 'details and particulars' of safety.

One consequence of this is that the analysis of incidents is not a tightly prescribed and formalised process and does not rely on formal risk-modelling methods. As one investigator reflected, "perception is very much in it, it is all in the eye of the risk assessor" (Si2-1). Another commented that, "it is an art not a science, but an informed art" (Si5-6). The key, of course, is what informs this 'art' of assessment: extensive operational experience and practical knowledge. Investigators believe that it is their operational experience and organisational knowledge that supports the early stages of interpreting incidents and analysing risks, and current methods and tools provide little support for this. "Really, if you take away the operational expertise, then the [risk matrix] tool itself doesn't do much. If you go to people in the street with it, it will be of no use" (Si5-13). Or, as another investigator wryly observed, when it comes to explaining the formalised risk analysis processes promulgated in common standards and guidelines, there are "lies, damn lies, and flow charts" (Si4-2).

For investigators, this reliance on their experience is natural and unremarkable. Indeed, the process of drawing on their experience and knowledge can explain the sense of 'gut feel' and 'intuition' that investigators are apt to ascribe to their analytical practices. On closer examination, these 'gut intuitions' are closely aligned with their detailed knowledge about prior safety issues, current investigations and emerging risks. Investigators draw on a diverse wealth of information and knowledge to piece together the meaning of an incident and to answer the following questions: Is this important? Should we worry? Is this unsafe? Or can we set this aside for the moment? Investigators work to make incidents meaningful by putting incidents into their organisational context. The risk implied by an incident, and what it means for safety, is interpreted through an interaction between what a report says and what investigators know. The resulting risk assessment is a construct that emerges from and depends on both of these. And investigators' reflexive understanding of this interpretive process is a key reason for the distinctive approach they take to their oversight work.

Organisational knowledge: Experience of operations and risks

Investigators make sense of incidents by drawing on a broad and general knowledge of organisational practices and risks. This knowledge comes from two key sources: their experience of managing safety and their practical experience of operations. Understanding the detail of operational incidents and 'reading between the lines' of what is being reported "is more from your experience on the front line" (Si3-4). Investigators typically work their way up, or sideways, from line operations into safety investigation and value that they are able to be "in touch" (Si5-14) with the operations that they are overseeing. Some investigators hold dual roles and continue to work 'on the line', as either seconded engineers or part-time management pilots. All investigators have experience of actually doing operational work. Their knowledge is not abstract, but first-hand and up-close experience of operational life. On reviewing incidents, investigators often refer to situations they themselves had experienced – a report of crew miscommunication during the aircraft engine start-up can provoke a knowing, 'I've done that'. Or they refer to their 'spanners and scratched knuckles' experience of knowing how particular maintenance tasks are actually done in the hangar. Their knowledge of risk and safety is therefore always grounded in an appreciation of operational specifics and practicalities. What is striking is the extent of this focus on practicalities and specifics.

Risks are always discussed with reference to concrete practices and specific incidents and events. These might include, for instance, some recent problems with the hydraulic systems on one particular fleet. Or, as discussed in the previous chapter, questions over which air conditioning pack ought to be shut off first on actioning the Quick Reference Handbook. Investigators certainly do not know the exact details and specifications of every last procedure or process. But they have a good working knowledge of what they expect these to look like:

> I don't have the skills to . . . make technical assessments that are beyond my expertise. But my experience and basic knowledge of the subject is adequate for me to decide or consider whether any level of action is required. (Si3-7)

Investigators' knowledge is characterised by breadth. They know enough about all areas of operational activity to understand incidents and make initial assessments of them. Investigators acknowledge that, "the expertise here is broad but quite shallow" (Si5-8). They are generalists. It is not unusual for a single investigator to have first-hand experience that spans several operational areas – whether on the flight deck, in the hangar or as part of cabin crew. Along with this practical knowledge, operational experience gives investigators an understanding and appreciation of what work is like 'on the line' – and often more importantly, 'up there' flying. The distinction between retrospectively reviewing events at a relaxed distance and the immediate pressures that are at play during an actual event is an important one for investigators. For instance, regarding one incident where a crew diverted because they had misinterpreted instrument and visual indications as signs that both engines – rather than just one – were showing a fault, investigators were sensitive to how this apparently simple error could have occurred:

First investigator:	You can talk yourself into anything under pressure.
Second investigator:	Yeah, it's all very well sitting at your chair at a desk, but it's a whole different matter up there (Si4-1/8).

Their operational experience provides them not only with practical understanding of operations and knowledge of organisational processes, but also with a sensitivity to the pressures and nature of this work. This is considered essential to properly understanding incidents and overseeing safety.

Investigators also draw deeply on their past experience of assessing risk and managing safety. Much of their knowledge of 'what's going on' comes, itself, from previous safety reviews and incident investigations. From this, investigators know what incidents and what sorts of events have occurred recently – and also in the past. They regularly recall and retell past organisational problems they have examined, and often refer back to the incident database to look up past events and clarify any specifics. Their knowledge is also derived from numerous analysis projects that are conducted either in response to incidents or for other reasons, such as assessments of proposed changes to operations or examining safety issues highlighted by events elsewhere in the industry. Producing regular quarterly, monthly or weekly reviews of incident data for board papers and company briefings also provides a rhythm of regularly reviewing and reanalysing recent incidents and monitoring trends. Investigators consider these important opportunities for maintaining and keeping on top of the 'broader picture'. The resulting briefings and reports are kept close to hand, and are frequently referred back to in the daily work of investigators, being used as reference points and "something of an aide memoir" (Si1-3).

Investigators particularly emphasise the awareness and knowledge that they gain from being immersed, day-to-day, in the ongoing stream of incident reports. They engage with this ongoing stream of incidents as an evolving story of the operational situation – describing it as 'watching a video' rather that just taking a static 'snapshot' of operations by plotting a graph. The richness of being immersed in this stream of information, as well as the richness of direct descriptions from the front-line, is highly prized by investigators: "every time you process the data you loose something" (Si4-3). Working amidst the flow of incidents continually being reported helps to connect investigators to the evolving status of operational safety, and provides an ongoing view of recent and past incidents that investigators draw on to interpret and assess current ones. Investigators believe it takes time to gain this experience:

> You've got to get in for a while. We notice when new guys come in that risk assessments change dramatically and we're changing them

back. They may have some knowledge and say, I don't see the problem with that. But we've seen more. (Si2-1)

It is this close experience of past events and past investigations that provides investigators with a large proportion of their general knowledge of organisational and operational "history" (Si2-1) of risk. Knowledge of this past history is considered central to interpreting current events. Knowing what has happened in the past is considered crucial to making sense of what is happening in the present.

Beyond the specific operational history within the organisation, investigators also draw on their extensive knowledge of previous accidents and major events experienced by other airlines. This knowledge, along with an awareness of the current safety issues being focused on by the industry, plays a central role in interpreting and understanding the important of safety incidents. Key sources of investigators' knowledge of operational risks are the published investigation reports on past accidents and analyses of flight safety issues and priorities, such as runway incursions and maintenance error. A huge amount of in-depth reports and investigations are produced and circulated within the aviation industry, most of which are widely available in the public domain – a situation in contrast to, for instance, healthcare or finance (Reason, 2004).

Past accidents are frequently referred to in discussions of risk. They are typically talked about merely by reference to a location – 'Tenerife' or 'Staines' – or a name – the '737 cabriolet' or 'QF1'. These brief terms are a common currency of communication amongst safety investigators, based on collective knowledge and cultural reference points. Investigators have an intimate knowledge of many of these past accidents and major incidents. To them, each is a cypher, signifying a range of particular errors and organisational failings: each captures a set of interacting risks and each is referred to in different situations as an exemplar of particular forms of organisational risk. Investigators continually use past accidents as referents to communicate about and understand their own organisation's incidents. Much of their experience of risk is, as such, vicarious and is based on their knowledge of what has happened to others.

Safety stories: The social circulation of experience

The collective knowledge of risk that investigators draw on is commonly shared and circulated in the form of narratives or stories. Accident and incident investigations are often condensed by investigators to a narrative of the key points and significant interactions. Stories are often used by investigators as a vehicle to share experience of risks and to summarise lessons about safety. The clearest instances of this concern the accidents and incidents of other operators. Investigators tell stories about these in a variety of situations. They use stories to explain specific incidents that have been reported to them and to describe the connections to more general organisational issues. And stories are often recounted about salient past events or troubling episodes in their organisation's history or their own experience. Narratives of past events or ongoing episodes are a regular feature of the daily work of safety oversight. These come in all shapes, topics and lengths. Most are exceedingly brief. They are told by one person in a few breaths, more as a short synopsis than a recognisable story. Others are more prolonged and might involve several investigators contributing to an account and embellishing it in their telling. But essentially all these contain two things: specific details – the 'facts' of the matter – and a sequence that relates them and links them together. As such, investigators do a lot with stories. They capture complex interrelations in operational processes; they trace out the history of a risk; they show how things changed over time; they relate antecedents and consequences; and they point to future implications.

Investigators tell stories that recount their own personal experience of operations, making that experience available to others and contributing to the collective knowledge of their colleagues and peers. As described in the vignette in Chapter 2, one investigator, for instance, recounted at length how tricky flight crew can find go-around manoeuvres – even though many consider these a routine operational event. The story was used to bring into question something previously taken for granted, and to emphasise how an event that may seem routine and frequent to investigators monitoring the incidents of an entire airline can actually be quite unusual and rare to an individual pilot. Likewise, other stories are told from personal experience about, for example, why pilots should never trust that air traffic controllers know what they're doing, and why flight engineers were valuable in the cockpit because they could ask the pilots apparently stupid questions:

First investigator:	When I was a flight engineer, you're not expected to know anything so you can ask dumb questions like, 'Oh, are we meant to be in Nav Mode now?'
Second investigator:	Yeah: 'Oh, the Flight Director's not working?' Oh no, I'm just cutting the corner. What! No,

	there's no departure route called 'just cutting the corner'.
First investigator:	It's like on an approach into Boston, we'd gone past the airport by about fifty miles at 3,000 feet, and so I say what's the safe altitude here? To be fair he got the map out and showed where we were, but you don't know . . . (Si4-1/8)

By telling short stories such as these, investigators can share their own experience, they can call into question current assumptions and they can reinforce the sense of what is appropriate or inappropriate for safety. In telling stories, investigators also circulate the experience of others, too. Much of the knowledge they have of risk is derived from what has happened to other airlines and to other people. Many of the stories that investigators recount are borrowed. Investigators pick these tales up from a range of sources: air safety seminars; industry forums; visits to and audits of partner airlines; accident reports; safety publications; and their personal contacts and colleagues within the industry. Countless accounts of events and close calls are circulated throughout the industry by these means, and are told and retold by investigators. A brief and simple example, for instance, is this short story told by an investigator to his colleagues, while reading another airline's in-house safety briefing:

Bloody hell, the landing gear doors were welded shut here, on a DC-10. The aircraft was struck by lightning, and on approach the front gear doors wouldn't open. After an emergency landing, the doors were found to have been welded shut by lightning! (Si4-2)

Investigators had not heard of gear doors being welded shut by lightning before. It was surprising and unusual, and they learnt something that they didn't previously know – specifically, that typically benign lightning strikes can have serious consequences. More generally, it reinforced and reproduced the view that an otherwise routine type of event can have non-routine, dramatic and surprising consequences.

The stories that are most commonly told are those that are found particularly unusual or interesting to investigators, and that reinforce their deeply held conviction that managing air safety is continually open to surprise. Their stories often depict counterintuitive or unexpected circumstances. And they are often vivid or dramatic, concerning disastrous or near-disastrous events. As such, stories typically function as small, focused and highly memorable case studies of organisational risk. They depict not only that something surprising happened – but more crucially why and how. Stories don't just describe events and transmit information. They carry lessons: they communicate what an event means and why it is important. On another occasion, for example, an investigator briefly retold a tale about a near-accident that had been shared by another airline at an air safety conference he had just returned from, the climax of which was dramatic:

First investigator: Basically the crew just lost it. The aircraft went from plus fifty degrees to minus forty degree bank in less than five seconds, headed into a 3,000 feet per minute descent less than 1,000 feet from the ground . . .

[Intakes of breath from the other investigators.]

Second investigator: Twenty seconds from death.

First investigator: . . . and they pulled up with 300 feet clearance . . . The conclusion was that it seems to have been a poorly performing Captain and a First Officer who was reticent and only involved in the final seconds . . . (Si4-3/5)

Clearly dramatic, this story and others like it emphasise how small slips and moments of inattention can quickly escalate to near-catastrophe. These accounts emphasise why such minor failures should be taken seriously. Telling them reaffirms to investigators that things like this can, and do, happen – and also provides insights into how and why. They reinforce investigators' perspective that they oversee the safety of serious, surprising and potentially catastrophic operations.

Telling stories is a process that forestalls investigators "forgetting to be afraid" (Reason, 1997, p. 199) and, although the circumstances of most major and recent accidents are well known by investigators, this does not prevent them being retold again and again. Some are retold loosely and at length, with new additions and highlights relevant to current problems or existing incidents that are under review. These sweeping narratives can range widely across many issues, and encompass numerous safety issues of the day, as is demonstrated by the extended (but still greatly curtailed) extract that follows. Here, two investigators retold the causes and implications of an infamous accident that another airline had suffered several years ago. It saw part of the roof of a Boeing 737 airliner rip off during flight, with the loss of a flight attendant – the '737 cabriolet':

First investigator:	It was loads of human factors that went into that. I was over in engineering then, and the millions that were spent on looking into that, looking at all this non-destructive testing to find cracks . . . But a guy who knew all about it reckoned the crack had to be like that [demonstrating several millimetres wide and several centimetres long]. It was up by the door, left number one, upper right side. You don't need tools to see that.
Second investigator:	Just a mark one eyeball.
First investigator:	Exactly. But when you get to engineering, they don't want to hear about human factors. They want to look at the tools, and get better tools . . .
Second investigator:	And it was on a real high cycle aircraft, it should have been one of their basic checks, they were a really high risk group.
Researcher:	With all the island hopping?
Second investigator:	That's it. Up and down, up and down, it's like a test, expanding and contracting it all the time . . . So they should have been checking it, and when they looked there was a history of pressurisation problems, leaky seals and things.
First investigator:	And one of the passengers reported seeing the crack, either on that flight or on one before.
Second investigator:	And there would have been sounds, but being close to the door people would just have said, yup, it's the door – leaky seal, that explains it.
First investigator:	That's right, if it had been right between the two doors people might have paid a little more attention to it. That's a good point, I like that. (Si4-1/9)

Retelling the story, investigators put it in the context of current concerns they had about incidents in their own organisation regarding routine checks on airframes. They discussed – as engineers themselves – the challenges of getting predominantly technical departments to 'buy-in' to human factors thinking. And they related it, again, to the problems of inattention to weak signals of threat and the risk of normalising and explaining away problems (e.g. Vaughan, 1996). So investigators use stories as a way to communicate knowledge and also to refresh it: to contextualise their current concerns with lessons from the past and to relate the past to current concerns. Stories and narratives occupy a central place in constituting and communicating investigators' knowledge of safety. They are the social and communicable form of safety knowledge that is collectively drawn on and reproduced in the work of risk analysis and safety improvement.

The challenges and risks of knowledge

At the heart of investigators' work of safety oversight work lies a set of nuanced and consequential beliefs on the relationship between knowledge and risk. One of the most fundamental assumptions is that knowledge of risk is always partial and limited. Latent risks will always exist beyond the bounds of current knowledge. Investigators equally consider their knowledge of risk to be permanently changing as new information or explanations comes to light. Because of this, their interpretation of an event yesterday might differ from today. Ultimately, they view the central risk of their oversight and analysis work as arising from the gap between their knowledge of risk and operational reality: a slippage between their interpretations and the facts on the ground – and in the air. This perspective underpins a distinct commitment to vigilance in their interpretive work.

Latent risks: The limits of organisational knowledge

One of the most basic assumptions of investigators is that their knowledge of risks is always partial and incomplete. They assume that they never have a full and complete picture of every current risk, and assume that that they never could. This epistemic challenge is a basic principle that incident reporting itself is based on. Reporting programmes are primarily designed to allow the identification of problems that lie outside the current base of knowledge: to find out about risks that aren't already known about and controlled. This is also a basic assumption of investigators regarding their own knowledge of risk. Much of safety management is viewed as a process of identifying risks and responding with planned defences and controls – but this process is always imperfect, which incidents routinely demonstrate: "We do our hazard identification and risk analysis and think we've cracked it. And then things happen: events" (Si5-6). Other investigators describe it more bluntly:

> You put your defences in place, and they are adequate, but they can't be one hundred percent. Then what you find is your defences

are not as robust as you originally anticipated . . . [so] incidents are in-your-face, direct audits. They are feedback. When incidents go wrong, they are saying 'You know all that stuff you planned? Well it isn't working. Because here is a report'. So it is feedback that is just saying, 'You got it wrong again. And again. And again. It still isn't working'. (Si3-7)

Incidents typically aren't planned or anticipated. Nor are they intended or expected. They are events that point to where investigators, and the organisation, have 'got things wrong' and where current knowledge of risk – and associated safety defences – aren't up to scratch. As investigators see it, the reality of their work is that they do not have comprehensive knowledge of every risk that currently faces, or could face, them. The continuous stream of incident reports continually reinforces this assumption. Much as investigators would have it otherwise, they consider their knowledge of the organisation, and of risk, to have fundamental and inherent limits. These limits are not permanent and absolute but, as Wildavsky (1988, p. 31) has argued, "in the sense that new and more powerful theories potentially will replace or alter the now known, knowledge is always incomplete." There will always be some set of risks that lie outside the bounds of current knowledge. These latent risks are those not currently known about or understood: they are risks that investigators, and the organisation, are ignorant of.

The basic limits to investigators' knowledge of risk are attributed predominantly to organisational complexity and change, which investigators see as inherent and irreducible features of organisational activity. First, investigators believe that the sheer complexity of organisations, and safety-critical high-technology organisations in particular, preclude complete and comprehensive knowledge of all risks. Organisations are too complex to have full knowledge of the possible occurrence and interaction of every possible failure, or of how these might lead to an accident. One investigator explained this with reference to how past accidents dramatically reveal gaps in their knowledge:

We always thought [this event] was back here in the chain, but then it can appear just one before the accident now. We hadn't thought about that. We didn't think that this would happen first, that would break down, and then that can happen. But if we could do that we would all be geniuses, and the thing with accidents is that they prove that we are not geniuses. They are where we have got it wrong and we need to learn. (Si3-7)

Investigators view accidents, and the numerous findings that inevitably follow, as indefatigable evidence of the inherent limits of organisational knowledge. They believe that there are always things that they haven't yet considered that could cause an accident – if they happened in a certain way, under particular conditions, or in conjunction with other specific events.

Second, investigators believe that continual changes in organisational arrangements and the broader industry give rise to new risks, even as they identify and deal with the current ones. Incidents are often considered a symptom that something has changed that they do not know about. One example, for instance, was when pilots initially started reporting indications of fumes on the flight deck: "We've been running those aeroplanes for years, so something must have changed – for us to be getting the problem" (Si2-3). Investigators believe that changes to operations can bring with them new risks that can render their knowledge out of date or invalid – and may leave them completely 'in the dark'. Change is, however, viewed as a certainty, the rule rather than the exception, as one investigator described at length:

> There's an awful lot of change at the moment. Engineering have offloaded a lot of their processes such as refuelling the planes, pushback too. These are the major ones, you know about them by doing a whole change process. But the minor ones you don't catch up with, and it happens all the time – who supplies the de-icing fluid, who does the de-icing? Things that you take for granted all of a sudden change, and you don't go publicising it because the manual stays the same . . . And all of a sudden it is ignorance. (Si3-8)

Organisational change can literally leave them ignorant of aspects of organisational activity and its associated risks. This view of ignorance is not a pejorative one, but is practical and pragmatic. Investigators aim to stay informed, aware and knowledgeable of the state of organisational safety. They know that risks could lie outside the current scope of their current knowledge. And they understand that organisational change and complexity are the primary sources of their perennially incomplete knowledge of risk. It is the relative ignorance of risks that renders them latent – and is particularly threatening.

Producing knowledge: Catching up with risks

Investigators' knowledge of organisational safety and risk is not a static entity. Their knowledge of risks changes with the occurrence of new events and as new information comes to light. The work of safety oversight is, in many ways, a process of knowledge production.

As investigators see it, developing knowledge is central to risk analysis. This orientation flows naturally from the assumption that their knowledge is perennially incomplete and liable to have become outdated: "We don't know what we don't know, and that is one of the delights of the job really, as you keep pushing back the boundaries and learning more" (Si3-5). Investigators believe that the extension and revision of what is currently known about risk is central to their work. They see themselves as aiming to 'push back' the bounds of their current knowledge – to find out and know about risks. And, as they see it, their knowledge of risk needs to change and advance because new organisational risks themselves are constantly emerging. As one investigator explains, changes in operations "are introducing new or variations on your risks that previously didn't exist. And your safety systems are managing, but you are playing catch up, because it is all a reactive system in the end" (Si3-7).

The work of safety oversight, and of incident analysis in particular, is understood by investigators as one of always 'playing catch up' with risks. Catching up with risks involves generating new knowledge or revising existing knowledge. Investigators believe that their understandings of risk, and of organisational activity, therefore 'move' over time – and crucially, with their evolving experience. Importantly, this means that they can interpret the same data differently at different points in time, depending on the current state of their knowledge. This is easier to identify in hindsight and investigators often discuss examples where very similar incidents are assessed in dramatically different ways because of changes in knowledge and understanding. One example, for instance, was a hypothetical incident where an unauthorised person gained access to the flight deck. Before a major incident many years ago – where a disruptive passenger fought with pilots and tried to crash a plane – and before the terrorist attacks of 11 September, 2001, the view of investigators would have been very different from now:

> Before [that] you'd say, he's drunk, take him away. No one would think he'd try and kill the pilot or something. Now you think we shouldn't have people on the flight deck full stop, so those factors come in. Your judgement of risk is dependent on what's happened in the past, it's not a fixed entity. (Si3-2)

A similar example relates to the findings from an investigation into a major safety issue regarding tyre failures:

> A tyre failure on [that aircraft type] now, you would go off the roof. But it is just a tyre failure like any of the other ones. Now it would be

bloody hell, we have had a failure of that tyre – it is not supposed to fail. But nothing has really changed in the incidents. (Si3-7)

Investigators are aware that near-identical incidents could be interpreted in radically different ways, depending on what they know and how their knowledge changed. The same incident data can be assessed in dramatically different ways at different time points, meaning that historical assessments of risk are likely to no longer be valid:

You couldn't look at last year's data and say, that was how the risk was scored then, that was how it's scored now, so there is an inconsistency. There isn't, because your knowledge has moved – and hopefully expanded. (Si3-3)

Changes in knowledge mean that things can be reinterpreted, and dramatically different meanings might arise from reviewing a near-identical event. Assessments of risk are not viewed as an objective and permanently valid measure of risk but as a pragmatic and temporary assessment based on current circumstances and understandings. That is, assessments of risk reveal as much about the current state of knowledge and understanding as they do about the nature of the event itself.

Assessments of risk are dependent on both the past data and current knowledge drawn on to produce them. In practice, this means that prior incidents are often reinterpreted by investigators in light of current events, or recent accidents, or new information – and this process takes place many times during investigations into an incident as more detailed information is gathered and pieced together. Equally, it means that the large database of past incident reports not only records data for trend analyses and the like. It also allows events to be kept for future reinterpretation, in ways that may currently be unimaginable, when investigators' knowledge of risk changes significantly in some area. The case of the issues surrounding the inadvertent selection of the autopilot switch, recounted in Chapter 2, provides a salient case in point.

The changing nature of what investigators know about risk is one reason why investigators consider their daily work so challenging. "It is not such a cut and dried subject. A different person on a different day, or the same person on a different day, they will shift something. They've heard one more thing that may shift it" (Si2-1). In this view, monitoring and assessing safety isn't simply the mechanical calculating and processing of information. Assessing risk is an active process of interpretation that is based on a continually shifting knowledge base. The work of safety oversight takes place at the sharp-end of organisational learning and the cutting-edge of knowledge generation, where the limits of knowledge are continually being confronted and overturned.

Interpretive slippage: Being caught out and surprised

For investigators, the persistent risk in their work of safety oversight is missing or misinterpreting signs of potential risks (e.g. Turner and Pidgeon, 1997). They worry, specifically, about succumbing to the insidious processes by which this could occur, a process that can be termed interpretive slippage. Their work involves creating a 'picture' of the ever changing safety situation in the organisation. It involves knowing about and understanding risks. So for investigators, not having known about or fully understood a risk before it manifests itself in some serious way is tantamount to having failed. As far as they are concerned, they ought to have found out about the risk earlier or when it was less serious. To investigators, missing the emergence of risks is deeply troubling:

> The ones that trouble you are the ones that come out of leftfield and you think, how did we get caught out like that? They are certainly small in number. You wouldn't want surprises every day. We hate surprises! A little bit of 'same old same old' is good: we know about this, and it doesn't have the potential to bite big time. (Si3-1)

Being 'caught out' or surprised by risks is to have already failed. Investigators believe that finding a serious weakness in the organisation – one with 'the potential to bite' – reflects on them and their own performance as much as it demonstrates there are problems elsewhere in the organisation. Discovering that safety is seriously degraded is therefore doubly troubling: they hadn't noticed or found out about it before. And while they know that risks are continually changing, they do not accept that serious problems appear overnight:

> To have something occur that is intolerable means that our systems not only have fallen down, but it has obviously been wrong for a long period of time. So if something comes up like that, that is intolerable. It means we have been derelict. (Si3-8)

This strong language is representative of how seriously investigators view situations where their interpretations of organisational safety and risk have gone awry. Investigators assume that their knowledge and understanding of risk is always limited in some way. They assume that they are often one step behind risks, playing 'catch up' with them. But they nonetheless do not want to fall too far behind, for too long, or only catch up with risks once they became manifest as seriously degraded defences. As they see it, their work is to find risks 'early', when they are 'small'. That means that the last thing that they want is to be surprised. Finding out about significant risks that they hadn't previously known about surprises investigators – and being surprised is considered too late. It means that they have already failed, by not finding out earlier. For investigators, it means that they have been ineffective in their work of monitoring safety. They haven't been doing their job properly:

> You've not done your job by flagging this back earlier. So if you get something that warrants action and soon, it surprises you. Horrify might be a better word. What! We can't be having this, and you're off to talk to someone about it. And if it comes up again then it's emergency meeting stuff. (Si3-1)

Investigators do not want to be surprised, shocked or 'horrified'. They believe that their role is to find new risks and constantly update their knowledge of organisational safety before risks surprise them. Surprises are not considered an effective way to identify risks. Surprises represent too great a disjunction between current beliefs and operational reality: smaller moments of disjunction are preferred. To investigators, surprises mean that their interpretation and understanding of organisational risks have been lacking to a serious degree and for a considerable length of time. This, in turn, means that addressing the risk is even more imperative, and holds implications for their own ability to analyse and know about risks.

> When we trip over it, that's where the intolerable occurs. So you have to immediately crawl all over it to understand why you can have a situation like that – and how you got into that situation in the first place, which is the more important one. (Si3-8)

These major risks – 'the intolerable' – partly deserve this label because they represent significant interpretive failure on the part of investigators – and the wider organisation. That such a situation could develop without being properly noticed or understood by investigators in itself represents a significant risk and a significant failure in their oversight work. An issue not receiving the appropriate attention and scrutiny is, to investigators, clearly a risk in itself. "If there is an important issue that is not being addressed and getting enough attention, then that in itself means that there is a high risk" (Si3-6). Investigators therefore adopt a reflexive view of organisational risks. Their assessment of organisational safety includes a consideration of their own role of monitoring and understanding it. In this sense, risk has an inherent interpretive dimension, represented by a failure to effectively know about or understand a problem. The risk is being caught out or surprised, failing in their job or being derelict. That is, they "risk losing touch with line reality" (Si5-14), where their interpretations of the nature and existence of risks become out of kilter with what is actually the case in the organisation – a near direct restatement of Turner's (1976a, 1994) view. The processes of interpretive slippage that lead to this situation deeply concern investigators. This concern reflects what they value and continually strive for – awareness and knowledge of risks.

One tangible issue that reveals investigators' concerns about missing and not knowing about risks is the failure of personnel to report safety events. Both 'unreported' mishaps, and more generally 'losing' a strong reporting culture, are two worries often dwelt on by investigators. Incident reports are a key way of uncovering risks. So when investigators start to see a slight drop-off in the overall reporting rate, they become uneasy about what it might mean. As one investigator explained, it could mean that there just aren't as many incidents occurring, so perhaps:

> ...you can give yourself that warm fussy feeling. On the other hand, perhaps your crews don't believe in your ability to fix anything, so they got pissed off telling you about things. There is always that bit when something goes wrong – 'Oh, that has always been happening'. But you never told us! 'Well, we gave you fifty reports about it and you never did anything so we gave up on it'. So that is the danger, that is the real risk. That is the dangerous one. (Si3-7)

Losing reporting is considered dangerous and 'the real risk', because it would potentially preclude them finding out about emerging safety problems. As such, it represents an interpretive risk, a threat to their analytical and oversight work: they simply might not find out about problems in the first place. This particular concern underpinned a prolonged focus by some investigators on ground damage to aircraft. Ground damage can be caused by the various vehicles and personnel that service aircraft on the ramp. In one instance, a small access door covering the ground power connection was found to be damaged. These doors are a few centimetres across and "not a problem to fly without"

(Si4-3). But the damage was found and reported by someone who hadn't caused it: it was therefore unreported damage and this was a serious worry. As one investigator had explained prior to that particular event:

> There is a tremendous amount of it [ground damage]. But as it stands it is not really a safety issue. It is unreported ground damage that is a big safety issue. So it is getting that culture right so that everyone says, 'Yes I did drive into the side of the plane, please go and mend it'. As, if you think you can get away with it and the aeroplane gets airborne, it may not fly. (Si3-8)

Unreported damage may not be discovered until it is too late. As far as investigators are concerned, it is the same for all other sources of risk. Not knowing, for them, is itself a risk.

Misinterpreting or not fully understanding risks might just as easily occur, investigators believe, from their own work being poorly performed. They believe that inattention or sloppiness on their part could quickly result in a divergence between their own interpretations of safety and operational reality. They consider that, according to accident reports, such interpretive slippage lay behind several high-profile accidents – such as the NASA Challenger accident (e.g. Vaughan, 1990, 1996). This is often referred to as a 'syndrome' that can easily be slipped into and that they try to remain wary of:

> The syndrome can slip in – and I'm sure we've done it as well – where things slowly but surely ramp down: where things that would have been an 'A' risk ten years ago are now a bloody 'D' risk. But they are not. The defences are just holding by a smidgen every bloody time, and no one's picking up on it because they get so friggin' used to it, until eventually, the last defence lets go . . . And everyone can do that. Because this tolerance may come in that we can accept lots and lots of dodgy approaches, because we are chipping away at every other one, so what is ten more this week? And that's why the isolated one-off is just another in a long, long sequence of isolated one-off events. (Si6-1)

Investigators worry deeply about the potential for interpretive slippage, where they could become 'oblivious' to possible risks. As another investigator described: "I put it down to the syndrome where if you go long enough without an accident, you almost become oblivious to the fact that you will have one" (Si6-7). This is variously discussed in terms of 'becoming immune' to incidents or 'deluding ourselves'. This is considered a slow, gradual, insidious process that investigators try to prevent. One investigator's computer screensaver scrolled the constant warning: 'Beware the incremental descent into poor judgement'. It is often described as a certain 'mentality' that they aim to avoid, where certain events gradually become accepted and ignored as they seem to be 'facts of life'. "It is a mentality we hope we avoid here. Some people may see it the other way – not maliciously, but, 'this keeps happening doesn't it, maybe it's just a fact of life'" (Si3-2).

Another investigator put it more bluntly. At the extreme, not acting on clearly repetitive or major safety incidents displayed carelessness or complacency:

> Incidents are slaps on the face telling you, you haven't got it right. And if you are having an accident it is more than a slap, it is a kick in the teeth. And if you are having repetitive incidents at that level, then fundamentally, something is wrong – something is seriously wrong. And if you are not acting on it, you are either complacent, in that you think you have it managed but think you have just been unfortunate. Or you are just being corrupt. You are ignoring the problem. Then you are careless. And if you are a service provider like us you will kill and injure people. (Si3-7)

Investigators consider the interpretive work associated with overseeing safety and analysing risk to be open, itself, to challenging risks. These risks are interpretive in nature: missing or misinterpreting signs of degrading organisational safety. These interpretive risks are considered as significant a threat to organisational safety as are failures in operational processes, and investigators take them – and their own role in producing and preventing them – seriously. Being shocked or surprised out of their ignorance is considered a serious failure of safety oversight, and is the ultimate risk that investigators work to continually avoid. How they do this vigilant interpretive work is examined in the next chapter.

6
Identifying and Constructing Risks

The early stages of risk identification are amongst the most critical but also the most challenging moments of safety management. It is, of course, only possible to analyse and address threats to organisational safety if those threats are identified in the first place. If the signs of emerging risks are misinterpreted, misunderstood – or entirely missed – then risk management can fail at this early stage, before it has barely begun. As explored in the previous chapter, investigators are acutely aware of the epistemic and interpretive challenges they face in overseeing safety and analysing risks. Investigators' assumptions and beliefs about the interpretive risks associated with their work underpin a distinctive approach to identifying and analysing risks, and shape their interpretive practice. This chapter examines both this approach to safety oversight and the common practices of risk identification through which investigators work to uncover emerging and previously unknown risks.

Investigators adopt a vigilant approach to their interpretive work and aim to remain alert and sensitive to weak signs of potential problems and emerging risks. They actively foster scepticism and doubt about the adequacy of their own interpretations of risk. And they adopt a cautious orientation to their own knowledge and understanding of organisational safety, regarding their analyses of risk as merely interpretations that might easily be flawed. This position of humility and caution is both a product of and continually reinforced by investigators' own experiences of failure. It is relatively common for investigators to encounter incidents that were previously unseen, to uncover risks that were previously unknown and to discover information that is at odds with what is currently taken for granted. As such, adopting an approach to safety oversight that emphasises interpretive vigilance seems natural and necessary to investigators.

At the core of this interpretive vigilance is a focus on identifying and actively seeking out indications of potential ignorance. The key resources that investigators deploy in this regard are their suspicions and doubts. Investigators scrutinise areas where the safety of organisational activity, or their knowledge of it, appears ambiguous, unclear and suspect: where they are no longer sure of safety. At this tentative stage, risk identification is a process of active construction rather than one of passive discovery. Investigators work to actively construct and piece together information, events and knowledge that might form a fleeting warning sign of a potential underlying risk. Investigators engage in an active and effortful process aimed at transforming moments of failure and fluctuations in operational performance into broader suspicions and doubts about the adequacy of organisational safety. These suspicions act as proxy markers for potentially new and previously unrecognised organisational risks. Warning signs of emerging risks are actively made by investigators, rather than thrust upon them.

There are four key ways that investigators work to develop and use suspicions to identify risks. These involve making patterns in operational mishaps, drawing connections between minor incidents and other major events, noticing new or novel types of occurrence, and perceiving a mismatch or disparity between current understandings and actual organisational activity. This chapter first examines the key features of the vigilant approach that investigators adopt to their interpretive work. Then it analyses the four main ways in which investigators aim to identify risks by marshalling suspicions around indications of potential ignorance. This approach and these practices can be seen as one particularly detailed arena of investigators' broader practical theory of safety: it concerns their own contribution to organisational safety and resilience.

A vigilant approach to interpretive work

Investigators adopt a vigilant approach to their analysis of incidents and identification of risk. Given their deep concerns about being surprised, and their aspirations to identify risks when they are still small, investigators seek to stay keenly alert and sensitive to early signals of emerging risks – signs which are often in the form of brief indications of possible problems and potential ignorance. The initial focus of their analytical work is to actively seek out where organisational safety may be compromised or is becoming problematic – where they can no longer be sure of safety. This vigilant approach is characterised by a persistent scepticism and suspicion. At base, investigators attempt to cultivate a sense of humility in the face of their potential ignorance. And they aim to maintain a healthy scepticism with regard to the current safety of operations, the information they have and their own interpretations of these. During the course of their work, investigators continually shift their attention to new suspect areas of safety, and work to create a shared representation of the currently problematic areas of organisational activity. Taken together, these aspects of investigators' work are the basis of what can be termed interpretive vigilance – a distinct approach to analytical practice that aims to both identify emerging risks at an early stage and arrest the processes of interpretive slippage.

Humble scepticism: Wariness of operations, information and knowledge

Humility and scepticism pervade the work of investigators and their attempts to keep alert to possible risks. Investigators are deeply aware of the catastrophic nature of the risks in their industry and the threats confronting them in their oversight work. As such, they approach their work with a degree of humility, appreciating the scope and scale of the challenges that are being faced and fostering a sense of scepticism and wariness, akin to Reason's (1997, p. 37) "chronic unease". This wariness is directed at the safety of operational processes, the information that they work with and their own knowledge of risk. Regarding the former, investigators are perennially sceptical of the safety of operations, and this view pervades their thinking on risk and safety, as described in the previous chapter. Investigators assume that operations can never be entirely safe, and that safety management is about continually "hoping for the best but planning for the worst" (Si3-5). This deep wariness was alluded to by one investigator who asserted that, "incidents act as a warning that they're out to get you – everyone. And if you believe that, you're alright" (Si2-1). They describe their approach as being based on a "healthy respect" (Si3-7) for operations and their potential for failure. Investigators are permanently wary of operations and safety is never considered to be certain or absolute.

Investigators handle information with an equal sense of humility and scepticism. They are intimately aware of the limitations of incident reporting data, and the flaws and influences it is open to. Primarily, as indicated previously, they are wary about not getting information at all. So a 'quiet' week is more of a cause for suspicion than for relief: investigators are sceptical that there have really been so few incidents. Instead, they suspect that they simply haven't heard about them. For example, after a few days that had seen particularly few incidents reported, one investigator joked wryly that a notice for their next weekly briefing should read that "due to the limited number of reports we are investigating whether the airline is still flying" (Si4-2). This humour indicates a deep assumption that pervades this professional culture – and mimics Reason's (1997, p. 195) idealised "state of intelligent and respectful wariness" that characterises informed cultures.

Investigators do not assume that if bad things happen they will hear about them. On the contrary they consider that, in this industry no news isn't good news, "no news means your radio's failed" (Si4-1) and therefore represents a double dose of bad news: that the communication system has failed, too. Moreover, investigators appreciate the limitations of the incident data that they work with. They only see the incidents that have been reported to them and so do not have a comprehensive picture of all safety-relevant events and risks. This is a key consideration for investigators, and they keep in mind that the incidents they do see could have implications for incidents that they don't see – events that haven't been reported. Investigators work with the basic assumption that, if this is what is actually being reported to them, it must be a whole lot worse out there. Investigators also appreciate that reports may be inaccurate – and occasionally entirely wrong – and provide only one perspective on what could be complex events. "Often the person who filed the report doesn't know what's wrong anyway. It may just say, 'Something went bang as we landed the aeroplane'" (Si3-6). Investigators are sensitive to the limitations and potential biases that may be inherent in even an individual incident report:

> Here we think that everyone is open to their own perspective and aims. A pilot may not know, or may have been limited by their perspective in how they understood an incident. And everyone will to an extent massage how much they report their own failures. (Si5-6)

So, while investigators emphasise the value of getting incident reports, they are nonetheless wary of the actual accounts given in them. They assume that reporters do not always have a clear view of what happened and temper their thinking with the caution that, in the case of flight crew for instance, "this is only their idea from the flight deck" (Si4-4). And investigators equally believe that when people report their own errors, they naturally play them down and may not provide an entirely balanced story. Investigators depend on reporters reporting incidents, but they equally treat what is reported with a degree of scepticism. Put simply, "the report is only as good as the reporter" (Si3-4). At base, investigators assume that 'early information is always inaccurate, and usually wrong' – and a poster to this effect hangs in one of their offices. All of these assumptions are continually reinforced by their own daily experience of analysing and investigating incidents:

> Where we fail is getting information early enough . . . Even sometimes from the individual bits of paper, it doesn't come out. You will get the report saying we had a fire warning in the cargo bay. Then you find out that it happened outside the cargo bay but the detectors inside detected it. Then you think this is serious, because we have a process to protect fires in the cargo bay – fireproofing and extinguishers. But this is outside, so you have a problem there, and the process escalates and you realise how much more important it is as you get more information. So the end result, we get the information, but it is very difficult to get that information early on. (Si3-2)

Investigators treat the information they receive with caution. Furthermore, investigators are aware – and wary – of how reporting policies and local work practices can influence which events become noticed, which are considered reportable, which are reported and therefore what contributes to the picture they see. They assume that a whole range of events are likely to be taken for granted by personnel, and considered 'normal practice'. Reporting of these is therefore unlikely, and they are therefore tough to find out about. In contrast, reporting policies or high-profile events are likely to raise awareness of an issue and increase the number of people who notice similar events, consider them reportable and therefore submit a report.

Issues that investigators highlight, or changes that they make to reporting policies, can dramatically alter the information they receive and can help to uncover risks that they previously had not known about. One case involved what became known as 'mapshift' events. On some aircraft, onboard computers continually calculate the speed and heading of aircraft and then regularly update the position of the aircraft on a digital map by checking with ground-based navigation beacons. In parts of the world where there are few beacons there is little opportunity for updating and confirming position, and so the map position can become erroneously displaced, "so on the descent the computer thinks they're trying to land where there is no airfield" (Si4-6) and gives the crew a false warning. Investigators noticed a small increase of these events being reported on one of their fleets, "so we put in a requirement for all crew to report mapshift. And suddenly the reports poured in" (Si4-6). As he explained further, "the thing with this is how it altered with no change to aircraft or the routes – just the [reporting] policy" (Si4-6). Investigators are fully aware – and often experience – that what is reported to them is not a direct representation of safety problems within the organisation, but is itself influenced and mediated by social and organisational processes. These include current reporting policies, the awareness amongst crew of what is important and relevant to report, and what gets noticed or ignored as 'normal' and therefore unremarkable and unreportable. This appreciation of the social sources of reported information in part underpins investigators' sense of humility and scepticism towards it.

Finally, but perhaps most importantly, investigators are sceptical of their own understandings and knowledge of risks. This is largely based on their deep appreciation and experience of the fallibility of their own interpretations; and that their assessments of risk necessarily result from these interpretive processes – and so are equally fallible. Investigators believe that they are only ever working with a representation of risk, a representation that they have produced and which could easily be incorrectly drawn. As one investigator bluntly acknowledged, "you can pull your risk graphs down with a stroke of a pen" (Si3-1). Investigators consider their assessments of risk to be a product of their own interpretations: a construct. As such, they don't consider these assessments to guarantee or "prove" (Si1-4) anything. They might be a useful way of communicating and prioritising problems, but "they're only as good as the people doing the analysis" (Si1-4). Investigators believe, "we could easily fool ourselves" (Si3-8) and attempt to maintain a degree of scepticism towards their own assessments and analyses of risk.

Investigators equally harbour doubts – a healthy wariness – about their own efficacy in managing safety. They quietly acknowledge that they prefer to view their historically low accident rates, and the fact that their airlines have not suffered an accident for a long period of time, as meaning they are long overdue for one – rather than that they have an excellent safety record. Likewise, they commonly discuss how they are uneasy about believing their own, or others', suggestions that they are doing well:

> There is always that risk that you start believing your own press releases, and away you go. You think, perhaps we don't need to put all that money into training and standards – because we are so good. (Si3-1)

Or as another put it:

> You've got to keep yourself honest and stop getting delusions of grandeur. That glossy magazine that we do – I've always had this uneasy feeling that it promotes us as being really good. And we aren't. (Si3-8)

Investigators are uncomfortable with apparent success and wary of its consequences, reflecting a deep humility towards their work. Likewise, investigators are quick to offer examples of where they have got things wrong and been caught out in the past. They aim for clear-eyed, dispassionate and 'independent' analysis, which in an ideal world would mean that they approach risk analysis in a way that "protects us from ourselves" (Si6-5), and tempers their "subjectivity" (Si6-4) and "biases" (Si6-1) in the process. These worries about being wrong, about their interpretations becoming 'skewed' and about losing their independence, run deep. As one investigator emphasised, "you've got to be sure you are right. And if you've got a vested interest in saying, well that defence is very, very robust – because you invented it – then the whole system is skewed again. Skewing is really easy to do" (Si6-1).

This deep appreciation of the fallibility – and fragility – of their own interpretations of risk leads investigators to hold their assessments of risk lightly (e.g. Weick, 1998b), considering their knowledge only ever provisional and always liable and open to change. They believe that their current understanding of risks will likely need to be revised in light of some future event or change of circumstances. And, because of that, they always want to make sure that they have "erred on the safe side" (Si4-3) in their judgements: "Your perception of risk may be pretty different to what I put in the box, but as long as it is equal to or higher, then that is just fine by me" (Si3-7). Ultimately, safety investigators are professional pessimists. They work hard to both maintain that pessimism and, as is examined in the next chapter, spread it around. They take a wary and cautious approach to their work that is based on a deep assumption of their own, and everything else's, fallibility. This wariness can be seen as an expression of the "chronic unease" (Reason, 1997, p. 37) that characterises effective cultures of safety. And the humility that it is based on is rooted in a deep appreciation of the inherent potential for ignorance in their work. By fostering scepticism and caution, investigators seek to remain alert and vigilant to the risks in airline operations – and in their own interpretations.

Identifying suspects: Representing problems and ignorance

A core focus of investigators is to identify where they can no longer be sure of organisational safety: where safety is suspect. Identifying suspect areas of organisational activity is how they monitor the adequacy of safety and aim to identify emerging risks. Investigators work to identify and focus on events that are disruptive or problematic to organisational safety, or their current understanding of it: "you're using them [incidents] to try and drive and recognise where your problems are" (Si3-2). Here, 'recognising problems' is a process of identifying suspect areas of safety: where there are gaps or inconsistencies in understanding. Many incidents are not interpreted as signalling that safety – or their understanding of it – has become problematic. In many cases, investigators believe that they understand the incidents and failures concerned, and believe them to be adequately defended against. In these cases, currently accepted beliefs about safety are not challenged or disturbed. As far as investigators are concerned, the large majority of incidents fall into this category:

> Most of them, you know enough to just fly through. [You] check and can say okay, it is not a problem... you're just flying through and they are standard. But as soon as you get into the contentious ones, you start talking about it. (Si3-1)

Many incidents are therefore dealt with routinely and, to a degree, automatically. Investigators are satisfied that they understand them, and that risk resilience is adequate in that area of operations. These incidents are not deemed to suggest possible problems or potential areas of ignorance, and the individual events concerned are frequently described as being "all part of normal operations" (Si4-3), and are effectively dealt with by the organisational processes in place. These incidents are considered – for the time being, at least – to be literally incidental, and are not suggestive of any deeper concerns. This conclusion is usually arrived at quickly and investigators review such reports rapidly, without provoking prolonged or in-depth consideration. But many events do provoke closer examination. These are the 'contentious' ones that are problematic in some way, and unsettle investigators' currently held notion that all is sufficiently safe and well in a particular area of operations. In these cases, investigators become suspicious and want to take a closer look to learn more: "Often it [risk assessment] is about going to get more information – if we are suspicious at all, then we get more information. It is better to ask questions and to see" (Si5-2).

To identify risks, investigators work to identify suspicions: where there is no conclusive evidence, but where they are no longer confident or sure about safety. Identifying where safety is suspect is the primary means of finding new risks – by uncovering the ignorance and false assumptions that pave "the path to adverse events" (Reason, 2004, p. 32). Becoming suspicious is the first step towards becoming aware of their potential ignorance and of a possible new problem. That is, in their role of safety assurance, not being sure of safety is a strong indicator of a potential problem to explore further. This can arise either from a perceived weaknesses in safety – or from a perceived gap in their own surety of it. Either way, these suspicions signal an area of potential ignorance which in turn is a proxy indicator of a potential risk. It is around these suspicions and potential problems that investigators 'ask questions' and 'start talking'.

Identifying where safety is suspect provides a point around which investigators actively scrutinise and examine the organisation and attempt to build or update their representation of safety. Suspicions trigger investigation, active processing and scrutiny; they provide a locus for learning. There is always a set of safety issues that investigators are currently suspicious of and worrying about. And it is suspicions, rather than surprise, that are used as the primary means of identifying gaps in knowledge and for directing reflection and learning. Suspicions are markers for some aspect of organisational safety that has become problematic, and that investigators want to actively explore and understand. Investigators often describe these as being where things have become "an issue, not just events" (Si4-3) and where things are being 'flagged up', 'focused on' or "have the spotlight on it at the moment" (Si4-4). Simply, these represent where current awareness and active attention is being focused:

> You want to monitor it, and be able to say I can see what they are doing. They have the manufacturer involved, or the QRH has been changed, and the crews have been trained accordingly. So then it slips back down into the ninety five percent. (Si3-1)

Focusing attention is the first step in working to build a representation or account of a particular area: to take previously invisible and assumed activities and make them visible and explicit and, in so doing, attempt to find out and piece together what is wrong – if anything at all. On some occasions, this can involve reinterpreting and revising beliefs about the adequacy of safety in that area. On others, it might mean re-establishing that safety is, in fact, still acceptable. But in all cases, it involves focusing on a problematic issue until it can be properly represented and deemed to be understood and resolved, when investigators are again sure that safety is acceptable. Then the issue moves 'back down' or 'shifts back' out of reflective focus. These processes closely represent Turner's (Turner and Pidgeon, 1997, p. 166) notion of a "continual cycle of assumption" in organisations, by which assumptions and beliefs about safety are checked and tested against operational realities through the "exposure of the limits of assumption; the subsequent revision of the assumptions; and their replacement by new ones" (Turner and Pidgeon, 1997, pp. 166–167). Here, this cycle is fuelled and initiated by investigators' suspicions.

When working in teams, investigators communicate amongst themselves to build a shared and common awareness of potential risks, contributing and sharing insights from their own experience through the course of regular discussions. The communication that supports this collective awareness takes a variety of forms. It can range from brief comments that simply let others know that something has happened, through general conversations about incidents and past events, to more formally established meetings in which the most significant risks and their ongoing investigations are reviewed. In their day-to-day work, investigators talk about incidents a lot. At a basic level, this simply takes the form of mentioning events to one another: "did you see this incident in . . ." (Si4-2), or "we've got another one of those . . ." (Si4-3), or "what about that event at . . ." (Si4-1). This is particularly the case for those events that investigators consider might indicate a particular problem or risk, those that they do not understand or those that relate to an ongoing issue they are already looking into or have discussed previously.

Mentioning such events might include, for instance, reading the first few words of a report aloud, often to the groans of disappointment from others. Or more cynically, "if I tell you the location, guess what happened" (Si4-8). These are small moments of communication that do important interpretive work. Through these brief remarks, investigators help to build a shared picture of 'what is going on'. What is remarked on – what is literally remarkable – establishes the basic foundation of investigators' collective awareness of risks and the accounts they build of safety. Their collective awareness is also built through the shared working records they keep of any events that are considered of particular significance. These records take various forms, including weekly briefings, monthly reviews or large ongoing review files (dubbed on several occasions 'The Bible') into which any suspect or significant events are noted, along with any other news that is deemed safety-relevant – as well as, of course, evolving investigations and ongoing analyses. Contributing to these records – and regularly reading and reviewing them – are important ways of building a basic shared awareness of risk. By both referring and contributing to these shared documents, investigators keep up to date with the incidents that their colleagues consider significant and troublesome. Though a small and seemingly trivial part of daily work, the making of these notes – again, literally about anything considered noteworthy – helps to keep investigators collectively informed and up to date.

Shifting attention: Representing problems

Investigators focus on a continually shifting set of suspect and problematic areas: Reason's (1997, p. 36) "one damn thing after another". Investigators aren't, and can't be, suspicious of everything all of the time. Being suspicious is the opposite of taking something for granted. It requires actively questioning and doubting some aspect of organisational safety, which in turn requires attentional and cognitive resources – resources that are finite. More tellingly, as far as investigators are concerned, questioning organisational safety based on every error and minor event is neither practical nor necessary. Most errors and failures are deemed to be a normal feature of operations that could be well dealt with. Moreover, in practice, the capacity of oversight departments to ask, and follow up, questions is not boundless. As a senior investigator described: "if [the department] was three times the size, we could ask six times the questions. That way we wouldn't take anything for granted" (Si3-8). Attention – like all other organisational resources – is finite. And in any case, to investigators many errors are 'normal' and unremarkable.

Investigators therefore focus their attention on those areas where they suspect something is currently wrong and needs better under-standing. This is seen by investigators as an ongoing process of shifting their attention from issues that have been resolved to those that have become newly problematic and suspect. The current set of concerns continually change, as one investigator described: "This is a bit of a pet [topic] at the moment. Awareness is high at the moment and everything shifts. Give it six months and it'll shift back. There are always flavours of the month" (Si2-1). This results in a continually changing set of issues that are of focal concern – bearing out Roberts and Creed's (1993, p. 252) suggestion that the most reliable organisations "are characterized by continually changing cultures striving to avoid a non-goal". For investigators, this is experienced as a process of "new issues coming up and being exposed" (Si3-2) by them, with continual revisions to the non-goals that they strive to avoid.

For investigators, having a set of issues that are being focused on at any point in time does not mean that everything else is being entirely ignored. As they see it, their work involves reviewing and attending to all events and then identifying those which are of prime importance.

Prioritisation lies at the heart of risk assessment. But investigators view their work as not only being about focusing on a small set of priorities, but as being about continually reviewing and identifying these priorities, from the mass of minor incidents. This process of identifying and shifting their attention to potential problems needs to be well managed, to avoid risky 'spotlights':

> You need a steady, measured approach to this. Otherwise you end up with this knee-jerk, incident driven society. Something goes wrong, drop everything to see what's happened, the wise men sit around for a week banging the table – and then something else will happen and you move on to that. (Si3-8)

What is important to investigators is that their attention, suspicion – and discussion – continually shifts to cover and track emerging risks in a 'measured' way. They aim to properly place and focus their pessimism on areas of the organisation that most warrants it – and so avoid the "misplaced optimism" that can precede accidents (Turner and Pidgeon, 1997, p. 89). These processes are determined by the ways they use their suspicion and doubt when reviewing the ongoing stream of incidents.

Producing and using suspicion and doubt

Suspicion and doubt are key resources of interpretive vigilance. Investigators use them to direct the focus of their unease and wariness. Investigators identify and develop their suspicions as a way of becoming aware of potential ignorance. Through their day-to-day interpretive work, they use their suspicions and doubts to actively construct safety issues and carve out areas of potential ignorance. There are four principle ways that investigators use suspicions to construct tentative signs of latent risks. These are:

- identifying patterns of failure, where events appear to have some underlying or systematic order;
- drawing relations between minor incidents and broader safety issues, or seeing connections with past major events;
- perceiving novel occurrences that have not been known before, or that current beliefs are inadequate to fully account for; and
- picking up on any apparent inconsistency or discrepancy in operational processes, or their own knowledge of them.

All of these ways of developing suspicions of safety involve identifying and making sense of necessarily weak, equivocal indications of risk. They are ways of constructing early signs of potential ignorance and possible problems. Here, producing suspicion depends on investigators putting incidents in a specific sort of context, such as that of similar incidents, past major accidents or as a reflection on the bounds of their own knowledge. Broadly, the former two processes of identifying suspicions are based on judgements of similarity – constructing patterns, making relations and matching like with like (e.g. Weick, 1995). The latter two processes are based on judgements of difference – finding gaps, disjunctions and discrepancies (e.g. Turner and Pidgeon, 1997; Weick and Sutcliffe, 2001). There is a degree of ease with which each of these processes can run into each other. In practice, none is entirely distinct from the others. For instance, once a pattern of failure has been identified and classed as an issue, this can then lead into connections being drawn between that issue and other more disparate and diverse events. Equally, seeing a novel or apparently new type of event can provoke a retrospective review of past events and reveal a previously unidentified pattern. This fluidity in the way that investigators create suspicions and develop their doubts demonstrates that, when working to reveal latent organisational risks, any suspicious starting point will do.

Making patterns: Constructing order in failure

Investigators believe that safety is suspect if they begin to see some sort of pattern in reported incidents. They constantly work to find connections and interrelations between individual events, however weak. Such patterns suggest to them that there is some common, underlying risk. As such, they aim to identify order in operational errors and failures – where events appear symptomatic of some persistent organisational flaw or organisational condition. These patterns are sometimes relatively obvious and easy to see. Most straightforwardly, they take the form of similar events being repeated:

> That is one of my prime triggers I think. You don't get enough of the really scary ones that you could work with, so you have got to start looking at interception at a lower level. And repeated events to me is an indication of a problem. You can use that to try and stop it early. (Si3-1)

Having near identical events 'repeat' is unusual but not unheard of. It is a strong indication of an underlying problem. One of these "repeaters"

(Si5-1), for instance, involved unrestrained cargo. Over a couple months, investigators at one airline had noticed several similar events involving pieces of cargo in the aircraft hold being found, on arrival, to be improperly fastened down – or not fastened at all. In the events, little more happened than the flight crew reporting hearing a 'thump' on occasion. But unrestrained cargo can be a problem if it moves around and affects the trim and handling of the aircraft. The concern was that pilots would "find out about it on landing and approach or take-off, when you'd least want to find out" (Si4-4). Three events had been reported in the first month, and then it went up to about seven in the second month, and investigators were concerned that they had been seeing "bigger lumps of cargo" moving around (Si4-4) into the bargain. Although the incidents were relatively small in number and had little actual impact, investigators flagged this up as a "minor issue snowballing" (Si4-4). These events presented a clear pattern to them, suggesting that something was amiss in the activities surrounding the loading of cargo. On further examination, investigators found that all the events could be traced back to the same terminal, reinforcing and localising their suspicion of an underlying organisational problem in the work practices there, and leading to a more detailed investigation.

Recurrent events do not always occur in such a quick or clear succession. But a series of similar events, nonetheless, still "jumps out" (Si4-13) at investigators. In the case of the parking problems described in Chapter 2, seven near-identical events were spread over a period of some five months. These all involved errors made by the crew marshalling aircraft towards the same terminal at the same destination. On one occasion this led to an engine being damaged as it came into contact with a loading jetty. All of these events happened on practically the same stretch of tarmac – to the increasing incredulity and agitation of investigators. These repeated events quickly convinced investigators of a clearly systematic problem with marshalling at that destination. Investigation primarily pinned this down to a simple yet persistent problem: stop lines for one type of aircraft hadn't yet been painted on the ground at the newly opened terminal. After the clear failure of previous attempts to put it right, this string of events also made investigators doubt the effectiveness of the general processes of safety management at that station – though this was something largely outside of their organisation's control. Seeing a pattern of repeating incidents shows that the processes to prevent recurrence – a basic principle of safety management – are not working. As such, patterns of failure represent something of a double failure to investigators. In this case, it led them to question why such a simple failure as missing stop lines (along with the concomitant ground crew training and education) could have 'slipped through' in the first place. Framing that question led them to discover that, while the airline had rigorous processes for assessing the safety of new destinations, it did not have any formal process in place to assess new extensions, such as this new terminal, at current destinations. This pattern of events therefore focused their analysis on this aspect of their own organisation and allowed them to identify and challenge a false assumption that they had previously taken for granted. It had made them ask, "do we just assume they are regulation stands and so are okay? Who does this in the organisation, dealing with new stands?" (Si4-6). So their suspicion of a deeper organisational inadequacy, on this occasion, was borne out.

Patterns are not always so easy to see. Events are not always clearly and obviously related. In many cases, investigators see patterns of failure based on more subtle relations. In these cases, investigators have to more actively construct and piece together the possible relationships between events. For instance, on reviewing an event in which a crew had been slow to disconnect the autothrottle – which resulted in a small eight knot speed exceedence for the flap setting – an investigator connected this failure with a set of apparently diverse events:

> This is a distraction-type one, we're starting to get pissed off with these. It's a flight management problem. If the auto-throttle didn't manage the speed then someone should be watching it . . . There were two last week. [Flipping to a copy of last week's brief.] Here, a crew taxied onto the runway – this sort of thing has killed lots of people, we don't want it. And a crew forgetting to set the altimeter out of QNH [the altitude mode valid only for landing and take-off, not cruise] giving a 400 feet error – that's putting them into situations where there's only TCAS [the traffic warning system] to save you. (Si4-1)

Soon after, another event was added to this emerging pattern, when crew reported flying a manoeuvre too slowly for the flap setting they were on, causing the investigator to wonder aloud:

> This is pilot handling, so is it part of a big picture, are we building up a risk? Is this something we need in the sims [simulators] or training – or a route check? (Si4-1)

Seeing a pattern of related events provoked a number of questions about whether there was an underlying, emerging source of risk that might connect these superficially disparate events, and they wanted to find out more. Perhaps these various events indicate that they were 'building up a risk' – in this case, where there seemed to be events accumulating around the issue of inattentive pilot handling and crew 'distraction'.

Identifying possible connections between events, that indicate an underlying risk, is a basic source of investigators' suspicions. The links between these events are not as clear as outright 'repeats'. Investigators often have to actively make these connections and creatively find ways that events might be related. This is more challenging interpretive work than that required to identify repeated instances, where the obvious similarity of events do much of the work for them. The basis of this interpretive work is therefore pattern making as much as pattern matching (cf. Klein, 1998). Patterns of failure are not always immediately obvious. Whether an event is part of a 'big picture' is not always self-evident. Investigators must actively build the big picture they suspect an event might fit into: actively hypothesising and imagining the underlying common circumstances that could link otherwise disparate events.

The patterns that investigators make are typically based on a small number of events. Investigators are terribly generous with the term 'trend', precisely because they want to find trends and fix them early. In the extreme, two events can indicate a trend. They are equally liberal with the term 'spate': three or four events can make one. Their suspicions, as such, are largely based on them "extrapolating" very small patterns – "a trend that you have picked up on" (Si3-1). They aim to identify trends when they are still small. As such, they knew that often, "you can't back it up with enough data. The bigger the trend the better, but the database won't always tell you that, because it is three examples that lead you to a conclusion" (Si6-5). The imperative to act early runs counter to the comfort of accumulating lots of data. Actively making patterns – and through that process, identifying risks – is therefore largely an interpretive rather than a statistical exercise. It is based on the construction and interpretation of a feasible pattern of failure, one that points to and supports an imagined underlying, common and systematic organisational weakness or condition. It is not based on the number or frequency of events reaching a certain predefined threshold or level.

Drawing connections: Relating major issues and minor events

Investigators develop suspicions by drawing a connection between an incident and a broader safety issue or past major accident. Making such a relationship, no matter how weak, leads them to doubt the adequacy of safety in the area concerned. Past accidents and broader safety issues – such as industry-wide problems identified by safety agencies or ongoing investigations – provide strong frames of reference that investigators use to interpret otherwise minor and equivocal events. References and allusions to past accidents while reviewing incidents are profligate. Incidents that cause most concern are often related by investigators to some major accident or event in the industry. As already illustrated, investigators' discussions of possible risks and safety events are full of references to past accidents. An incident could be "like Taipei" (Si2-1), or was "Tenerife all over again" (Si4-3), or "stinks of Milan" (Si4-4) – all references to past major air accidents. These connections are made on the basis of any perceived similarity between the organisational processes that underlay those past accidents and those implicated in an incident.

For instance, in one incident a crew reported that they had nearly used the full length of the runway to land. It had been raining, and there had been a brief moment of confusion over the windscreen wiper. As a result, they had inadvertently left the autothrottle engaged and failed to select idle reverse thrust, actions which they had planned to do and had briefed for prior to their descent. Without selecting reverse thrust the aircraft had less stopping power on the runway, and so took a longer distance to slow down. To investigators, this was immediately deemed "a bit of a QF1" (Si4-1), referring to the flight code of another airline's aircraft that had overrun a runway under similar – though far from identical – conditions several years before. Relating an incident such as this to the broader frame of a past major accident leads investigators to question aspects of organisational safety more broadly, and more seriously, than an event on its own would reasonably justify. Connecting an otherwise minor event and a past accident is one way that investigators extend and expand their concerns beyond the immediate incident reported. Investigators consciously use and draw on their knowledge of past accidents as an interpretive resource:

> It's quite specific, what we try to do is see what other operators are doing. So if we see the results that another operator has gone that one step further, and we think we're only one step back from it, then we will try and use that. If we have exactly the same procedures, do everything the same – but we haven't been unlucky enough to do the last bit. (Si3-1)

Past accidents are used as interpretive tools by investigators, to identify possible risks in their current organisational activities. Making these connections suggests ways in which their operations may be unwittingly exposed and poorly protected against risks. Investigators continually work to relate their knowledge of organisational accidents to reported incidents, believing that essentially, "we know all the basic ways to crash an aircraft, they've all been done before. The thing is to recognise when you're getting into that situation and to stop it" (Si4-8).

Investigators aim to recognise signs that aspects of their current operations are similar to the processes and conditions involved in past accidents, however 'tenuous' those connections may be. One investigator, for instance, reviewed an event where a coupling of a fuel line failed during refuelling, causing a spillage. He was concerned about this because the year before, a similar failure had resulted in a serious fire and the death of a member of ground crew. This event seemed "exactly the same scenario" – though with just this one incident being related to that one past accident, he explained that it was nonetheless a "tenuous link" (Si4-4). Tenuous though these links may be, such connections provide a key basis for identifying suspect areas of safety. Importantly, making these connections serves to illustrate the reality of such risks. It shows that, "they are not impossible. They have gone past being theoretical, it pushes the potential into an actuality, even if it is someone else's [accident] – like after that deep landing [linked to a similar runway overrun accident]" (Si2-1).

Past accidents therefore provide two key moments and opportunities for learning. The first is when they initially happen. Accidents in the industry spark a review by investigators of their own processes and systems: to actively "put yourself in someone else's accident" (Si6-1) and retrospectively review the incident database to identify similar events in their own operations. The second opportunity for learning is when a reported incident suggests that operations might be going in the same direction as a previous accident in the industry. These two opportunities to learn from the experience of others are heavily exploited by investigators. They provide 'free lessons', a term often used by investigators, as they come without the costs of an accident – though they are "not free to those who had the accident of course" (Si4-1).

Similar interpretive processes are used in relating incidents to other safety issues and the broader concerns of investigators. There are always a range of high-priority issues that investigators are looking to make connections with. "People have hot potatoes or current high priority issues they are watching out for, like unstable approaches or runway incursions. So incidents with similar operational effects are of special importance because of that" (Si2-3). These current 'issues' arise from a variety of sources. Sometimes they emerge from particular accident enquiries within the industry. This included the 'runway incursion' issue, where several accident investigations and a series of near miss-events within the industry had highlighted the risks of aircraft colliding during take-off or landing due to an aircraft crossing an active runway without permission. Sometimes issues emerge from analysis work or special reports produced by safety agencies or regulators. This includes the 'unstable approach' issue, where approach and landing accidents are continually ranked as a top risk by several safety agencies. Equally, issues can arise from investigations or analyses conducted within investigators' own organisations. This is particularly the case for any ongoing or active investigations, or problems that investigators can't seem to get to the bottom of and that form part of the current set of active risk issues. This includes, for instance, the pattern of pilot 'distraction' that investigators had previously identified: "this is an issue not an event now" (Si4-3). It had become a persistent worry to investigators, specifically in conjunction with missed checklist items, and they were finding it hard to understand and resolve. It had become an active risk issue and one that could be re-activated and strengthened by even the most apparently minor of related events. For example, one investigator drew this connection while reviewing a report describing how an incorrect altitude level was entered into the computer prior to take-off – an error attributed by the crew to 'high workload', extended delays and bad weather. But as the investigator explained:

> We're just getting into that pilot distraction thing, not much, but with lots going on with lots of changing runways, that's when they should be checking those little things. It's a small thing but it's part of a bigger picture. (Si4-1)

Drawing out where 'small things' such as this are part of a 'bigger picture' is one mechanism through which investigators develop and amplify doubts about the adequacy of organisational activities in that area of operations. Moreover, as in this case, connecting various minor events to a central 'issue' extended the boundary of investigators' suspicions: it is the means by which investigators 'generalise' and 'expand' errors to have broader consequences for the organisation. Events that otherwise would be considered largely unremarkable can, if seen to relate to some broader issue, become deeply problematic, both enlarging the importance of the incident and equally enlarging the scope and range of the issue itself. This process of relating minor events to more major issues is a key tactic used in investigators' interpretive work to identify emerging risks.

Perceiving novelty: Seeing the new and revising the old

Investigators doubt the adequacy of organisational safety – or their knowledge of it – if an event is perceived to suggest some new or previously unrecognised facet of organisational failure. Recognising new ways that operational processes might break down is a key indicator of potential ignorance for investigators. It involves perceiving signs of new and previously unheard of forms of organisational weakness – either by seeing new forms of failure or by seeing new implications of known failures, such as novel ways that they might occur and develop:

> It could be either a new kind of condition or a condition you have had for a while, but you will suddenly see it as a major link in a chain . . . a new link in a chain that gives us an unease. (Si4-7)

Perceiving new organisational 'conditions', or previously unrecognised implications of existing ones, raises investigators' unease and suspicion. Recognising novelty is a simple and direct way of exposing the limits of current knowledge. This process is as much about reflecting on their own knowledge as it is about examining organisational processes. So while making patterns and drawing connections involves a 'big picture', perceiving novelty is more about identifying where there is either no picture or holes in the picture. It depends on investigators identifying a gap or inadequacy in their current understanding of organisational safety. Signs of novelty suggest to investigators that their knowledge of the specific organisational activities surrounding some event is lacking.

Some incident reports represent events that have not been encountered before by investigators. They involve new forms of failure that have not previously been heard of or foreseen. Investigators find these fairly straightforward to identify because, simply, it is obvious that they don't already know about them. For instance, in one incident the flight crew, on their pre-flight check of the aircraft exterior, noticed a stream of water from a drain at the rear of the aircraft. The crew asked an engineer to investigate it, and on closer examination a puddle of iced water was found in the bay area underneath the vertical stabiliser fin, partially submerging some flight control cables. Investigators immediately identified this event as "an interesting one" (Si4-6) that was "obviously serious". It was obvious to them that the water could freeze on a long flight, and may interfere with the flight controls running through the area. And it was interesting to them because they had not seen a specific event like this one before, where the 'stabiliser bay' had become flooded. As a result, they wanted to track down where the water had come from, how long it had gone unnoticed – and why – as the first steps to understanding any gaps in the organisational activities involved.

In this case as in others, signs of novelty are typically perceived in terms of the specifics of organisational activities. In investigators' day-to-day work, novelty is perceived with regard to the specific forms that organisational weakness can take or the particular ways that a failure could come about. In the example above, neither leaks from fluid systems nor water freezing around flight controls were entirely new or unheard of failure modes. What was novel was the leak at that specific location onto those particular flight control cables along with – investigators presumed – the associated weaknesses in the specific organisational activities that surrounded those activities and allowed them to occur. Although signs of novelty can at times be straightforward to recognise, these signs are commonly both subtle and specific. They involve sometimes modest but nonetheless important 'variations on your risks', in terms of some slightly different or new facet of degraded resilience.

A similar example concerned the reporting of momentary 'sticking' of flight controls during cruise. On further extensive investigation this turned out to have resulted from de-icing fluid accumulating in crevices of the aircraft, re-hydrating on warm, humid days and then freezing at high altitude – later discovered to be an industry-wide problem (e.g. Wastnage, 2005). On its own, problems with flight controls are clearly considered a 'bad thing'. But importantly these events also signalled a gap in investigators' knowledge regarding the organisational activities that created this situation. Here, for instance, investigators had uncovered a new and previously unknown risk associated with de-icing, a risk that was initially indicated by way of minor incidents of momentary stiffness of the flight controls. This novel risk, and the novelty of the underlying sources of the risk, had not been identified by other means. As one investigator described, "the audits say: de-icing procedures – all in place and complied to" (Si5-6). Surfacing novel and previously unrecognised sources of risk therefore requires a nuanced and subtle view of novelty, and a close engagement with the specifics of operational activities.

Incidents can provide early descriptions of unexpected operational events, and are actively used by investigators to discover new aspects and variations of organisational risk. Nonetheless, investigators do not expect risks to present as entirely new or radically different forms of failure. As explained on numerous occasions, most types of events and forms of failure have been seen before:

> People are always trying to find new ways to kill themselves, even though a lot in aviation is stuff that has happened before. (Si3-3)

And,

> People always try to invent new ways to crash aeroplanes, but it is very difficult to do so. (Si3-9)

Although,

> We do amaze ourselves at times with our creativity in creating new ways to do things incorrectly. (Si3-7)

In general, most broad categories or types of failure have been seen before. Incidents that lie entirely outside the range of experience are not common, though they do occasionally occur and can stand out strongly when they do. As such, investigators mostly work to discern where otherwise routine events might suggest some nuanced and subtle element of novelty.

Remaining open and sensitive to slight aspects of novelty is a particularly challenging aspect of analytical work – it involves remaining open to signs of new threats emerging in areas of operations that have previously become taken for granted and invisible. It is not practical for investigators to 'take nothing for granted'. But investigators nonetheless aim to avoid 'stereotyping' incidents or "becom[ing] general or bland in my application of risk" (Si4-7). Each incident reported, whether of a well-known type or not, is considered an opportunity to reconsider whether the underlying safety of organisational activities may have changed – and whether current beliefs are in need of revision. Differentiating new risks by identifying novelty depends on attending to the details and specifics of operational events. Novelty is not apparent when analysing broad categories or trends in general event types. It requires a close examination of specifics and particulars. One striking example of novelty being revealed in apparently routine incidents involved a type of event that had been seen regularly by investigators – the erroneous selection by pilots of the autopilot activation switch instead of the disconnect switch, described in Chapter 2.

This switch automatically applies full engine power, either for take-off or for conducting a go-around, which if erroneously engaged can cause a surprising and inappropriate application of power in the final stages of landing. As previously described, this type of error was well known to these investigators and was usually committed by pilots who have recently moved from one fleet to another, where the switches are located in a different position to their location on other aircraft. Investigators estimated that they had seen about one of these events every couple of months since the aircraft had been introduced. One summed up their position:

> We've investigated this to death, and unless [the manufacturer] changes the ergonomics we'll keep getting them. So it's a grass cutting exercise . . . It's not unsafe. It's a known problem, we know what it is, and the fix really is just educational. (Si4-6)

The accepted belief was that, although it was essentially believed to be "design-induced pilot error" (Si4-1), the rate of events was being monitored by them and crews were sufficiently trained and aware of it. Investigators therefore considered that operations were adequately protected in this area: crews were trained to avoid the error, they were appropriately prepared for it when it happened and could recover effectively. They either "catch it and keep [the approach] stable" (Si4-6) or abort the landing attempt and complete an unplanned but routine go-around manoeuvre.

The incident that dramatically changed this view was initially only seen to be slightly different to all the others previously encountered. The crew, while recovering from a switch mis-select error, let their air speed decay a little and, although they didn't get a stall warning, they deviated from the target speed for the aircraft. This degraded safety margin was what investigators immediately noticed and became concerned about in the incident report. Through the investigation, they further found that the whole recovery and go-around had been performed poorly, with a range of tasks out of sequence:

First investigator: The recovery was a problem, they totally lost it on all of it – the gear was still down, flaps [were set incorrectly], the nose was up.

Second investigator: The problem was they had two different mental models of what they were doing.

First investigator: And there were no plans in there, they were pulling
                        things left and right. (Si4-1/6)

Bluntly, as far as investigators were concerned, what started as an error
became a mess. This incident resulted in considerable doubts about the
adequacy of numerous organisational activities that surrounded and
defended against these switch mis-select errors – and more broadly,
go-around manoeuvres in general. It was subject to prolonged investigation and actions on "a whole bunch of issues beyond the physical
selection of the switch" (Si4-6), such as sharing mental models, crew
communication, go-around training regimes in the flight simulators and
the efficacy of crew briefings for such situations. The reinterpretation
and re-examination of this event dramatically challenged a previously
established view of safety. "We thought selecting [this switch] was not in
itself an unsafe action. This altered our view that it was unsafe" (Si4-6).
Investigators uncovered a latent organisational risk by identifying
novelty in a routine event, and in doing so overturned their previously
accepted beliefs of organisational safety.

Sensing disjunction: Finding inconsistency and discrepancy

Investigators suspect that safety may be inadequate when they identify any apparent inconsistency in organisational activities, or their
own knowledge of them. These inconsistencies and discrepancies are
where things don't seem to properly match up or fit together – either
in organisational activities or in how investigators understand them.
They are often subtle signs, and their precise nature or cause is rarely
immediately obvious to investigators. These signs are "the little nig-
gling things" (Si2-1) that they sense in events, the things that 'irk'
them, where it seems that there is "something not quite right" (Si3-3),
but they typically don't know exactly what. A simple example of this
concerned a report that described an apparent mismatch between the
'ECAM' (Electronic Centralised Aircraft Monitoring) warning drill and
the 'MEL' (Mandatory Equipment List) procedures for dealing with a
fuel pump pressure warning prior to take-off. This provoked immediate
concern: "Anytime we see a disagreement between ECAM and MEL it's
very worrying, as the manufacturers write both. And generally the crew
follow the ECAM. So we definitely need to understand this" (Si4-6).
In this case, due to this procedural conflict, the crew ended up having
to go against the ECAM procedures in order to prevent fuel cross-
feeding into an inappropriate fuel tank. So this event signalled that

there was an inconsistency in the procedures specifying this particular set of crew actions (between the ECAM and the MEL), and that there was also a discrepancy with how investigators understood crews to normally act – here, by going against the ECAM. Discrepancies like these worry investigators, and they consequently want to understand them further.

In initially finding organisational disjunctions like these, investigators rarely know which – if any – side of the mismatch is the 'correct' one. And it is partly this relative ignorance that augments their suspicion. On a different occasion, another procedural confusion was flagged up by investigators as warranting further scrutiny. The incident involved confusion between the flight and ground crew about when in the arrival sequence chocks should be placed under the aircraft wheels – a seemingly minor point that demonstrates the extent to which organisational activities are specified and proceduralised:

> I'll stick this one in [to the significant events log]. I'm not sure about the procedures, but these two people clearly have different understandings of this procedure. It doesn't matter who's wrong, but that they believe the procedures are different. (Si4-8)

Organisational inconsistencies such as these, involving even minor disagreement between the way two people understood a procedure or activity, are interpreted by investigators as weak signals of potentially more serious problems. These sorts of operational discrepancies are relatively easy to spot. More challenging for investigators is identifying where organisational activities may be missing certain elements, or have been omitted entirely.

Noticing omissions is more critically dependent on the knowledge, experience and expectations of experts doing the noticing (Klein, 1998; Weick and Sutcliffe, 2001). Investigators become suspicious when they perceive some sort of slight discrepancy between what they would expect to happen and what is actually reported in incidents. A noteworthy example of this that has already been briefly mentioned concerned an incident where a take-off had been aborted at low speed due to an engine overspeed warning – a warning that signals that one of the compressor fans in the engine is spinning too fast, reducing thrust. The flight crew immediately contacted the engineering control centre, and were advised to check the engine with a stationary engine run and, as that was clear, to depart as planned. While rejected take-offs are considered part of normal operations, the investigator became suspicious about the advice given to the flight crew on this occasion. He wasn't sure, but "thought they would have done other checks before restarting" (Si4-3) with that particular type of warning. He decided to have "a dig around" (Si4-3) and made a few phone calls, and found out that the powerplant engineers "weren't happy" (Si4-3). They confirmed that it was a 'red' EICAS (Engine Indicating and Crew Alerting System) warning that required maintenance checks be conducted. The general performance of engineering control on this occasion was consequently called into question, and was subject to further investigation. Picking up on small discrepancies between the way investigators believe things should be and the way they appear to occur in incidents therefore allows investigators to identify potential emerging risks. Suspicions are developed based on identifying where their expectations are challenged or violated by events, even in the weakest of ways.

Incidents can also suggest that some discrepancy in an organisational activity exists merely by virtue of their occurrence. Merely that an event has happened can sometimes be enough for investigators to identify some sort of mismatch between their understanding of operations and the actuality. Instances of flight crew reporting smells of oil in the cockpit is a case in point. Over time, this developed into an ongoing issue that was being actively investigated by a number of airlines, manufacturers and agencies – but that had resisted adequate explanation. It was still not well understood. Continuing to experience these events reaffirmed to investigators that, despite any progress they believed they had made in the investigation, a discrepancy remained between their knowledge of the problem and its stubbornly hidden causes. In such cases, incidents are used as a way of confirming there is still some unknown but persistent discrepancy in understanding that needs to be accounted for to regain control. These incidents are used to try and further bracket and refine where that discrepancy might lie. For instance, as mentioned earlier, at one point in this ongoing investigation investigators believed that oil servicing and maintenance may be one of the most likely suspects. This suspicion led to closer scrutiny of those processes, which in turn revealed further questions – at root, that there seemed to be so many different standards and so much conflicting evidence relating to these practices. That is, investigators came to doubt their own – and others' – understandings of what had previously been considered a well-known and simple process of measuring and servicing aircraft oil levels.

By sensing discrepancies, investigators can come to suspect both the adequacy and efficacy of organisational activities, and their own knowledge of them. Developing suspicions around discrepancies is one of the core ways that investigators attempt to uncover previously latent organisational risks. These moments of ignorance act as focal points around which investigators organise attempts to understand, investigate and represent potential organisational risks. The work that investigators do to initiate and coordinate these activities of safety investigation and improvement are the subject of the next chapter.

7
Improving and Evaluating Safety

How do investigators address risks and enact safety improvement? And how do they determine where to focus those efforts? The answers to these questions are complicated by the organisational arrangements within which safety management is conducted. Investigators, like many risk managers, are typically based in independent safety oversight departments with no executive authority or direct operational responsibilities. This separation between safety oversight and operational control is common in many risk management systems and is designed to encourage the reporting of safety incidents and other safety information, and to provide an independent, impartial and critical view on matters of risk and safety. But this separation also dramatically influences how investigators can act on risks and improve safety. With no direct control over operational departments, investigators work in more subtle ways to initiate, coordinate and shape safety improvement activities. This chapter examines how investigators respond to and address organisational risks. It explains how investigators view the purpose and objectives of their safety interventions, what forms those interventions take and how appropriate action is evaluated, decided upon and carried out.

Action and improvement are at the core of investigators' practices. Investigators believe that acting to address risks and improve safety is the ultimate and overriding purpose of overseeing safety and analysing risk. But as they have no direct authority to take or enforce action in their oversight role, the focus of their work is largely targeted on getting others to engage in safety improvement and participate in risk management. Investigators aim to influence and effect safety improvement through several different routes. These include setting and communicating a clear safety agenda, initiating investigations and publishing regular reports. These are designed to reveal risks to relevant personnel, shaping their awareness of risk. A primary improvement tactic of investigators is therefore communicative and symbolic: to pose questions about safety and to publicise signs of potential problems. This is done to prompt local specialists to examine and review the organisational activities that are implicated in their own areas of responsibility.

In the case of more complex risks, attempts to generate action and improvement on a specific safety issue can involve bringing together networks of experts from different organisational departments, operational areas or even across multiple organisations. Investigators use the posing of questions and the publicising of problems to produce accountability and responsibility for safety improvement. When presented in front of peers, questions require a response and problems require a solution. By publicly highlighting and bracketing risk issues, investigators aim to ensure that the appropriate personnel take ownership of a risk – and are accountable for its resolution. By co-opting local specialists to reflect on and re-design organisational activities, investigators coordinate widely distributed activities of safety improvement and organisational learning. This learning is participative. Knowledge is developed and change is effected through the active participation and engagement of personnel in reflecting on, representing and redesigning organisational activities. That is, investigators work to manage risk and improve safety by creating *participative networks* of improvement around risks.

Evaluating the potential benefit of these interventions is a key aspect of investigators' work. In order to determine where to focus attentional and organisational resources, investigators evaluate the likely value or worth of taking action to improve safety. Assessments of safety value are central to how investigators understand and analyse risk. Safety value is commonly assessed in terms of three facets: the potential for learning and improvement; the efficacy and extent of any current organisational response; and the practicality of achieving a beneficial result. Investigators consider these three aspects of safety value to determine whether, and what type of, intervention would be most beneficial in a particular situation. This chapter first examines investigators' understandings of the purpose of action in their oversight role. It then explains the organisational nature and form of their action. Finally, it details how investigators appraise if and what action is appropriate and worthwhile to improve safety.

The nature of oversight and improvement

Investigators believe that acting on incidents – and risks – is the ultimate purpose of safety oversight. The purpose of collecting and analysing incident reports is to act: to use incidents to improve organisational safety. However, in their role of independent oversight, investigators do not have any executive control. They cannot demand or implement action. As such, investigators aim to guide and influence the activities of others to take ownership of risks and improve safety.

Using incidents: Applying resources and getting things done

A core belief of investigators is that, ultimately, the purpose of safety oversight and risk assessment is to improve safety. Reports of incidents, as such, are a basis for action and not an end in themselves. Incidents are used to provoke and trigger deeper investigation of risks, to focus organisational resources on problems and, essentially, to effect organisational change and safety improvement. As investigators see it, what matters most is what is actually done with incidents and how they are used to improve safety. Investigators emphasise that oversight and analysis are of no tangible use unless they achieve something. "In the end it is what you do with this stuff that counts. The corporate response is the most important bit in the end" (Si3-7). Incident reporting and risk analysis is deeply oriented to action and improvement: "It is what you do with the output that is important. If you spend a whole year in analysis and then do nothing, it is a year wasted" (Si3-8). Analysis is only considered worthwhile if it can be acted on – if something can be 'done' with it. A common criticism of many formalised analytical approaches and methods is that they take too 'academic' or 'purist' a view of risk. They are too complex, require more information than is feasibly available and provide analytical specificity beyond that which can be practically acted on – and therefore more than is practically useful for improvement. Instead, investigators say that they "take the pragmatic approach" (Si3-8). Analysis needs to be sufficient for organisational action – but only sufficient. Beyond that, more detailed analysis is regarded as being too 'academic' to be practically useful, and may even distract from taking practical action:

> They may have trouble with making [safety] recommendations, as they are a purist rather than a pragmatist . . . Purism has to be tempered with pragmatism even when it comes to risk assessing these things. (Si3-8)

And:

> It is a purely academic exercise unless you do something with it. So the question is, what are you doing with the risk, and how does that influence the organisation? (Si6-5)

This distinction drawn by investigators is essentially between analysis that attempts to produce a certain fact and analysis that allows them to effectively act. Their analytical efforts are always oriented to action, and risk analysis is a pragmatic process that is engaged in to achieve safety improvement:

> The risk rating is not, 'is it right or wrong', but is it helping you identify the areas where you need to put your resources? In its broadest terms, change processes and people, time and money – whatever it takes to reduce the risk. As long as it is doing that then it is working. It may not be 'pure' risk, but surely the whole raison d'être for this is being fulfilled. And that is all you can ask it to do. (Si3-7)

For investigators, analysing incidents is intimately tied to the management of risk: it does practical work within the organisation. When risk analysis is 'working', it allows investigators to allocate organisational resources to the problems that most need addressing. Assessments of risk are a prioritisation tool that generate action – a 'corporate response', as this investigator continued, "The purpose you do [analysis] is . . . because you want to understand the appropriate corporate response. It helps you focus your resources on the appropriate areas to bring about the change that will hopefully get rid of that problem" (Si3-7).

In this sense, what a risk assessment *means* is what it *does* in the organisation. Assessments of risks are used to get things done: to initiate investigation, focus resources, effect change and enact improvement. As far as investigators are concerned, that is the core purpose of their assessments. In practice, the line between analysis and action is not just blurred, but is in many ways indistinguishable. Investigators describe any attempt to separate analysis from action as something of a "chicken and egg" (Si3-7; Si3-3; Si5-11): analysis drives action and that in turn generates information to feed back into analysis. Investigators would be in a "grey area" without assessing the risk of incidents, simply because ". . . my job is [that] I need to get the right resources on the problems, and I have got to make sure that we are dealing with the big problems" (Si5-7). Analysing and assessing the risk of safety incidents is explicitly used to prioritise and drive action within the organisation. Effectively acting on risks is seen as the ultimate goal of incident reporting. At one level, this pragmatism is driven by the brevity of incident reports: reports provide so little information that anything of concern invites further investigation.

Pursuing incidents: Opportunities for investigation and improvement

Incidents reports rarely give investigators all the information they need to make a first assessment. Investigators' first response to reports is often that they need more information, as "the report didn't tell us what we want to know" (Si4-4). They expect incident reports to be "usually one-liners anyway" (Si3-8) and anything of interest will need to be followed up. As such, incidents are taken as small 'triggers' or 'flags' to pursue something further, to a greater (or lesser) depth: "All incident reports do is flag up that something has gone wrong . . . But you have the report, and that is your trigger to go out and find out what is really going on" (Si3-3). To investigators, incident reports invite action and investigation. Incidents are not seen as data to be analysed in depth, but as an opportunity to go and examine some facet of the organisation more closely. As the initial reports are considered to rarely provide the necessary information to support detailed or extensive analysis, passive analysis conducted at a distance will not do: incidents need to be acted on and 'chased up'. In the first instance, this action often takes the form of asking operational personnel for more informa- tion. The response of one investigator to a 'spate' of mis-set altimeters is typical:

> We've had another mis-set altimeter. We've had five or six of those, I'm going to find out what they are doing . . . But the five or six reports are bland. Most of them say due to distraction. What is a distraction? Why a distraction? What is happening? The reports don't tell you. So you've got to go there and ask questions and dig underneath . . . They are wonderful in that they are one-liners saying, 'Oi! Look at me'. And you may look at you, and think I'm interested in that and go and ask for more. But they don't give me a lot. (Si3-8)

Identifying a potential risk is considered an opportunity to take a closer look at a particular area of operations, to have a 'dig' around – to ask questions and review assumptions. But the information in the incident reports themselves rarely provides a sound basis for this. Incidents need to be acted on and further information needs to be gathered – something that is unavailable when reporting programmes are designed solely for the analysis, rather than the investigation, of incident reports (e.g. Wallace, Ross and Davies, 2003; Macrae, 2008).

The work of safety oversight is, in large part, bound up with chasing up incidents and finding out more about them: it involves investigating.

These are, after all, safety investigators. As such, assessments of risk and moments of suspicion are considered to be triggers for action. They signal that something has to be done. Indications of risk "should trigger a reaction in the organisation because that is actually a day-to-day meaningful application of risk; it triggers something" (Si6-5). As another investigator described, a signal of risk is "an internal thing to trigger us to do something . . . You can call it red, green, blue, whatever you want. But it's just an internal thing to trigger us that something has to be done" (Si6-7). As such, investigators commonly apply formal assessments or categories of risk to incidents as a means to communicate where they want to take a closer look at something, find out more and create action. Incident reports are viewed as opportunities to actively investigate and act on risks, and assessments of risk are used by investigators as a tool to guide and effect that action.

Independent influence: Guiding organisational action

Investigators are based in organisational units that have no direct authority over personnel. This is a typical arrangement for those professionals charged with managing incident reporting programmes and for risk management in general. This establishes safety oversight as a function separate from operational or production pressures and also from enforcement or disciplinary powers. But it also means that investigators have no power of executive control. Being independent, they can advise and make recommendations about safety improvement, but they cannot order or instruct. Investigators consider that their modes of action are more reliant on persuasion and influence. They work to shape the thinking and guide the action of others:

> We try and herd people into the position to get the job done right. We can't make them safe – we try and get others to make themselves safe. We can't turn around and say do it that way, as if they say no, we disagree with your recommendations – then what? (Si4-5)

Investigators are well aware that they do not have any executive authority, and have to work in partnership with those who do. For investigators, getting organisational action is therefore about influencing and guiding people to do things: they act to get others to act. "We can only lean on them more and more. It relies on them actually doing it" (Si4-3). Investigators cannot directly change a procedure, say, or alter crew training. But they can influence others to and much of their work is about persuasion and facilitation, and making sure that appropriate people throughout the organisation are taking ownership of safety:

> Happily we have got rid of the notion that '[the safety department] owns safety', but then the question is how do we exert an influence? And much of it is persuading people. It is about persuading others that your ideas are their own . . . We facilitate good decision-making and intelligence. Those are our two aims, safety facilitation and safety oversight, and it is keeping the two balanced. (Si5-6)

Investigators cannot effect change by imposition, "edict" or "decree" (Pidgeon, 1997, p. 11). They have to influence and persuade. Assessments of risk do not just need to be produced; they need to be actively sold to those who must act on them. As investigators depend on these 'softer' means of persuasion to assure safety, they work to maintain good relations with those they are overseeing. They believe it is more effective to exert their influence subtly, with diplomacy and tact. But occasionally they do have to be firm: to harangue, cajole and "shoot from the hip" (Si6-6).

Though they have no formal powers of enforcement, the role of oversight provides investigators with "subtle power" (Si4-5). Investigators regularly report on the adequacy of safety and its management publicly within the organisation and directly to those in the upper echelons of the organisation – to senior managers and directors. This provides a social mechanism of control. Investigators offer opinion on and account for the actions of others, both in public and private forums where reputations are at stake. "Each [area] is responsible for their own safety. So we help them, but we report on them too. So it is a white-hat, black-hat situation" (Si5-13). The position of independence provides investigators with the legitimate authority and organisational position to hold people accountable for safety improvement. Investigators, crucially, are also the key conduit to external safety regulators, who wield considerable power and authority. The authority of safety investigators is buttressed by the invisible hand of external regulators. The ultimate recourse for investigators is the regulator, carrying the implicit threat that "if you don't like our [safety] recommendations, then their's are going to be with knobs on" (Si1-2).

Investigators use these sources of authority and their independent position to influence operational departments and indirectly generate and guide organisational action. They believe that much of their influence comes from their independent facilitation, advice and investigation, where they work co-operatively with those responsible for safety.

But they know that their influence also arises from their powers to report on safety issues – and by implication, on those responsible for resolving them – to senior executives, peers within the organisation and ultimately to external regulators. They both 'herd' and 'lean on' people and use these forms of influence strategically, to actively guide and shape the risk management work of personnel throughout the organisation.

Creating networks of participation around risks

Investigators work to engage and guide the safety improvement activities of organisational personnel. They make personnel aware of risks by posing questions and publicising signs that point to potential problems. In doing so, investigators seek to get operational specialists to examine problems in their local area. And, by questioning and publicising safety issues, investigators actively create systems of accountability. Their actions subtly but purposefully require responses from those responsible for resolving risks. Investigators centrally oversee and coordinate widely distributed and locally owned activities of safety improvement, and use a range of social mechanisms to achieve this.

Revealing risks: Publicising signs and posing questions

Investigators seek to influence organisational personnel through effective communication. They work to make people aware of risks. The regular briefings and the incident investigation system are used to reveal new risks to personnel and to keep current risks visible. Investigators do this in two related ways: by asking questions and by publishing signs of risks. Both are intended to call some aspect of organisational safety into question. To investigate particular incidents, questions are put to operational specialists regarding the operational processes involved. And investigators' briefings and board papers are compendiums of recent events that are used to communicate significant or troubling warning signs that personnel should be aware of – and should address. In these ways, investigators' actions are predominantly aimed at influencing other peoples' ideas about, and understandings of, safety. Investigators shape awareness, guide attention and raise the profile of risks throughout their organisations. This work is in large part interpretive and symbolic, aimed at shaping the culture and understanding of safety throughout an organisation.

For investigators, the most immediate tasks of risk management largely concern determining who ought to be informed of what. Their thinking around an assessment of risk looks much like this: "I want to see it going to this board, and it is going to be on the minutes of that meeting, and oh God he's a major player, I better have a brief for him . . ." (Si3-7). In working to keep people aware of risks, investigators are creating and maintaining an informed culture (Reason, 1997; 1998). At base, having identified a risk, they aim to "flag it up, and say these are the things you should be looking at today" (Si6-1). They set and continually revise a safety agenda: what people should be aware of, attending to, thinking about – and acting on. This agenda is communicated by way of established organisational mechanisms: primarily the incident investigation system, the distribution of weekly briefs and the weekly meetings in which they are reviewed, and the quarterly board meetings. By these means, investigators engage in what Turner (1971, p. 125) calls "the management of awareness". Here, investigators seek to actively manage the organisational awareness of risks.

Investigators guide organisational attention by asking questions. Questions are put to specialists who have expertise and responsibility in the area of a particular risk. Assigning an 'action' in the incident investigation system invariably means asking someone a question. At their broadest, these questions simply request an appropriate person – such as a flight technical manager or a station manager – to "carry out an investigation and report on actions taken to prevent recurrence" (Si4-D). More specifically, investigators ask for particular information to be provided and reviewed, to clarify what has happened and why. For instance, regarding a report of a late landing, where the aircraft landed further down the runway than was usual, an investigator might want to know how long the runway was, how far down it they landed and whether they followed the appropriate procedures. In other cases, they might ask for further analysis of the event to be conducted by having the Flight Data Recorder 'trace' reviewed and the flight crew debriefed. Or they might ask a flight technical manager to review the processes and procedures through which airport charts and plates get updated.

The purpose of these questions is not merely to request information but to structure and guide the thinking and activities of the technical specialists and operational personnel responsible for resolving a risk. So, even when requesting quite specific information, investigators frame their questions broadly. While their questions relate to specific and quite localised operational incidents, the queries are typically open-ended and question the general adequacy of safety in that area. For example, in one event an aircraft was landed with close to only the reserve amount of fuel left onboard. Investigators found it curious that, during the approach, the crew had received – and cancelled – a ground proximity warning. They surmised that the warning may have been caused by a non-standard flap setting, a setting that is specified in the 'low fuel' checklist – and that the checklist may not have included an instruction to override the warning system to avoid the chance of an unnecessary go-around resulting from an erroneous ground proximity warning when the aircraft had little fuel remaining. Their suspicion was therefore highly specific and focused, and yet the question they put to a flight technical manager on the fleet was strikingly general. Having discussed the details of all this, one investigator simply advised another: "he's a good place to start, ask him if there are any issues about fuel there" (Si4-7). The first question put to the manager accordingly asked if there was any sort of 'issue' regarding fuel planning, and to please review the checklist omission. The purpose of these questions is not to pre-empt the findings and investigation of operational specialists but to initiate, guide, shape and oversee this local investigative activity and reflective enquiry.

On the basis of a specific occurrence, investigators question more general processes. By asking questions about incidents, investigators focus the attention of specialists in an operational area on a particular aspect of the operations that they are responsible for – but they do not presume or prejudge the answer, and they do not seek to prematurely shut down the search for sources of risk. These questions arise from investigators' suspicions, and help to represent and frame the gaps in their knowledge. What is more, by using these questions to direct the attention of specialists, investigators operationalise their suspicions: ignorance is made practical and used to do work in the organisation. Ignorance is spread around. Framed as questions, suspicions are used to guide the attention, awareness and enquiry of others. Questions focus attention on some aspect of organisational activity, both making it an object of enquiry and specifying what is not known about organisational safety. Questions bracket issues to be reflected on and inquired into.

Investigators guide awareness in the organisation by publicising incidents as signals of risks. Investigators report on significant safety events in various briefs distributed to board-level executives, directors, senior managers and operational personnel, and create brief narratives of risk and ignorance around these incidents. In one airline, for instance, investigators publish two complementary weekly briefs, a monthly review and two sets of quarterly board papers that present the most recent significant events in varying levels of detail, as well as a quarterly magazine and contributions to crew newsletters and briefings.

Incidents are described in these briefings to keep people informed of risks, and as a basis for closer attention and review of the associated risks by those closest to the relevant operational activities. Investigators actively use these briefings to these ends. Particular incidents are often included because investigators want them, for example, to "filter down as a reminder" (Si4-3) to the supervisors in an area. Or, in the case of an unsecured pallet of cargo being found several months after that particular issue was considered resolved, "it is just a heads-up that this has happened again" (Si4-4). On other occasions, an odd flight crew error was included, "just so that the training guys know about this" (Si4-1) over in the flight simulator team. Or they "put it in as Ground [Operations] should know about this" (Si4-2).

In this role of raising awareness and shaping knowledge of risk, investigators believe that their communications directly counter an inevitable and deeper organisational risk – the selective filtering of information as it passes up a hierarchy. Such filtering is, of course, a necessary component of organising (Turner, 1971). But biases in these filtering processes can create cultural blind spots and risks (Vaughan, 1996; Turner and Pidgeon, 1997), as investigators are well aware: "Senior management in any company like good news more than bad news, I am sure it is no different here" (Si3-1). By communicating incidents widely, such as distributing their 'significant incidents' weekly brief to the operations directors and senior managers, investigators seek to actively counteract this. They select incidents and issues that they believe might otherwise be overlooked:

> It's not just a long list but a good list too. It means it gets to people. With the best will in the world, the directors wouldn't have time to go in to [the database] to search himself, and so someone would be doing it for him. So if they aren't telling him the good stuff, then we are. So that stops the filtering. (Si4-1)

Incidents are publicised to make sure that the people who should know, do. Further, investigators often use briefings to more actively point to the existence of a risk. For example, they include groups of events to demonstrate a pattern, as was the case with a few incidents attributed to slips in flight management: "when we've got a couple more we'll bunch them together [in the brief]" (Si4-2). They include incidents to show that risks haven't gone away, but still, apparently, persist – as was the case with switch mis-selection errors: "that's going in, with what's been going on recently" (Si4-3). And they include even minor incidents that suggest that a problem may, for instance, be broader than currently thought. Investigators explain that these incidents are often included in the brief because of the 'general risk' or issue that they point to, rather than the specific events themselves. Again, investigators are putting their suspicions to work: they publicise the incidents that have led them to suspect safety, and they use this as a way of both communicating their awareness of risks and provoking similar questions and suspicions in others. In order to provoke action, the descriptions of incidents publicised in weekly briefs are kept purposefully short and brief. Like the questions that investigators pose, they use them to pique the interest of the relevant experts, bracket areas of ignorance and provoke active and closer scrutiny of safety throughout their organisations.

Engaging experts: Enacting local and distributed enquiry

Investigators inform people of risks for a purpose: to prompt the relevant specialists around the organisation to examine and review the implicated organisational processes. Investigators initiate and coordinate these investigations. Major investigations are large and lengthy, involving teams of specialists seconded from operational departments and led by several investigators. But most investigations are smaller in scale. These might involve only one operational specialist responding to a simple query. For example, any incidents implicating the 'sleeping receiver' problem previously discussed would be sent to an avionics engineer working on the investigation: "We push all of these his way. He's the guru on it, and we tend to leave it to the experts" (Si4-3). Or, risks might equally require more extensive investigation by specialists in several different operational areas, requiring investigators to involve a range of different personnel in the investigation of an incident. Investigators also provoke other processes of enquiry around the organisation, that are only loosely overseen by them, based on the briefs and reports that they publish.

Investigators work to engage local experts in examining suspect areas of safety. They want to 'get people thinking' about particular risks and to generate distributed processes of enquiry into risks around the organisation. This is the principle motivation behind including an incident in one of their briefs. An investigators' response to an incident of unrecorded maintenance work demonstrates this well: "Hmm: 'Unrecorded, unauthorised work carried out by unknown staff'. Let's put that in to get someone thinking about that" (Si4-1). Investigators aim to initiate enquiries into the adequacy of organisational safety by the experts and operational specialists who know most about the activities involved and who are best placed to investigate and improve them. That is one reason why they keep questions broad and the information in their published briefings short. They want to provoke closer scrutiny by others, rather than providing the answers themselves.

Investigators include only the barest minimum of information on incidents in their regular briefings, so that managers have to go and find out more about them. They are pleased when a weekly brief "sparks various actions, and they [the senior managers] do their homework before going to the briefing [meeting]" (Si4-6) to discuss it. On one occasion, an investigator recounted with some satisfaction an encounter earlier that day with one director: "He passed by my desk and said, 'Your brief! It's so long. We spent hours on it'. And then he just trudged away, looking depressed" (Si4-6). It isn't just that investigators liked to see their pessimism spread around – although they certainly do. It is that they want to prompt people to closely review incidents and examine the risks associated with them. They consider that providing the answers themselves is neither their place – "these guys are paid to do that and trained to do that and would be considered the experts. They are the competent person which, legally, I am not" (Si4-6) – and that it would blunt the spur of enquiry for others. This is as much the case with board papers as it is with the widely distributed briefings. For instance, having identified an increasing trend in checklist and standard operating procedure violations, one investigator explains, "We'll use this at the board to prompt discussion – we'll present it as, this is what we've spotted, rather than providing answers" (Si4-4).

Investigators ask challenging questions, not only of their own understandings of safety, but of everyone else's, too. They work to initiate and guide the enquiry and attention of experts who are distributed throughout the organisation. But they do not have complete and direct control over these enquiries. They can only prompt and shape them to a degree. As such, the activities they engage in are processes of social enactment, in Weick's (1995) terms, rather than of social control. Enactment is "acting that sets the stage for sense-making" (Weick, 1979, p. 147). Here, investigators act to provoke and shape the sensemaking of others around risks – to make them consider whether defensive processes are adequate and whether things can still be taken for granted or need to be revisited and revised. The activity of investigators is part of an ongoing interaction with specialists and personnel throughout the organisation. Investigators work to influence how the sensemaking of others proceeds. And how that sensemaking unfolds in turn shapes the circumstances that investigators themselves must then to respond to – according to what those enquiries reveal, whether improvement actions are considered appropriate, or whether they cause a surge of similar reports to 'flood in', as described previously. Investigators distribute the task of investigation to experts around the organisation to both draw on the knowledge of local specialists and engage them in safety improvement. Investigators do not seek total control over how these investigations progress. What they do seek, however, is to ensure investigations are conducted effectively and that the investigative and improvement activities of local experts from different organisational areas are properly connected and integrated. Investigators use incidents and their underlying risks as boundary objects that span organisational departments and engage different professional groups (Star and Griesemer, 1989; Wenger, 1999), and around which specialists from various operational areas are connected and work together to examine risks and improve safety. For investigators, this can involve mediating the interactions between, for instance, a powerplant engineer in Singapore who is concerned about an engine check being missed, the manager of an aircraft fleet and the manager of the engineering control unit at the airline's operational headquarters. In this particular instance, the investigator asked the flight crew for more details on the conversation they had had with engineering control; he requested that "powerplant give their opinion more formally", and then forwarded all this to the engineering control unit "to ask why their understanding was different" (Si4-6).

Investigators connect and coordinate distributed processes of enquiry throughout the organisation. They work to actively create these connections in the organisation, around these small yet concrete incidents and the indications of risk that these events symbolise. Incidents are transformed into symbols and tokens of risk, around which enquiry, diagnosis and investigation – that is, epistemic work – are organised. By enacting local and distributed enquiries into risks, investigators guide and shape an intelligent, informed (Reason, 1997) and reflective (Pidgeon and O'Leary, 1994) culture throughout the organisation – they actively create and maintain a culture that scrutinises itself. As such, investigators' work directly aims to counteract the risks that can result from strict organisational 'silos' (Hopkins, 1999; 2005), organisational fragmentation and communication barriers (Turner and Pidgeon, 1997), where sections of an organisation operate as distinct units that are largely ignorant of each other.

Further, though the specific tasks of investigation are conducted by a distributed and broad range of operational specialists, investigators retain an overview and composite picture. Their role is to "bring all the elements together" (Si5-14) and attend to 'the full picture'. As one described, because all the investigative actions are coordinated and recorded in the incident reporting system, "the incident [and investigation] report gives you a chance to go back over the whole story. You have an audit trail so you can see what people think about it and what they're saying, and you get everybody to add bits and pieces to it so you get the full picture" (Si3-9). Investigators coordinate the reviews of local specialists, retaining central oversight of these distributed and participative processes of investigation. The operational experts are the experts in their specific area, and are relied on for the details. But investigators attend to the big picture and how this fits together: they provide the view that encompasses the broader, organisational implications of a risk and any interactions across operational areas. This echoes Hopkins' (1999) recommendation that major, catastrophic risks are best monitored and managed by centralised units, as local personnel often neither have direct experience of them, nor would they be able to see the connections between problems in their area of the organisation and others. The central coordination of distributed processes of enquiry and investigation elegantly puts this into practice here.

Actioning accountability: Assigning ownership of improvement

Questioning safety and publicising risks is as much about creating accountability as it is about awareness. Investigators make risks visible to those responsible for responding to them and improving safety. Passing an incident to specialists to review also passes them ownership of their part of the risk, along with a concomitant responsibility to act. Likewise, incidents published in briefings serve to highlight risks to those who are responsible for resolving them. These processes make the ownership of risks visible, as much as the risks themselves. They are an invitation to act: "[We] don't take the decisions, we invite the departments to – to take ownership of safety . . . It is making them accountable, and it is their decision" (Si5-6). Asking questions of safety in a particular area of the organisation invites responses from all those who are responsible for managing it – the relevant line managers and operational specialists.

Investigators facilitate a process of allocating and distributing responsibility for resolving risks and improving safety. They work to get the appropriate personnel to take ownership of risks and to act on them. This ownership does not imply blame. Investigators are not concerned with determining a 'culprit' who is responsible for causing a risk – and, as far as they are concerned, there very rarely is one. Rather, investigators work to ensure that risks, once identified, are taken ownership of – that whoever is responsible for resolving a risk and improving safety is identified and held accountable for taking action. In posing questions and publicising events, investigators seek to remain impartial and independent. "It is not meant to be judgmental. We just say, this has happened . . ." (Si3-8). For instance, investigators were pleased to see how the morning after they had highlighted a number of incidents in their weekly brief, that those events that had not previously been acted on were all 'cleared up' in the airline's incident reporting and investigation system, and investigations had begun. Assigning ownership is seen as a necessary prerequisite to getting risks investigated and safety improved. Investigators create accountability for the improvement of safety through the organisational work they do: posing questions and making risks publicly visible within the organisation. Both put an onus on those responsible for acting on the risks to account for themselves and their action, and create a "regime of mutual accountability" (Wenger, 1999, p. 81) around improvement efforts.

Investigators do not just create spaces in which to investigate and represent risks. They also shape the organisational processes through which people determine what needs to be justified and explained and what needs to be accounted for – and then ensure that it is. Their 'awkward questions' help to both create accountability and motivate action, and are designed to ensure that people are talking about and acting on the right things: "It comes back to culture I guess. You do need to have this knowledge that someone who isn't necessarily on your side is going to ask you awkward questions, and your only defence against that is to do the best thing and the right thing in the right order. You need it, human nature being as it is" (Si3-7). Investigators aim to ask hard questions as that "keeps people honest . . . is a good health check and discipline. And that discipline filters back down through the organisation" (Si3-7). Despite being independent and with little formal power or means of direct control, investigators nonetheless oversee and manage some of the key mechanisms through which people are held accountable for safety. Investigators use these mechanisms as resources for shaping action and priorities.

Briefings of significant incidents, and their associated risks, are publicised not only to those responsible for resolving them – but to their seniors and peers within the organisation. These briefs are reviewed in weekly meetings in which senior representatives from all operational departments are present. Publicising significant events in their organisation therefore creates a form of public accountability. Likewise, the actions taken by managers on incidents published in board papers are subject to close scrutiny in board and committee meetings, and those responsible for dealing with them are held to account – literally producing public explanations and accounts of how a risk has been addressed and the reasons for believing that safety has been improved. And, as already quoted, the details and responses that get appended to incident report investigations in the safety management and information system by specialists form an 'audit trail', identifying who has done what. This allows investigators to oversee and challenge those actions, and also holds specialists accountable for those actions. Actions to address risks can be challenged by investigators, who retain oversight of the adequacy – or not – of organisational action on risks. As discussed previously, insufficient or ineffective action is treated by investigators as a troubling failure in itself. As such, investigators' relationship with operational experts is not one of complete deference. While the expert views and actions of specialist personnel are mobilised to manage risk, and their expertise and close proximity to operations is respected and made use of, authority does not reside entirely with the experts involved (cf. Rochlin, 1989; Weick and Sutcliffe, 2001). In contrast to current theory on high reliability organising, it is responsibility and accountability – rather than authority – that 'migrate' to those with the requisite knowledge.

Operational experts and technical specialists throughout the organisation are made accountable for risks, and their actions are reviewed by investigators. The accountability that investigators help to create is a key source of their 'subtle power', and is used to influence organisational action where they would otherwise have no formal or executive control. One example, for instance, arose when reviewing an event where a birdstrike resulted in noise and vibration from an engine, yet the crew opted to continue their short flight. Investigators were concerned at this decision, and yet the question posed by them to the fleet management remained neutral:

> Why did they continue, with noise and vibration? Why did they carry on? It's not acceptable to me. One dodgy engine on a two engine aircraft. You should ask them why: "do the fleet consider it a valid decision to continue?" (Si4-3)

This was presenting a tough – though non-judgemental – question: 'do the fleet consider it a valid decision to continue?' And yet questions like this demand a response – a response that is reviewed by investigators as to its adequacy and completeness. In this instance, the investigators were later satisfied that the fleet management had acknowledged and acted on the issue both broadly and appropriately, but when this is not the case, and investigators do not see what they believe to be appropriate action being taken, they escalate or 'ramp up' an issue.

There are various means available to escalating a safety issue. In the first instance, they "like to deal with it directly" (Si4-6) with those involved, ideally by setting further investigative tasks and posing more detailed or wider ranging questions. On other occasions they may feel it is necessary to include incidents in the weekly brief to "have a prod at" (Si4-2) the department involved – to bring to bear a broader form of peer review. They consider this to be somewhat 'underhand', involving 'picking on them' in the brief for a few weeks with any related incidents to build up pressure and attention – but it is nonetheless seen as a legitimate and useful strategy. It is also possible to emphasise and escalate issues through investigators' roles on various safety committees and operational meetings. For instance, one investigator reported back to his colleagues that at the weekly operational review meeting, "I had a good old whinge and did my impression of a grumpy old man . . . To be fair [the Fleet Captain] took it on the chin, and they are feeling the heat about it and doing something about it" (Si4-5). Such public demonstrations of dissatisfaction are rare. Investigators do not want to unnecessarily damage their working relationships with line management, and it is only on rare occasions that any 'table thumping' is used. More typically, investigators resort to pushing an issue further up the organisational hierarchy. As one describes, "No one intentionally makes these mistakes . . . [But] if they are not responsive, or it is felt they don't have the ability or the skills to act on the situation, then we can go to management and it becomes a long-trouser issue" (Si4-6). Investigators can 'pull rank' and pass an issue to more senior managers and directors. Or they might put an issue up for review by the 'long trousers' at a board meeting, "who can apply pressure and motivate them that way" (Si4-6).

Ultimately, investigators are well aware that, if disaster struck, a range of personnel would be "standing up in a court of law" (Si4-6) explaining their actions. This recourse to legal responsibility is rarely directly acknowledged but provides an undercurrent to many discussions about safety. Safety is a serious business with serious professional consequences:

I remember the last time there was an accident. I was in the seat of the guy who left after that . . . Where his name had been on the paper [signing off the problem]. After an accident there will be a trail there. (Si4-9)

In extreme circumstances, investigators know that the ultimate arbiter for them and others would be state agencies, regulators – and ultimately may be the law. As such, investigators' use of accountability to 'motivate' people is not always a pleasant, collaborative affair. Safety investigations and improvement activities are not always harmonious and peaceful. Issues may be contentious – especially where risks are concerned – and disagreements can arise. And, while investigators have no formal authority, they use people's accountability for safety, and their responsibility for resolving risks, as powerful forces to drive action.

Coordinating learning: Effecting participative reflection and change

By shaping awareness, enquiry and accountability around risks, investigators coordinate distributed processes of organisational learning and improvement. This learning is done through the active participation of operational specialists. Investigators guide the investigative work of others, around specific indications of risk. In doing so, knowledge of safety and risk is developed collectively, by both investigators and by personnel in the affected operational areas. Investigating risks and improving safety is a social, participative process. It emerges from dialogue, discussion and interaction around risks between managers, operational personnel, technical specialists and investigators. Investigators consider this participation of operational personnel essential, because those personnel hold much of the expert knowledge – and because those personnel are also the ones who have to implement the practical changes. Working with local specialists is considered essential to understanding the detail of operational issues. "In [incident] analysis you pick up on a lot of issues, but without speaking to people you may miss what they really mean" (Si3-4). It is also necessary to ensure that safety improvements are practical and workable:

> When we make recommendations here we don't just sit in a room and lock the door. We go out and talk to the recipient, and say this is what we think you should do. Is it possible? They may say no, so there is give and take. (Si3-8)

Investigators actively include people in the process of finding out about and resolving risks. They see the assurance of safety as a collective, participative endeavour, connecting the individuals who report incidents, line managers, operational specialists, senior executives, front-line personnel and themselves. All of these people are routinely involved in acting on risks and improving safety. It is typical for the reporter of an incident to be contacted to contribute further detail and information. Line managers and specialists do much of the ground work. And the front-line operational crews are those who have to get to grips with the resulting new ways of working. These participative processes that maintain safety are continuous and ongoing. Consider this example:

> If there is a spate of missing something on a checklist, or something like that, that will get picked up by us, it will get picked up by Flight Ops, the fleet will see it, I am sure it will be on the Monday brief and there are two of those. I'm sure the fleet will jump on it, and the sims [flight simulator training] will be pushing that sort of stuff. And then you watch, and the next week they are not there. And then another one will pop up in a month's time, so it will come back, and it will go in [the brief] as well. It might be just one, but awareness has to be raised again. (Si6-1)

Investigators work to ensure full participation in safety improvement. Actively involving personnel throughout the organisation in dealing with risks is, essentially, empowering them to effect organisational change. Investigators don't solve problems; personnel are encouraged and helped to solve problems themselves. This participation and empowerment of the workforce is a key theme in concepts of effective safety cultures and risk regulation regimes (Hopkins, 2005; Reason, 1997). Investigators facilitate this through their ongoing creation of diverse networks of participants, who are brought together to examine and resolve the risks indicated by incidents. Risks are used as the focal point of multiple conversations and investigations in which personnel reflect on and work out how to improve organisational safety. By guiding the nature and focus of these enquiries, investigators connect their own interpretive activities with those throughout the organisation. They work to coordinate and organise organisational learning, by asking questions, highlighting risks and bringing people together in processes of collective enquiry. Their aim is literally to educe organisational safety: to draw out and elicit solutions from those closest to the problem.

Learning is not just about shaping knowledge, reflection and thinking. Nor is it solely about dialogue and deliberation. Crucially for investigators, it is about action and improvement. Generating participation is ultimately about effecting "material change" (Si4-6) in organisational practices and processes. It is about improving organisational safety by changing how things are done and improving processes so that similar events can be better dealt with in future: "Some incidents have touched practice and process in so many different areas of the organisation that you think, that's been a really useful learning process. It's almost, well thank God we had that event as now we can stop it happening again!" (Si3-5). For investigators there is an imperative to effect action and organisational change – to stop things happening again. Reflection and deliberation are valued, but only as steps in that direction. So, while the diagnostic work involved in investigations is important, for investigators the networks formed around risks are crucially about acting on those diagnoses and implementing change.

For instance, having received another report of a crew taxiing without flaps prior to take-off, an emerging trend identified in one airline, one investigator decided to "fire one off to the fleet" (Si4-6) – a question – asking a fleet manager for a "debrief from the crew to get more details" (Si4-6) about what happened. His colleague explained that this was part of an ongoing "grass cutting exercise" (Si4-4), in which they were trying to keep on top of the occurrence of these events and pull together as much information as possible, while a high-level Flight Ops standards group was working on the problem. In the mean time, any related incidents were being publicised in the brief, it was being emphasised in simulator training, and "they keep reminding crews" (Si4-4) in monthly crew newsletters. Responding to the investigator's question, the fleet manager came back outlining further interim action they were taking. As the investigator recounted, "they agree there's a trend in this area. They're aware of it and they've launched a 'Flap Selection Awareness Drive', of all things" (Si4-4). Flight crew distraction is a particularly persistent, challenging and slippery problem to address. Nonetheless, in practice there is the imperative to act on – and not just analyse – risks. Investigators believed that the issue had not yet been addressed at a fundamental level. But, in this instance, they were satisfied that appropriate actions were being taken towards that end. In this way, incidents, and the risks that they point to, provide a focus around which reflection, and crucially action, can become organised. They provide the material around which ongoing and incremental processes of "cultural readjustment" can be coordinated (Turner and Pidgeon, 1997, p. 70), in which cultural beliefs and practices are continually reshaped in response to emerging risks.

Appraising the value of safety improvement

An important aspect of how investigators manage risk and improve safety is their assessment of the potential value of acting on a specific risk. Investigators evaluate how worthwhile and beneficial to organisational safety it would be to act on a risk and attempt to improve safety in an area of organisational activity. Assessments of the value of action have three key features. These concern the potential gain and improvement in safety, the current level of organisational activity, and the practicality of effective action.

Safety value: Assessing the worth of improvement activity

A key aspect of investigators' analyses of risks is a consideration of how valuable or worthwhile it would be to investigate and address them. For investigators, assessing risk is about allocating and prioritising organisational resources. They aim to apply finite resources where these would be of most benefit and result in the most significant improvements to safety. The idea of value, or safety value, is inherent to their understanding of risk. In practice, there is an intrinsic evaluative component to judgements of risk and analyses of incidents. This evaluation runs throughout their interpretive work. Contrary to normative models of risk assessment, it is not simply some separate or final stage at the end of a linear analysis process (e.g. Eduljee, 1999; Institute of Risk Management, 2002). As already discussed, assessing risk and determining action is something of an 'egg and chicken' process, and assessments of risk are shot through with a notion of value, which in practice is tied to action. "[Risk assessment] is the value added . . . where to prioritise resources. It's bangs-for-bucks stuff" (Si2-6). Appraisals of safety value concern where they can improve safety and what it is worthwhile trying to do. Investigators work to identify where they should practically focus organisational resources and investigative action for greatest gain:

> We get so many reports that we need to see where we are going to get best value . . . We have investigation criteria, whether the incident is to be investigated or not. For instance, birdstrikes are not normally investigated. We consider the potential gain of investigating. (Si5-14)

A key element of investigators' analytical work is identifying which risks appear to be most worthwhile investigating and acting on. Investigators evaluate where safety gains and improvements could be made through participative action. Another term used by investigators is that of the "safety return" (Si3-8) they could expect to get from an investment of organisational resources. In this sense, analyses of risk are in large part framed by an evaluation of positive and beneficial outcomes in terms of potential safety improvement – rather than predictions of future adverse outcomes.

For investigators, risk analysis is not based merely on preventing the intolerable and resolving the unacceptable. Instead, risk is used by investigators to signal where investigative efforts could and should be most profitably focused to improve safety. This premise reflects investigators' deep assumption that incidents and errors are inevitable, and so they are best used as opportunities for learning. This focus on improving safety is equally aligned with their interpretive framework of assessing where safety – or risk resilience – is below par. Appraising potential safety value provides investigators with a more pragmatic and finer evaluative gradation for assessing risk than more traditional judgements of acceptability. Moreover, in day-to-day practice, risks that are considered intolerable or unacceptable – the risks that require mitigation in normative approaches to risk analysis – are relatively few and far between. More regularly encountered are circumstances deemed slightly less than adequate: activities that are not as resilient as they could be. More subtly, while tolerating and accepting risks suggests an orientation of passivity, attempts to find value and safety gains reflect an active and creative search for safety and resilience.

In practice, investigators differentiate and evaluate risks by using positive judgements of the likely safety value, benefit or improvement that would accrue from action being taken. There are three key facets to these evaluations:

- the potential safety benefits and improvement that may result, in terms of strengthened resilience and reduced ignorance;
- the extent to which current organisational activity is already addressing the risk; and
- the practicality of addressing the risk and achieving actual improvements.

Investigators assess the likely value of enacting improvement and shaping participative action around a risk, in terms of these three facets of safety value. Each is considered in turn below.

Potential improvement: Gaining resilience and knowledge

In assessing risks, investigators consider the potential to improve, or the learning value, that a risk presents. This is evaluated in terms of two of the key concepts that characterise investigators' understanding of organisational safety: resilience and ignorance. The potential for learning and improvement depends on judgements of the possible gains in risk resilience or the creation of new knowledge that would result from acting on a risk. Judging improvement potential is therefore intimately tied to their investigators' core analyses of resilience and ignorance, as detailed in the previous chapters. More simply, "it is the likelihood we will discover something new, or the likelihood we can make a recommendation to stop it happening again" (Si5-2). For example, one investigator identified improvement potential on reviewing an event where some unknown chemical powder had been spilt in the cargo hold of an aircraft. He explained that, "they tested it for anthrax and everything, but did it damage the aeroplane? . . . we're concerned about the effect on flight safety – and that no one else seems to have worried about that" (Si4-4). In this instance, they were worried that safety was being 'crowded out' of the picture by an increased emphasis on security threats. To them, this incident suggested a clear opportunity to re-emphasise flight safety to ground personnel by highlighting the safety issues surrounding potential corrosive substances coming into contact with aluminium airframes. Acting to highlight this and bringing attention back onto it were considered to offer the potential for improving safety, in this small and localised way. Likewise, the potential for improvement that surrounded the problems involving the servicing of oil systems was clear to investigators. This potential was largely based on a perceived need to clarify the current uncertainty and confusion that was 'clouding' the issue of what lay behind the problem. In a more focused way, the work done on the go-around and switch mis-selection problems, discussed in Chapter 2, was deemed to provide significant and urgent learning potential – both in terms of increasing knowledge of this previously misunderstood risk and in terms of improving organisational resilience to it. Accordingly, the actions taken around this event were lengthy and broad-ranging.

Current activity: Existing action and its efficacy

As part of their appraisals of safety value, investigators consider the level and effectiveness of any current action being taken to address a risk. Essentially, they consider whether 'the normal processes' could adequately deal with a risk or whether they need to get more actively involved themselves. They assess whether the current organisational response to a risk is, in their view, appropriate and proportionate – and crucially, whether it is working. For instance, the problems experienced with aircraft marshalling at a new terminal of a foreign airport, discussed in Chapter 2, was an issue that was initially considered under control. After the first events, the investigators were satisfied with the actions being taken. They believed that managers in Ground Operations had drawn up adequate plans with their counterparts at the foreign station and were dealing with the problem: as they said at the time, "these guys are on top of it" (Si4-4). But when more events occurred they quickly changed their mind. It became clear that the actions being taken were ineffective and it was worthwhile them getting involved.

Investigators believe it is most beneficial to intervene and guide action onto areas where current improvement activities around risks are judged to be inadequate. Conversely, on many occasions investigators determine that their involvement would be of little additional value. These are situations where problems are considered to be already 'in hand' or where there is adequate and effective investigative work already ongoing. For instance, on receiving further reports of suspected 'sleeping receiver' events, investigators were comfortable that an extensive investigation was already going on. It was, "rumbling away. There's already action in hand so [intervening further] wouldn't achieve anything more. There'd be no gain" (Si4-6). Where organisational action is deemed to be effectively underway, investigators see little value in them raising the issue for further attention. In these cases, investigators consider awareness to already be high, with investigations or actions progressing effectively. As such, these issues are rarely publicised or followed. They monitor them and would start highlighting the issue again "if it goes quiet again" (Si4-3) and the impetus of current activities seems to slow. Investigators' assessments of the value of them acting are therefore partly based on their knowledge of what actions are going on elsewhere in the organisation and the potential value of their involvement relative to this.

Pragmatic practicality: Achieving results and improvements

Investigators evaluate the extent to which they think it would be practically possible for them to achieve safety improvements. This is another side to what they term their 'pragmatic' approach. Some risks that they face are simply beyond their control. They couldn't reasonably expect to resolve them. For instance, air traffic control services in some parts of the world are known to be exceedingly and persistently poor. Flight crew are well aware and regularly reminded of this. But it is not considered an issue that a single airline is able to solve. They contribute to action being taken by international agencies, but it is, to all extents and purposes, a risk that they do not practically expect to resolve. "Going into [an African airport] you know that half the approach lights aren't going to work because they've stolen the bulbs. Point it out, they put the bulbs in and within a week they're gone again . . . That's life. You've got to take the pragmatic approach" (Si3-8). The pragmatic approach in this case being to ensure that crews are being prepared and trained as best as they can and then to move on to tackling an area where they can more reasonably expect to achieve improvements in safety. Investigators keep one eye on the practicality of them initiating organisational action that would improve safety and defensive activities. Put another way, "we only inject resources if we see we can gain from the investigation" (Si5-3). In most instances, investigators do consider this to be the case – but to varying extents.

Some risks are considered to be very simply addressed, with practical and straightforward solutions. For instance, this included the problem of drinks containers becoming wedged under rudder pedals. Investigators thought this should be relatively easy to solve – introduce a check for debris by flight crew and ensure the additional checks are complied with – giving immediate improvements in resilience. In other cases, any further improvement gains from their action might be considered to be limited because, for the time being, a problem is in the hands of another organisation. A problem with faults on a certain type of engine became cause for concern in one airline – but the task of investigation and any subsequent modification was quickly handed over to the engine manufacturer. Similarly, in one event a pilot's seat moved forward on its rails during landing – not a helpful feature: "He practically ended up on top of the controls . . . This is potentially quite nasty" (Si4-4). Investigators were concerned by this event, as these sorts of problems could dramatically interfere with a pilot's control of the aircraft on take-off and landing. Flight Ops and Engineering were asked to investigate, and responded that the rails were not blocked, as suspected, but appeared very slightly worn, and circulated digital photographs to demonstrate where. Following this inconclusive finding, seat rails on the rest of the fleets were checked and the problem was referred to the airframe manufacturer, and the investigators then waited on a resolution, a 'Tech Bulletin', from them. Further action within the airline was considered unlikely to contribute any further, and so it was not considered worthwhile pursuing the problem in more detail until the manufacturer had completed their investigation and made their recommendations.

In other cases, investigators might take the view that incidents reflect a risk that their organisation has little practical ability to act on – as with the persistent problems with air traffic services in certain localities mentioned above. In these instances, the problems are viewed as best dealt with at an 'industry level'. They are simply 'too big' for a single airline to resolve on their own, and beyond their reasonable control, no matter how basic or simple they may seem:

> [Many things] are things that are not rocket science to put right but are totally out of our control. There is not a lot you can do about them. You can spend your life going around, but the output will be limited. (Si3-8)

A key element of investigators' assessments of risk is based on this assessment of where the results from acting are likely to be limited and where the results of acting are likely to be valuable. The determination of what is likely to be practically achieved forms a key component of investigators' assessments of the potential benefits and safety improvements their action might yield. In this way, assessments of risk are grounded both in the practicalities of managing risk and in investigators' beliefs about the practical capabilities of their own, and their organisation's, mechanisms to improve safety and organise resilience.

8
Organising Resilience

This book has sought to answer a practical and specific set of questions: how do airline flight safety investigators interpret incidents, identify risks and improve safety? Answering these questions requires understanding the practical theories that shape how investigators think, along with the situated practices through which they interpret and act. Flight safety investigators represent a particular type of risk manager: one that works at the heart of safety management systems that are designed to capture moments of organisational risk and transform these into sources of improvement and resilience. Understanding the practices of flight safety investigators lifts the lid on the challenging and complex world of airline safety management, a world in which knowledge and control are amongst the most valued and highly prized attributes of organisational performance. Picking apart these practices also offers deeper and broader insights into the practical work of risk management, the nature of safety and resilience in complex sociotechnical systems, and the role of incidents, errors and close calls in both manufacturing and managing risk – issues which this chapter turns to shortly.

More immediately, the work of flight safety investigators reveals the fundamental but often hidden ways that the analysis and investigation of safety incidents can create invisible infrastructures for improving safety and organising resilience, and embed these activities deep into daily organisational life. When viewed from a distance, reporting and analysing safety incidents can sometimes appear little more than administrative activities directed at collating and aggregating data on organisational failure. Indeed, in some cases that is all that these systems become: it can be easy for attention and resources to be lavished on the information systems and the technological infrastructures of data collection and analysis, while overlooking the less tangible cognitive and social infrastructures that act as the engines of learning and improvement in organisations. Remove these complex networks of social organisation and collective sensemaking, and incident reporting systems become little more than passive data repositories – or 'very expensive filing cabinets', as investigators would have it.

Analysing investigators' risk management practices reveals that safety incident reporting and investigation systems can support widely distributed cognitive and social infrastructures within which the limits of organisational knowledge and control can be continually tested and revised. Safety investigators organise distributed networks of experts who are called on to collectively interpret, analyse and address risks. Operational incidents are used as a resource to challenge and reshape cultural assumptions and practices around safety. Safety investigators work to activate, organise and maintain the social infrastructures within which small moments of organisational life can become transformed into wide-ranging programmes of organisational renewal and improvement.

Investigators sit at the heart of these infrastructures of improvement, and it is in large part their patterns of thinking, their practices of analysis and their organisational interventions that give shape to how risks are understood and managed within their organisations. The work of safety investigators is defined by a continual struggle for knowledge and control in the face of uncertainty, complexity and change. These themes deeply shape investigators' practice. Safety investigators are preoccupied by gaps in understanding, failures of organisational activity and weaknesses in learning. These preoccupations with ignorance and error structure investigators' practical work of risk management: they provide a focus for interpretation, attention and investigation. The practical work of investigators is organised around finding and addressing gaps – gaps in how risks are represented and understood, and gaps in how safety is organised and improved. By leveraging the social infrastructure supported by incident reporting systems, safety investigators are able to use fleeting moments of failure to identify doubts, produce disruptions and organise widely distributed activities of reflection and change throughout their organisations.

Another way of saying this is that operational incidents are used by investigators as opportunities to re-examine, re-codify and re-engineer organisational practices; incidents are used to generate affordances to reflect on and account for current organisational practices. In short, incidents are used to do epistemic work. Brief moments of organisational life are bracketed and turned into objects of collective and productive enquiry. Incidents do not do this of their own accord. Investigators work hard to transform otherwise fleeting fluctuations, variations and anomalies within organisational activities into symbolically disruptive and challenging events with far-reaching cultural implications within their organisations – and sometimes beyond. In doing so, investigators transform events that typically have had little or no material impact on organisational activity into events that carry deep symbolic significance and that challenge and test current assumptions regarding the limits of knowledge and control. Operational incidents are transformed into epistemic incidents by investigators: incidents that are used to test and develop knowledge about organisational safety.

The use of incidents to drive safety improvement represents both a subtle subterfuge and a deep irony. The subterfuge is that, on the one hand, investigators work to continually ensure that operational mishaps can only happen far from the realm of near-disaster. But at the same time, investigators communicate risks and organise improvement by actively constructing close calls, near-misses and organisational disruptions: they work to convince people that, in encountering an incident, their organisation has come dangerously close to something it should desperately avoid. The irony is that organisational safety is perhaps best understood as a dynamic non-event (Reason, 1997; Weick and Sutcliffe, 2001) – a dynamic process of continual adjustment and adaptation that produces a non-event of no materially adverse outcome. But the engine that drives safety is events. Investigators deploy a set of practices that seek to continually create and actively produce disruptive events, and then use those events to symbolically provoke the dynamic adaptation, organisational learning and cultural readjustment that underpin safety. In this sense, organisational safety may be better described as an ongoing series of dynamic events that collectively produce a non-outcome.

Characterising cultural practices is inevitably inelegant work. The practices of airline flight safety investigators have been explained in the preceding chapters through a theoretical account and set of core concepts that have purposefully aimed to remain descriptively close to the practical work of investigators, offering a series of lenses onto the interconnected features of practice and the conceptual tools of the trade that investigators use to analyse, organise and improve flight safety. The first of these, risk resilience, captures the nuanced meaning of risk and safety for investigators in this safety-critical setting, along with the professional judgements and organisational properties through which safety and risk are assessed. The second, interpretive vigilance, concerns the central use of knowledge – and ignorance – in identifying risks and interpreting incidents, including the ways that indications of potential ignorance are constructed and used by investigators as a tangible proxy for risk. And the third, participative networks, explains how investigators understand the organisational processes of investigating and learning from risks, their own place in initiating and shaping this activity, and how the worth and value of such action is evaluated. Taken together, this multilayered explanation provides a number of views onto the fundamental practices of risk management and safety improvement. These concepts also sketch out the mutually reinforcing practices and beliefs that sit at the core of a professional culture of resilience, vigilance and improvement.

The theoretical account developed in this book nonetheless remains partial and limited. There are many things that this book does not try to accomplish. Primarily, the concepts and ideas developed here do not claim to represent a final and complete theory. Rather, they present a stage in a theorising process (Weick, 1995) that, by capturing and revealing the rich empirical grounding of this analysis, aims to offer an invitation for further exploration. The three core concepts and their numerous components attempt to provide an initial structure and set of guiding characteristics through which the practical work and cultural practices of risk management can better be explained. This theoretical account emerged from studying practice and it aims to explain practice, but it should not be taken as suggesting that the investigators or organisations studied here had in some way attained a state of perfect and perpetual interpretive vigilance, nor that the organisations involved produced immaculate renditions of participative networks – or, indeed, that they collectively worked with a complete and coherent theory of safety as risk resilience. The investigators would, in any case, be the first to disagree. These theoretical concepts, and the discussions that elaborate them, aim to bring a degree of clarity to capture and examine important facets of risk management practice. They do not claim to represent that such clarity has been – or perhaps ever can be – achieved in its pure form in practice. This analysis also makes no empirical claim to represent widespread and ubiquitous practices found across the entire aviation industry, or in other industrial domains. The aim here has been to produce a closely grounded theoretical account of this specific and particularly challenging corner of risk management practice. Such work requires empirical and strategic compromises (Turner, 1983). Focusing on depth and detail of explanation necessarily sacrifices breadth, and this is especially the case in qualitative, ethnographic work aimed at exploring organisational practice (Weick, 1979). My analysis here is necessarily a representation of a relatively small corner of the airline industry at one unique moment in time.

Accepting those limitations, this close study of the work of airline flight safety investigators raises a range of interesting implications, both specific and expansive. Understanding the practical theories and situated practices of investigators provides an opportunity to challenge, elaborate and revise current models and theoretical perspectives in the field of safety and risk. These implications concern five key areas: the nature of organisational safety and practical sources of resilience; the diagnosis of organisational risks and emerging threats; the production and use of organisational ignorance; the use of symbolic disruptions that initiate and guide improvement activities; and the practices of high reliability organising and the oversight and organisation of resilience.

Practical sources of safety

Organisational safety is an ongoing accomplishment that requires continual attention, effort and care. Safety must be continually monitored and re-accomplished, otherwise it degrades. Sociotechnical systems change and gradually decline into disorder: entropy inevitably does its work. Accomplishing safety in complex organisations depends on a deep understanding of what safety looks like and what practical resources and capabilities it is based on. Airline flight safety investigators confront the challenge of understanding and analysing safety every day, and the practical theory they draw on has interesting implications. One of the most striking implications concerns the idea of safety defences and the complex networks of practice that this idea represents. The notion of safety defences is a foundational concept in many theories of organisational safety and methods of risk analysis (e.g. Reason, 1997; Hollnagel, 2004). The idea is widely used by investigators, but to them safety defences are complex and emergent properties of organisational practice: they are the elements of organisational activities that keep those same activities within acceptable, understood and safe confines. Accepting that defences do not exist separately or apart from organisational practice – but rather are the self-correcting and self-regulating features of organisational practice itself – is a subtle but consequential shift. It is a shift that indicates how fragile and complex, but also how flexible and adaptive, the organisational substance of safety may be. Safety defences must be performed: no matter how heavily specified, planned or engineered a particular defence may be, it still requires practical, interactive work to be performed in the moment it is needed in order to bring that defence into existence. If defensive activity is not performed at the moment it is required – when an unexpected fluctuation in activity must be compensated for or when an unintended event needs identifying and addressing – then a safety defence essentially does not exist. A safety defence must be brought into reality at the moment of demand through adaptive, practical work.

The practices that produce a particular safety defence are not only those that are performed at the specific moment of threat, but run across an organisation – and other organisations – and take many forms. The work that creates and sustains any particular safety defence at any specific moment is widely distributed. In an airline these activities stretch from policy making and crew training to piloting aircraft and repairing hardware. Each 'defence' is produced and reproduced through a distributed constellation of interrelated communities of practice. Pilots, engineers, ground crew, training staff, technical managers, designers, regulators: each group contributes in their own way, through their own specialised knowledge and specific set of practices, to the continued maintenance and upkeep of a particular defence – even if it is only the most proximal and immediate actions that are typically noticed and labelled, for convenience, as the 'defence': the activation of an automated warning, for example, or the completion of a checklist item. Understanding these distributed sociotechnical sources of safety requires understanding the practicalities of and interconnections between constellations of diverse defensive practices that are widely separated in space and time. The analytical role of investigators is primarily one of exploring, understanding and mapping these practical interrelationships. Analysing organisational safety requires investigators to act much like ethnographers and anthropologists as well as engineers, paying close attention to the socially distributed beliefs, habits, norms, practices and cultural contexts that shape the networks of organisational activity that produce safety.

The idea of safety defences is commonly viewed as the bedrock of precautionary, anticipatory approaches to controlling risk: future threats are assessed and defences are designed to prevent or protect against them. But viewing the nature of safety defences as interactive, sociotechnical practice highlights the inherent interaction between anticipatory and more resilient modes of organising (Roe and Schulman, 2008). Predesigned procedures, plans, protocols and the like can create an illusion that they are themselves safety defences or risk controls. But those plans and procedures are not, in themselves, safety defences. They are merely images of and preparations for defensive activity of some sort. Likewise, those plans and specifications for practice can imply that the practices they refer to are fully understood. But there is always some degree of gap or mismatch between procedures and performance, and between plans and practices (Suchman, 1987; Wenger, 1998). Plans are merely resources for action (Suchman, 1987). To bring a defence into being requires action – a defence must be enacted and reproduced by bringing together resources from past moments of socialisation (procedures, training, plans, routines) and combining those with the materials at hand at a specific moment (information, awareness, judgement) to negotiate the particular and specific demands of the current situation. Defensive practices therefore represent a constant interaction between anticipated, designed organisational resources that are prepared to deal with foreseen operational risks, and the resilient, adaptive performances that are required to translate those preparations and put them into practice in the unique and specific situations confronted by personnel when risks are actually encountered. Safety is always an integrative performance: an interactive duality of anticipation and adaptation; prior planning and current practice; risk and resilience.

This practice-based view of safety has consequences for common safety analysis methods and models, and particularly the way that safety defences – and the operational hazards that they purportedly defend against – are currently defined. It is typically assumed that defences are designed to keep 'bad' things 'out'. Like the concentric fortifications of a castle, safety barriers stop hazards – fire, say, or explosions perhaps – coming into contact with valuable and fragile assets, such as people or property. These are the assumptions that 'barrier' theories of safety, Reason's 'Swiss Cheese' framework (Reason, 1997), as well as common models of risk analysis, are based on: adverse events are the result of hazards penetrating system defences and causing damage (e.g. Hollnagel, 2004; Svenson, 1991). But when defences are viewed as emergent properties of organisational practice, safety defences can no longer be reified as a distinct barrier that separates an 'asset' from a 'hazard'. (It is striking that traditional notions of external and individuated 'hazards' barely feature in the thinking of investigators.) Instead, the threats to be defended against are the inherent potential for organisational activities to break down and for mechanisms of self-regulation and control to degrade. That is, defences don't stop a hazard getting 'in'. They stop organisational activities getting 'out' – out of the controlled, normal, understood range of activity (e.g. Rasmussen, 1997; Amalberti et al., 2006). Defensive practices keep organisational activity within safe, understood and manageable confines and protect against organisational activities drifting into uncontrolled and unchartered waters.

Organisational proximity and diagnosis

At the heart of risk analysis stands the dilemma that Turner (1976) articulated so many decades ago: how to distinguish the boundary between acceptable safety and relative risk and, in so doing, determine what to pay attention to and what to ignore. Or, put another way, how to know where the 'edge' is without falling over it (Reason, 1997). Safety is sometimes simplistically equated with the avoidance of harm, and the metaphors of close calls and near-misses implicitly carry with them the idea that risk in some way involves coming within seconds or centimetres of a harmful outcome, while safety implies keeping one's distance. Examining the interpretive practices of airline flight safety investigators reveals that, in their analytical work, the reference point and boundary between acceptable safety and relative risk is displaced. Harmful outcomes are no longer the benchmark for distinguishing between safety and risk. The marker of acceptable safety is shifted and occupies a point some distance from the actual occurrence of any adverse outcome. Close calls, near-misses and even worst cases are no longer defined as events that come dramatically close to a harmful outcome. The moment at which organisational activities pass into the realm of unacceptable risk instead occupies a point some considerable distance from an actual accident. This is because the reference point for assessing risk is not defined in terms of adverse outcomes and adverse events. Instead, the reference point is defined in terms of organisational safety: the limits of organisational knowledge and control. Close encounters with risk and harm are transposed into close encounters with the limits of organisational capacities for knowledge and control. The benchmark and metric for risk is not a harmful outcome that might result, but the loss of understanding and control. The limits of safety can be uncoupled from the occurrence of adverse outcomes.

This is the hidden principle that underpins precautionary and proactive approaches to safety assurance. It is the degradation of safety itself – rather than the outcome of harm – that is the risk to be managed and avoided. Coming close to the limits of knowledge and control in itself represents a risk, and is perceived as a close brush with danger. It is safety itself that is at risk. This line of reasoning begs a further question. What constitutes the 'space' that produces safety, the reduction of which results in the 'proximity' of close calls and near-misses? The answer revealed by investigators' practice is that this space is thoroughly organisational. The 'distance' that assures safety is produced by the human, social and technical controls and comprehension that prevent small mishaps snowballing into major breakdowns. Returning to a brief example is illustrative. Airline emergency fuel reserve requirements act as a safety margin against an unforeseen emergency – to ensure there is always some reserve of fuel left in the event of an unexpected problem. But that safety margin needs to be actively maintained. The flight crew must effectively plan their hold fuel requirements, monitor changing weather conditions and make early decisions to divert to an alternate airport if required; air traffic controllers must monitor and communicate any expected delays; and a vast array of social and technical infrastructure is required to support these activities. All of these activities, when performed effectively, ensure that organisational activities operate well within the boundaries of effective control and comprehension with regard to this specific safety margin. It is as these organisational capacities for control break down that activities move closer to the limits of safety, and become worrisome for investigators. In another case, airline safety investigators worry about events where there is no geographical or temporal loss of separation between aircraft but where the controllers and crew in question did not appear to be fully cognisant, aware and in control of the situation, that is, where the organisational space between aircraft had been reduced. Organisational safety is not predicated on the mere existence of technical safety margins but on the organisational and interpretive work that goes into actively creating, maintaining and protecting those safety margins. It is where this work breaks down that organisations risk breaching their predefined limits of safety and so experience proximity to risk: close calls and near-miss events.

As dramatic encounters with risk become increasingly rare in many industries, risk managers develop more precautionary and expanded boundaries of safety, against which small moments of organisational life can be transformed into consequential encounters with risk. This approach to the analysis of near-miss events and organisational safety therefore represents a process of active production rather than passive discovery of risk. As the boundaries of knowledge and control expand, events with seemingly trivial outcomes are reconstructed as proximal and threatening brushes with the limits of safety. In this sense, near-miss events are made rather than thrust upon us. Uncoupling ideas of risk from adverse outcomes and linking them instead to capacities for organisational knowledge and control not only shifts the boundary between acceptable safety and relative risk, it also shifts the framework for analysing risk. It redefines risk in organisational terms, much as Turner (1978) and Reason (1990) redefined accidents in organisational terms. Rather than predicting the likelihood and severity of future outcomes, the work of risk analysis becomes more focused on diagnosing organisational weaknesses: where defensive practices and organisational knowledge are showing signs of degradation. Taking this line of thinking further, organisational risks come to be defined in terms of the nature and degree of weakness in the capability of organisational activities to comprehend, respond to and contain disruptions, rather than purely in terms of the extent and scale of the adverse outcomes that might result from those disruptions (e.g. Reason, 1997; 2000). In this case, the analytical skills brought to the fore are not those of calculative precision regarding future adverse outcomes but rather those of the sensitive diagnosis and interpretation of the underlying organisational capabilities for control – and weaknesses therein.

This perspective carries with it implications for various tools of risk analysis and technologies of incident reporting. In particular, the tool of risk assessment typically applied to safety incidents is the common risk matrix or risk map illustrated in Chapter 2 (e.g. Breakwell, 2007). Within incident reporting systems these risk assessments are typically applied to one incident at a time (e.g. National Patient Safety Agency, 2001; Institute of Risk Management, 2002). This sits uneasily with the practices of organisational risk analysis examined throughout this book, where assessments of risk are pitched at a different level – and type – of analysis than predicting outcomes of individual incidents. In practice, risk assessments are targeted at and reflect the extent of an underlying set of organisational weaknesses and inadequacies, of which a specific incident is merely a superficial and transient symptom. The ways in which risk assessment tools and methods can function as more sensitive diagnostic instruments in the ongoing oversight and monitoring of safety needs particularly careful thought. At the least, the use of risk matrix tools ought to be uncoupled from the assessment of individual incidents. Risk ratings should, instead, be explicitly tied to the underlying organisational sources of risk that they represent. Otherwise, there would seem to be a gap between the specification and the practice of risk assessment – of the type that investigators worry so much about elsewhere in operations.

Ignorance and early warnings

Encounters with uncertainty, the unexpected and surprise are defining features of risk management – and of organisational life more generally – and ignorance is a major theme that runs through organisational theories of both accidents and safety. Knowledge of risk is always partial and incomplete in complex organisational settings that depend on advanced technologies and highly specialised personnel. In such settings, analysing risk and overseeing safety are activities that present distinctly epistemic challenges. The work of safety oversight represents an ongoing effort to continually test, maintain and update current knowledge of the state of organisational safety, and the early and most critical stages of risk analysis are directed at efforts to notice and piece together weak signs of potential – and previously unrecognised – threats. The most fundamental interpretive efforts of risk management concern identifying where organisational safety, or current knowledge of it, is suspect – where there are grounds for scepticism, doubt or unease regarding the adequacy of safety. Risk analysis is commonly viewed as a process of managing, organising and reducing uncertainties. Examining the work of investigators suggests that, on the contrary, the earliest and most tentative stages of risk analysis depend on the active production and amplification of uncertainty through the construction and enlargement of specific areas of ignorance. Ignorance and doubt are actively produced and used to bracket areas of organisational activity that warrant further investigation, attention and improvement. Markers of ignorance serve as proxies for latent risks.

Close calls and safety incidents provide opportunities for risk managers to reflect on and identify the limits of current knowledge. They provide the source materials to interrogate the unknown (Wildavsky, 1988), test current assumptions (Turner, 1978), invalidate expectations (Weick and Sutcliffe, 2001), become aware of ignorance (Smithson, 1990) and undergo experience (Downer, 2011). That is, they can act as epistemic incidents that reveal gaps in current knowledge, models and assumptions about the safety of organisational activities – before those gaps are revealed in catastrophic organisational accidents. But incidents do not do this on their own. The work of flight safety investigators indicates that, in response to safety incidents, a range of interpretive tactics can be activated to apply and test current organisational knowledge in an attempt to produce early warnings of risk. These interpretive tactics are based both on judgements of similarity – making patterns and drawing connections – and judgements of difference – perceiving novelty and finding discrepancy. An important implication of this is that warning signs and signals of threat are not present unambiguously 'in' incidents and events, to be merely found, noticed or missed by risk managers. Rather, early warning signs must be actively constructed and produced through a process of interrelating current events, prior knowledge and future expectations.

It is common after a major accident for a string of 'missed warnings' or signs of impending disaster to be identified, the underlying implication being that early warnings are simple, self-contained and unequivocal events that are there for the taking – and are simply not noticed in the run-up to an accident. But this examination of investigators' practice indicates that events only act as early warnings if they are placed within a broader frame of reference that renders them meaningful and threatening in some way: if, for instance, they suggest troubling gaps in current beliefs or practice, or can be linked to some past pattern of catastrophic failure. The earliest stages of risk identification are therefore productive and creative processes of interpretation that involve actively constructing and piecing together early warnings. Weak signals and early warnings are actively and intentionally constructed from an ongoing stream of ambiguous and otherwise inconsequential incidents through processes of interpretation and sensemaking. As such, the critical activities of risk identification appear to occur at a much earlier and more tentative stage than the simple perception or recognition of a warning sign. Few, if any, normative models of risk management make any provision for these subtle and critical processes, and this early and tentative stage of risk analysis remains largely invisible to and unsupported by current analytical methods and tools.

Fleeting doubts about the adequacy of organisational safety – or knowledge of it – constitute some of the earliest and most tentative warning signs of previously unknown risks. The occurrence of unexpected events that violate expectations and reveal gaps in assumptions are often accompanied by surprise and a considerable degree of confusion (Turner and Pidgeon, 1997; Weick, Sutcliffe and Obstfeld, 1999; Downer, 2011). Identifying and using surprises as indicators of previously unrecognised problems is posited as a defining feature of high reliability organising (Weick and Sutcliffe, 2001). However, examining the interpretive practices of flight safety investigators suggests that surprise may not be the most suitable form of ignorance to act as a proxy for latent risks. Surprises are things that force themselves on the unsuspecting. To be surprised is to be caught out – which, in the eyes of these investigators at least, is tantamount to failure. Investigators aim to avoid surprises by actively constructing more tentative forms of ignorance: suspicions and doubts that can be investigated *before* an event surprises them. Flight safety investigators work to actively create and carve out areas of potential ignorance. Investigators work to tackle ignorance before it tackles them, by producing and localising doubts, suspicions and a sense of unease – all of which are more subtle, equivocal and tentative forms of ignorance than surprise.

Risk analysis is a process of producing organisational ignorance for a specific purpose (Smithson, 1989; Miettinen and Virkkunen, 2005). By specifying and representing gaps in knowledge, ignorance can be made 'usable' by providing a focus for further inquiry, investigation and analysis (Merton, 1987; Ravetz, 1987; Macrae, 2009). The notion of uncertainty is core to most models of risk management, but this is largely in terms of estimates of the probability or likelihood of predicted future events. In practice, flight safety investigators rarely attempt to predict the future. Their work is instead shaped by, and focused on, ignorance of a different kind: gaps in knowledge of current organisational activities or misunderstandings about the adequacy and quality of defensive practices. Framing risk analysis simply in terms of the severity and likelihood of predicted future adverse outcomes, as is done by most normative risk management models, seems an extraordinarily narrow deployment of the concept of ignorance. It is a framing that marginalises important aspects of organisational diagnosis and interpretive practice – from the active production and enlargement of doubt to the interrogation and testing of current assumptions about safety.

Uncertainty, doubt and ignorance are produced in light of what is currently known and taken for granted: they represent moments of absence, ambiguity or confusion in relation to existing assumptions and beliefs about how organisational activities unfold and how effectively those activities can handle disruptions. The nature and source of the knowledge that is drawn on in the work of overseeing safety and managing risk is deeply practical. It is practical knowledge of organisational work: how that work is actually conducted and performed and how it fits together and interacts across organisational boundaries. In particular, overseeing the ongoing operations of complex organisational activities requires a particularly deep appreciation of the social aspects of sociotechnical practice and a sensitive understanding of the practical demands and operational realities that exist for front-line personnel. Advice can be sought on specific engineering and technical issues from specialists in those fields. But the analysis of operational incidents and the oversight of organisational safety depends on a close understanding of the practical and socially interactive work that underpins the use of complex operational technologies.

The work of safety oversight both develops and draws on knowledge that is rooted in the practicalities of organising. It requires something of the skills and perspective of a social anthropologist as much as those of an engineer. Narrow, technical or abstract expertise is necessary but not sufficient for the oversight of organisational safety (Roberts, 1990;

Hopkins, 1999). The knowledge drawn on to interpret incidents must be integrative and broad ranging – while also being deeply concrete and practical (e.g. Weick, 1995; Cook and Brown, 1999). This suggests that to improve safety management, organisations – and organisational theorists – ought to pay much more attention to where different forms of knowledge come from, how these are produced, reproduced and circulated, how knowledge of safety can be represented and communicated to others – and ultimately, how it can be invalidated, tested and continually revised.

Examining the work of flight safety investigators reveals that a huge stock of knowledge is captured in narratives of safety occurrences, and these continually circulate in investigations of accidents and stories of near-miss events. These narratives provide many of the broad frames of reference within which incidents are interpreted and risks identified. Despite their importance, these practical sources and forms of knowledge are largely absent in most formal considerations of safety oversight, and receive little explicit acknowledgement or support in risk management systems. The broader frames of reference drawn on to interpret and analyse risk could be more explicitly supported and developed as a central part of risk management work, and could be more visibly incorporated into the formal processes of analysing and representing risks. Rather than a risk matrix that aims to visualise estimates of the potential outcomes of individual events, it could be extremely valuable to visualise the network of connections and relationships between safety incidents and the broader frames of reference that render them meaningful as early warnings or indications of risk – a risk nexus, perhaps.

Disruptions and epistemic work

The ultimate objective of risk management – and incident reporting and analysis – is to address underlying threats to organisational activities and to bring about improvements in safety. Improving safety ultimately means adapting practices and technologies on the organisational frontlines, where the operational work gets done. Safety improvement is therefore an inherently cultural and practical process: it requires reengineering work routines, changing shared expectations, developing new tools, shifting collective beliefs and redesigning existing technologies. Investigating and responding to safety incidents creates mechanisms of organisational change, through which risks can be resolved and safety improved. The work of flight safety investigators demonstrates how safety incident reporting systems not only provide a means to monitor and analyse organisational safety – they provide a social infrastructure through which epistemic work can be organised, knowledge can be produced and organisational culture and practice can be examined and refashioned. For the most part, the outcomes of the sorts of safety incidents routinely reported to investigators are rarely harmful or materially adverse. These events are not, in and of themselves, materially disruptive to organisational activities – they merely represent an ongoing stream of mishaps, errors, defects, failures, variations and fluctuations in operational performance. Using materially inconsequential events to effect organisational change requires them to be transformed into culturally significant and symbolically disruptive events which can legitimately challenge current assumptions and collective practices within an organisation.

Investigators use safety incidents as source material to produce narratives of proximity and doubt that are circulated through the organisation, highlighting ways in which organisational safety may be degrading and current knowledge may be flawed. In precautionary systems of risk management, it is not materially disruptive accidents but symbolically disruptive incidents that drive the continual cycle of testing and renewing assumptions – a cycle that is at the heart of cultural processes of readjustment to and learning from failure (Turner and Pidgeon, 1997). Safety improvement and organisational adaptation become organised around imagined weaknesses and symbolic threats, rather than in response to materially harmful or actual adverse outcomes. This represents a process of precautionary adaptation, in which organisational activities are redesigned in light of perceived weaknesses rather than materialised impacts. Resilience is activated by and enacted around symbolically disruptive risks, rather than materially disruptive accidents. Narratives of cultural disruption are actively manufactured and circulated by safety investigators, and safety incidents are actively used by investigators for organisational purposes. Incidents are transformed into moments of risk and markers of ignorance, around which diverse operational specialists are connected and brought together to examine and improve organisational practices.

In this sense, an assessments of risk is an interpretive device that is used to do epistemic work. Risks are conceptual constructs, constructed for the purpose of directing attention, focusing resources and organising action – akin to Smith's (1988, p. 1492) definition of 'problems' as "conceptual entities defined as a way of allocating attention to unsatisfactory aspects of reality that one hopes to improve through action", and Miettinen and Virkkunen's (2005, p. 438) definition of epistemic objects that "embody what one does not yet know. At the time of their inception, they are still relatively undefined". Risks are created and used to organise the epistemic work that underpins safety improvement, providing specific and practical foci for socially distributed processes of investigation, reflection and analysis throughout the organisation. Incidents are transformed into risks, which then function as boundary objects, facilitating communication about the safety of organisational practices that otherwise may not take place. And incidents provide specific, concrete cues that act as focal points for operational personnel, technical specialists and managers to reflect on, and enquire into, the safety of organisational practices and their own assumptions about them. By transforming fleeting incidents into troubling risks, organisational practices are turned into objects of collective enquiry (Miettinen and Virkkunen, 2005), around which are organised the activities of reflection and learning that are critical to effective cultures of safety (Pidgeon and O'Leary, 2000).

The work of flight safety investigators points to the specific and practical ways that safety can be managed by creating and maintaining an informed culture (Reason, 1997). Openly distributing information on multiple small and particular instances of organisational failure, coupled with targeting relevant information at designated personnel who have specific responsibilities for safety in their area of operations, allows locally informed cultures to be managed in the particular and the specific. In this sense, following Turner (1971), safety incident reporting systems allow the creation and maintenance of multiple overlapping informed *sub*-cultures, each formed around specific indications of risk. By actively targeting and engaging specific operational specialists in the analysis and investigation of incidents pertaining to their local area of organisational practice, a small group of safety investigators can lead, coordinate and oversee widely distributed processes of safety improvement, cultural change and epistemic work across their organisation.

In this sense, risk analysis is often targeted at identifying opportunities to influence and shape local culture and improve knowledge and practices. In the professional field of health and safety, risks are commonly assessed and defined in purely negative terms – stopping the unacceptable and preventing the intolerable. But, in the work of flight safety investigators at least, it is productive to view risk assessment at least in part as an evaluation of potential sources of safety improvement. Assessments of risk represent not only where safety is potentially degrading and knowledge is doubtful but also where there is greatest potential for learning and for improving resilience – where safety value is likely to be produced. These evaluative aspects of improvement are almost entirely unacknowledged and unsupported in traditional models of risk and safety management. More explicitly incorporating these positive appraisals of value into risk analysis methods – in terms of the potential for learning, improvement and the likely gains from intervention – could result in more sensitive and targeted methods for identifying and managing incremental improvements to safety.

These observations also hold implications for the skills required to oversee safety and manage risk, and particularly reaffirm the importance of social skills in assessing and managing risk (e.g. Weick and Roberts, 1993; Weick, Sutcliffe and Obstfeld, 1999). Organising safety improvement is a process of persuading and influencing as well as challenging and recommending. In particular, the practical ability to disrupt existing cultural assumptions by framing and posing challenging questions, along with the ability to influence and shape the thinking and enquiries of others, are key and easily overlooked skills of safety oversight. The ability to follow up those questions in ongoing and robust conversations is just as important. Likewise, the ability to craft compelling and engaging narratives of risk, and to create and target messages that resonate with, challenge and disrupt the thinking of different professional audiences, is key to organising the epistemic work of safety improvement.

Rethinking resilience and high reliability

Many current efforts to understand and manage safety in complex and trying organisational settings focus on ideas of organisational resilience and high reliability. Images of high reliability organising provide a rich set of principles and ideas that describe how organisations grapple with issues of safety, complexity, knowledge and ignorance. Theorising the practices of investigators presents a range of implications for how principles of high reliability and organisational resilience can be refined and operationalised, particularly when they confront the messy and ambiguous realities of organisational life, and when the focus of explanatory attention extends to practices of management, analysis and oversight in safety-critical systems, in addition to the immediate operational activities of front-line personnel.

The principles of remaining sensitive to front-line operations, focusing on failure, avoiding oversimplification, organising around expertise and continually aiming for resilience (Weick and Sutcliffe, 2001), provide something of a shorthand description of the deep assumptions and analytical practices of the flight safety investigators studied here. Examining the practices of flight safety investigators reaffirms many of these principles, and also extends and refines them in important ways. In particular, it helps to answer the question – what next? And, how? For instance, a preoccupation with failure is at the core of both the practical work of investigators and the design and operation of incident reporting and investigation systems. Rather than facing a situation in which "failures are a rare occurrence . . . [and managers] are preoccupied with something they seldom see" (Weick, Sutcliffe and Obstfeld, 1999, p. 92), in practice, most risk managers will in fact routinely encounter failure events and reports of masses of operational failures. Error is normal and failures are the bread and butter of risk management systems. The challenges in practice therefore more commonly focus on discerning and distinguishing which failures matter, which carry deeper implications for the safety of organisational systems and which do not. Every defect is not always a treasure (Davidoff, 2012). Many are decoys (Turner, 1976a). And differentiating between the two is one source of the many close calls that risk managers have to make in their routine analytical work. Drawing on nuanced practical theories of organisational safety and deploying mental models of defensive practices provide one route to address this challenge, and allow investigators to make sense of safety in organisations that routinely encounter failures but rarely experience catastrophic accidents.

Likewise, the interpretive practices of investigators represent a close approximation to the idealised principle of developing sensitivity to operations: being focused on the practical work that is conducted on the organisational front-line, being able to draw on their own experiences of that work, and working to avoid or unpick bland abstractions and generalisations. But beyond that, the pressing questions in practice relate to how this operational sensitivity can be socially distributed, organised and enacted across an organisation by a core group of safety managers. The organisational arrangements and information technologies of incident reporting and investigation systems allow a small group of safety professionals to draw on the specific operational insights of a widely distributed networks of specialists, and then integrate and circulate that operational sensitivity widely. Safety investigators, working within a distinct social and cognitive infrastructure, produce and distribute operational sensitivity both across organisational boundaries between different departments, and directly up and down organisational hierarchies to executives, senior managers and directors – people who otherwise might find themselves working at some distance and some level of abstraction from operational reality. Equally, the practices of investigators suggest that overseeing and interpreting safety involves a continual interpretive struggle – not merely to avoid simplifying interpretations of risk but to actively complicate, elaborate, test and challenge those interpretations. Incident reporting and investigation systems provide a social infrastructure within which multiple voices, perspectives and views can be brought together to debate and create rich collective narratives of risk.

Incident reporting and investigation systems, and the work of investigators, represent processes and activities that closely match the high reliability principles of deference to expertise and the underspecification of problem-solving structures. Safety investigators organise and coordinate the distributed investigative activities of local specialists. Those people closest to the problems, and those with the most relevant and practical knowledge, are expected and encouraged to take ownership of those risks. Delegating analytical and improvement activities to operational specialists not only allows problems to migrate to those with the most appropriate expertise and skills to solve them, but it also actively creates and sustains networks of participation, building local knowledge in particular aspects of safety, as well as cultivating local capacities for investigation and improvement. Within these architectures of participation problems do not spontaneously migrate to experts, but rather are reviewed by safety generalists – the investigators – and then intentionally allocated and distributed to specialists. Moreover, investigators do not fully defer to the judgement and decisions of experts. Rather, they retain oversight of these experts and the processes of investigation. Investigators challenge and test the professional opinions and the data that are provided, and they integrate those with the insights and evidence provided by others experts around the organisation and beyond. Critically, through these activities of oversight it is not simply problems that migrate to experts, but accountability migrates too. Investigators work to create and maintain local accountability for safety improvement across their organisations. Circulating signs of risks in professional forums, reporting on incidents and investigations to boards, and documenting and recording opinions and improvement actions within the safety information system ensure that experts publicly account for their actions. Safety oversight is a process of distributing and organising accountability for improvement, as much as it is a process of circulating signs of potential risks.

The idea of organisational resilience is mired in definitional and conceptual problems. These problems have not been much helped by the idea's recent ascendance in both popular and policy-making discourses. Organisational resilience has come to mean many things to many people (Sutcliffe and Vogus, 2003; Hollnagel, Woods and Leveson, 2006), but the core principles of responding to disruptive events, learning from trial and error and adapting to failure run deeply through the work of flight safety investigators and their thinking on risk, and underpin the risk management strategy of resilience – and of incident reporting and investigation.

Examining the practical work of investigators reveals some new variations on the theme of resilience, and in places offers a degree of clarity regarding some of the more troublesome complications inherent to the idea of organisational resilience. Three of the common complications typically present in discussions of resilience are outlined and addressed by Comfort, Boin and Demchak (2010). These relate to the moment of resilience, the severity of the triggering event and the state to which an organisation returns. That is, does resilience refer to the preventative activities that occur before a disruption or to the recovery activities that occur after it? Does resilience refer to activities that unfold in response to major and devastating events or also to more routine interruptions? And does resilience represent activities that ensure organisational systems 'bounce back' to a previous state, or that support adaptation and change? The effects of these definitional complications run through much of the literature on resilience. They lead, for instance, to the conflicting propositions that high reliability organisations can't use trial-and-error learning as the first error might be the last trial, *and* that high reliability organisations are exceptional in the ways that they learn from their errors and critically depend on past experiences of failure (e.g. La Porte and Consolini, 1991; Weick and Sutcliffe, 2001). These complications also help to explain some of the more expansive and liberal definitions of resilience that at times appear to encompass and occasionally conflate all aspects of organisational adaptation, learning, flexibility, forward planning and anticipation as characteristics of resilience (Hollnagel et al., 2010).

The definition provided by Comfort, Boin and Demchack (2010, p. 9) to clarify these positions is a helpful one: resilience is "the capacity of a social system . . . to proactively adapt to and recover from disturbances that are perceived within the system to fall outside the range of normal and expected disturbances". This blends both the proactive and the reactive, as well as activities of adaptation and recovery. This definition is also deeply cultural, relative and incremental. It hinges on what is perceived as normal, expected and disturbing within a particular community – perceptions that can presumably change and evolve over time as the boundary of expected and understood events evolves. Yet several complications persist beyond this definition, and can be addressed by this examination of investigators' patterns of thinking. One of these issues concerns the nature of the disturbances and disruptions that activate resilience, and how those are perceived and produced in organisations. In essence, this concerns the question, resilience to what? For flight safety investigators, the disturbances that provoke attempts to investigate and adapt organisational practices take the form of risks: symbolic and cultural disruptions that represent breaks with current assumptions and existing knowledge, but that are associated with minimal – and usually no – materially disruptive outcome. In a cultural and symbolic sense, the identification of potential risks and imagined threats can cause dramatic revisions to how organisational activities are understood and enacted – whilst also resulting in no materially adverse impact. As such, in the terms of Comfort, Boin and Demchak (2010), it is hard to determine if these activities of resilience that are activated by cultural and symbolic disruptions occur 'before' or 'after' the moment of disruption: investigators appear to be organising recovery and adaptation after cultural disruptions, at the same time as they are organising adaptive prevention before material disruptions.

This complication is also present in distinctions posited between proactive and reactive modes of resilience (Boin and van Eeten, 2013). 'Precursor' resilience represents the ability to accommodate change without catastrophic failure, while 'recovery' resilience represents the ability to respond to, and recover from, unique disastrous events (Roe and Schulman, forthcoming). Elaborating these distinct modes of resilient organising is helpful, particularly when it reveals specific sets of organisational practices that can be better monitored, managed and supported within organisations. But these distinctions can implicitly reinforce the assumption that the ultimate reference point is a materially catastrophic accident or disaster: activities of resilience happen either before or after a harmful catastrophe. Many of these complicating distinctions and ongoing debates regarding precisely 'when' resilience occurs and how 'big' a trigger is needed can be clarified by uncoupling the material and the cultural components of disaster (Turner, 1978), and accepting that the disruptions that occasion resilience can be primarily cultural and symbolic in nature, as much as they can be material. In particular, the practices of flight safety investigators point to the value of privileging the cultural and interpretive aspects of our models of organisational resilience. They indicate the value of examining events not in terms of the severity of their material consequences, "but according to their unexpectedness in the view of prevailing institutionally accepted models of the world" (Turner, 1976b, p. IX 26). That is, resilience, adaptation, learning and cultural change can be provoked by cultural disruption alone – materially adverse outcomes may be sufficient, but are not necessary.

The practices of flight safety investigators, and the social and cognitive infrastructures that incident reporting and investigation systems support, suggest other ways in which current debates on organisational resilience might be extended. One in particular is the degree to which resilience can be organised and assured. The idea of organisational resilience as a strategy of safety assurance and improvement can find itself caught between two opposing ideals, namely between central oversight and local adaptation. On the one hand, the risk management strategy of resilience is commonly associated with a set of ideals that celebrate improvised, distributed and decentralised approaches to adaptation, which depend on locally specific knowledge and emergent interventions that are sensitive and specific to their local context (Rochlin, 1989). On the other hand, it is argued that risk management requires strong and centralised control to provide standards, an integrated picture of risk and to circulate and institutionalise the lessons learnt from previous failures. Charles Perrow (1999, p. 331) pithily termed this the 'Pushmepullyou' problem, referring to a creature from the Doctor Dolittle stories that has a head at both ends and wants to go both ways at once.

Incident reporting and investigation systems provide cognitive and social infrastructures that balance and in many ways dissolve the tension between widely distributed, locally led adaptation and learning on the one hand, and centrally coordinated and organised improvement and standardisation on the other. The work of investigators involves overseeing and integrating widely decentralised activities of learning and adaptation. Investigators occupy a central coordinating role in a widely distributed infrastructure of improvement. They oversee and integrate locally developed knowledge and locally applied solutions to locally identified risks, and ensure that those emergent adaptations are adequate, fit together within the broader organisational system, and ensure that knowledge of risks – and improvements – is not hidden in pockets but is circulated widely and reflected in organisation-wide standards. This activity supports widely distributed local safety improvement work while also allowing changes in practices to be centrally monitored, assured and integrated into a broader picture of organisational safety. This integrative activity also at least partially addresses the risks of professional specialisation and organisational silos – or the problem colloquially known in the passenger cabin of airliners as 'not my aisle' (Macrae, 2010; 2013).

The practical theory of flight safety investigators equally stands at odds with models of resilience that emphasise the improvised, haphazard and locally emergent practices underpinning resilience – the "organisational messiness" of resilience (van Eeten, Boin and de Bruijne, 2010, p. 159). For flight safety investigators, organisational safety depends on assured, organised and reliable processes of local adaptation and accomodation, a commitment that is captured in part here by the idea of risk resilience: a widely distributed organisational capacity to protect operations from the potential of operational mishaps and disruptions developing into catastrophic and disabling organisational breakdowns. Resilience to risk captures the duality that is at the heart of organisational safety. It is predicated on the existence of assured, established, reliable and persistent organisational capabilities that stand ready to adaptively catch and responsively organise around both operational and symbolic disruptions – before those disruptions escalate into disorderly situations that require improvised, experimental or messy interventions to recover control. The ideal of organisational safety that emerges from and structures the risk management practices of flight safety investigators represents a state of reliable and assured control, based on organised and persistent capacities for adaptive performance in the face of unexpected, unintended and unaccepted events. This perspective guides flight safety investigators in their ongoing efforts to transform moments of risk into sources of resilience.

Coda

Explaining the work that is done to interpret close calls and analyse and improve flight safety in airlines is necessarily a story about the work of flight safety investigators. This book lifts the lid on the interpretive and analytical work that is required to make sense of safety, piece together the early warning signs of risks and then use those signs to organise and coordinate productive enquiry and collective improvement efforts. If nothing else, a clearer understanding of this practical work brings some of the earliest and more subtle aspects of risk management into plain sight, and offers implications regarding how incident reporting and investigation systems might be better designed, operated and supported. If these practices have more general characteristics – if they represent more generic practices of risk management and safety improvement – then the implications raised through this exploration of risk management practice are significantly broader. In particular, they raise implications for how organisational resilience is defined, conceptualised and put into practice as a strategy of safety management, as well as how the principles and ideals of organisational safety and resilience can be elaborated and translated into practical tools that help organisations address the nuanced, messy and pressing challenges of practical risk management work.

The practices and practical theories of risk resilience, interpretive vigilance and participative networks may help to define core features of effective cultures of safety and high reliability, and may offer an expansive and wide-ranging framework within which to understand and organise systems of risk management, safety oversight and organisational improvement. The extent to which that is the case is both an empirical and a practical question. The value and utility of the explanations developed here will be revealed in practice over time: what works and what doesn't; what is applied and used; what is elaborated and what is not. This theoretical account of the risk management practices of flight safety investigators, and the concepts that have been developed to structure and organise it, are themselves epistemic objects around which future productive enquiry and interpretive work might be organised in the pursuit of organisational resilience and safety. The most pressing goal for flight safety investigators, though, is to keep uncovering latent risks and pockets of ignorance, and to keep improving the safety and resilience of airline flight operations. For them, close calls, safety incidents, risk, ignorance, resilience and practical theories of safety are simply means to that end.

References

Amalberti, R., Vincent, C., Auroy, Y. and de Saint Maurice, G. (2006). Violations and migrations in health care: A framework for understanding and management. *Quality and Safety in Health Care*, 15, i66–i71.

Australian Transport Safety Bureau. (2004). *ATSB Human Factors Course*. Canberra: Australian Transport Safety Bureau.

Boeing. (2012). Statistical Summary of Commercial Jet Airplane Accidents: Worldwide Operations 1959–2010. Accessed online 20th August 2012 at http://www.boeing.com/news/techissues/pdf/statsum.pdf

Boin, A. and Van Eeten, M. J. G. (2013). The resilient organization: A critical appraisal. *Public Management Review*, 15(3), 429–445.

Braithwaite, G. R. (2001). *Attitude or Latitude? Australian Aviation Safety*. Aldershot: Ashgate.

Breakwell, G. M. (2007). The Psychology of Risk. Cambridge: Cambridge University Press.

British Standards Institute. (1996). *British Standard 8444-3:1996. Risk Management – Guide to Risk Analysis of Technological Systems*. London: British Standards Institute.

Cabinet Office. (2002). *Risk: Improving Government's Capability to Handle Risk and Uncertainty*. London: Cabinet Office Strategy Unit.

Carroll, J. S. (1998). Organizational learning in high-hazard industries: The logics underlying self-analysis. *Journal of Management Studies*, 35 (6), 699–717.

Civil Aviation Authority (CAA). (1996). *CAP 382: The Mandatory Occurrence Reporting Scheme*. Gatwick: Civil Aviation Authority.

Collingridge, D. (1996). Resilience, flexibility, and diversity in managing the risks of technologies. In C. Hood and Jones, D. K. C. (eds), *Accident and Design: Contemporary Debates on Risk Management*. London: Taylor and Francis.

Comfort, L. K., Boin, A. and Demchak, C. C. (2010). *Designing Resilience: Preparing for Extreme Events*. Pittsburgh: University of Pittsburgh Press.

Cook, S. D. N. and Brown, J. S. (1999). Bridging epistemologies: The generative dance between organizational knowledge and organizational knowing. *Organization Science*, 10 (4), 381–400.

Cooke, R. M. (1991). *Experts in Uncertainty: Opinion and Subjective Probability in Science*. Oxford: Oxford University Press.

Cox, S. and Tait, N. R. S. (1991). *Reliability, Safety and Risk Management: An Integrated Approach*. London: Butterworth-Heinemann.

Crotty, M. (1998). *The Foundations of Social Research: Meaning and Perspective in the Research Process*. London: Sage.

Daft, R. L. and Weick, K. E. (1984). Toward a model of organizations as interpretation systems. *Academy of Management Review*, 9 (2), 284–295.

Davidoff, F. (2012). Is every defect really a treasure? *Annals of Internal Medicine*, 156 (9), 664–665.

Downer, J. (2009). When failure is an option: Redundancy, reliability and regulation in complex technical systems. ESRC Centre for Analysis of Risk and

Regulation Discussion Paper 53, London School of Economics and Political Science, London.

Downer, J. (2011). '737-Cabriolet': The limits of knowledge and the sociology of inevitable failure. *American Journal of Sociology*, 117 (3), 725–762.

Eduljee, G. (1999). Risk assessment. In P. Calow (ed.), *Handbook of Environmental Risk Assessment and Management, Vol. 1. Environmental Impact Assessment: Process, Methods and Potential*. London: Blackwell Science.

Emerson, R. M., Fretz, R. I. and Shaw, L. L. (1995). *Writing Ethnographic Fieldnotes*. London: University of Chicago Press.

Fischhoff, B., Lichtenstein, S., Slovic, P., Derby, S. L. and Keeney, R. L. (1981). *Acceptable Risk*. Cambridge: Cambridge University Press.

Flight International. (2004). Editorial: Holes in the cheese. *Flight International*, 7–13 September, 5.

Glaser, B. G. and Strauss, A. L. (1967). *The Discovery of Grounded Theory*. Chicago: Aldine.

Gould, J. H. (1998). Evaluation of the likelihood of major accidents in industrial processes. In P. Calow (ed.), *Handbook of Environmental Risk Assessment and Management, Vol. 1. Environmental Impact Assessment: Process, Methods and Potential*. London: Blackwell Science.

Harford, T. (2011). *Adapt: Why Success Always Starts with Failure*. London: Hachette Digital.

Hale, A., Wilpert, B. and Freitag, M. (eds). (1998). *After the Event: From Accident Analysis to Organizational Learning*. London: Pergamon.

Health and Safety Executive. (2001). *Reducing Risks, Protecting People: HSE's Decision-Making Process*. Sudbury: HSE Books.

Heinrich, H. W. (1931). *Industrial Accident Prevention: A Scientific Approach*. London: McGraw-Hill.

Hollnagel, E. (2004). *Barriers and Accident Prevention: Or How to Improve Safety by Understanding the Nature of Accidents*. Aldershot: Ashgate.

Hollnagel, E., Braithwaite, J. and Wears, R. (eds). (2013). *Resilient Health Care*. Aldershot: Ashgate.

Hollnagel, E., Paries, J., Woods, D. and Wreathall, J. (eds). (2010). *Resilience Engineering in Practice: A Guidebook*. Aldershot: Ashgate.

Hollnagel, E., Woods, D. D. and Leveson, N. (eds). (2006). *Resilience Engineering: Concepts and Precepts*. Aldershot: Ashgate.

Hood, C. and Jones, D. K. C. (eds). (1996). *Accident and Design: Contemporary Debates on Risk Management*. London: Taylor and Francis.

Hopkins, A. (1999). *Managing Major Hazards: The Lessons of the Moura Mine Disaster*. St Leonards: Allen and Unwin.

Hopkins, A. (2000). *Lessons from Longford: The Esso Gas Plant Explosion*. Sydney: CCH.

Hopkins, A. (2001). Was Three Mile Island a 'normal accident'? *Journal of Contingencies and Crisis Management*, 9 (2), 65–72.

Hopkins, A. (2005). *Safety, Culture and Risk: The Organizational Causes of Disasters*. Sydney: CCH.

Hutchins, E. (1996). *Cognition in the Wild*. London: MIT Press.

Hutter, B. (2001). *Regulation and Risk: Occupational Health and Safety on the Railways*. Oxford: Oxford University Press.

Hutter, B. and Power, M. (eds). (2005). *Organizational Encounters with Risk*. Cambridge: Cambridge University Press.

Institute of Risk Management. (2002). *A Risk Management Standard*. London: IRM, ALARM and AIRMIC.

Interdepartmental Liaison Group on Risk Assessment. (1996). *Use of Risk Assessment within Government Departments*. London: Interdepartmental Liaison Group on Risk Assessment and the Health and Safety Executive.

Klein, G. (1998). *Sources of Power: How People Make Decisions*. London: MIT Press.

Koorneef, F. and Hale, A. (1997). Learning from incidents at work. In F. Redmill and Rajan, J. (eds), *Human Factors in Safety Critical Systems*. Oxford: Butterworth-Heinemann.

La Porte, T. R. (1994). A strawman speaks up: Comments on *The Limits of Safety*. *Journal of Contingencies and Crisis Management*, 2 (4), 207–211.

La Porte, T. R. and Consolini, P. (1991). Working in practice but not in theory: Theoretical challenges of high reliability organizations. *Journal of Public Administration Research and Theory*, 1 (1), 19–47.

Learmount, D. (2013). A very good year for safety. *Flight International*, 47–54, January 15th–21st 2013.

Lewin, K. (1951). Problems of research in social psychology. In D. Cartwright (ed.), *Field Theory in Social Science: Selected Theoretical Papers*. New York: Harper & Row, 155–169.

Macrae, C. (2007). Analysing near-miss events: Risk management in incident reporting and investigation systems. ESRC Centre for Analysis of Risk and Regulation Discussion Paper 47, London School of Economics and Political Science, London.

Macrae, C. (2008). Learning from patient safety incidents: Creating participative risk regulation in healthcare. *Health, Risk & Society*, 10(1), 53–67.

Macrae, C. (2009). Making risks visible: Identifying and interpreting threats to airline flight safety. *Journal of Occupational and Organisational Psychology*, 82, 273–293.

Macrae, C. (2010). Regulating resilience? Regulatory work in high-risk arenas. In Hutter, B. (Ed), *Anticipating Risks and Organising Risk Regulation*. Cambridge: Cambridge University Press.

Macrae, C. (2013). Reconciling regulation and resilience. In Hollnagel, E., Braithwaite, J., and Wears, R. (Eds), *Resilient Health Care*. Aldershot: Ashgate.

Maitlis, S. (2005). The social processes of organizational sensemaking. *Academy of Management Journal*, 48 (1), 21–49.

Maurino, D. E., Reason, J., Johnston, N. and Lee, R. B. (1997). *Beyond Aviation Human Factors: Safety in High Technology Systems*. Aldershot: Ashgate.

McIntyre, G. R. (2002). The application of system safety engineering and management techniques at the US Federal Aviation Administration (FAA). *Safety Science*, 40, 325–335.

Merton, R. K. (1987). Three fragments from a sociologist's notebooks: Establishing the phenomenon, specified ignorance and strategic research materials. *Annual Review of Sociology*, 13, 1–28.

Miettinen, R. and Virkkunen, J. (2005). Epistemic objects, artefacts and organizational change. *Organization*, 12 (3), 437–456.

NASA. (2013). *Aviation Safety Reporting System Program Briefing*. Moffett Field, CA: National Aeronautics and Space Administration ASRS.

National Infrastructure Protection Centre. (2002). *Risk Management: An Essential Guide to Protecting Critical Assets*. Washington, D.C.: National Infrastructure Protection Centre.

National Patient Safety Agency. (2001). *Doing Less Harm*. London: National Patient Safety Agency and the Department of Health.

National Transport Safety Board (NTSB). (2001). Survivability of Accidents Involving Part 121 US Air Carrier Operations, 1983 through 2000: Safety Report NTSB/SR-01/01. Washington, D.C.: NTSB.

O'Leary, M. and Chappell, S. L. (1996). Confidential incident reporting systems create vital awareness of safety problems. *International Civil Aviation Organization Journal*, 51, 11–13.

Perrow, C. (1984). *Normal Accidents: Living with High-Risk Technologies*. New York: Basic Books.

Perrow, C. (1999). *Normal Accidents: Living with High-Risk Technologies* (2nd ed.). Princeton: Princeton University Press.

Pidgeon, N. (1988). Risk assessment and accident analysis. *Acta Psychologica*, 68 (1–3), 355–368.

Pidgeon, N. (1991). Safety culture and risk management in organizations. *Journal of Cross-Cultural Psychology*, 22 (1), 129–140.

Pidgeon, N. (1997). The limits to safety? Culture, politics, learning and man-made disasters. *Journal of Contingencies and Crisis Management*, 5 (1), 1–14.

Pidgeon, N. (1998). Safety culture: Key theoretical issues. *Work and Stress*, 12 (3), 202–216.

Pidgeon, N. and O'Leary, M. (1994). Organizational safety culture: Implications for aviation practice. In N. Johnston, McDonald, N. and Fuller, R. (eds), *Aviation Psychology in Practice*. Aldershot: Ashgate.

Pidgeon, N. and O'Leary, M. (2000). Man-made disasters: Why technology and organizations (sometimes) fail. *Safety Science*, 34, 15–30.

Power, M. (2007). *Organized Uncertainty: Designing a World of Risk Management*. Oxford: Oxford University Press.

Rasmussen, J. (1997). Risk management in a dynamic society: A modelling problem. *Safety Science*, 27 (2/3), 183–213.

Ravetz, J. R. (1987). Usable knowledge, usable ignorance: Incomplete science with policy implications. *Science Communication*, 9(1), 87–116.

Reason, J. (1990). *Human Error*. Cambridge: Cambridge University Press.

Reason, J. (1995). A systems approach to organizational error. *Ergonomics*, 39, 1708–1721.

Reason, J. (1997). *Managing the Risks of Organizational Accidents*. Aldershot: Ashgate.

Reason, J. (1998). Achieving a safe culture: Theory and practice. *Work and Stress*, 12 (3), 292–306.

Reason, J. (2000). Safety paradoxes and safety culture. *Injury Control and Safety Promotion*, 7 (1), 3–14.

Reason, J. (2004). Beyond the organizational accident: The need for 'error wisdom' on the frontline. *Quality and Safety in Health Care*, 13, ii28–ii33.

Reason, J. (2008). *The Human Contribution: Unsafe Acts, Accidents and Heroic Contributions*. Aldershot: Ashgate.

Rijpma, J. A. (1997). Complexity, tight-coupling and reliability: Connecting normal accidents theory and high reliability theory. *Journal of Contingencies and Crisis Management*, 5 (1), 15–23.

Rijpma, J. A. (2003). From deadlock to dead end: The normal accidents-high reliability debate revisited. *Journal of Contingencies and Crisis Management*, 11 (1), 37–45.

Roberts, K. H. (1990). Some characteristics of one type of high reliability organization. *Organization Science*, 1 (2), 160–176.

Roberts, K. H. (ed.). (1993). *New Challenges to Understanding Organizations*. New York: Macmillan.

Roberts, K. H. and Creed, W. E. D. (1993). Epilogue. In K. H. Roberts (ed.), *New Challenges to Understanding Organizations*. New York: Macmillan.

Roberts, K. H., Rousseau, D. M. and La Porte, T. R. (1994). The culture of high-reliability: Quantitative and qualitative assessment aboard nuclear-powered aircraft carriers. *The Journal of High Technology Management Research*, 5 (1), 141–161.

Rochlin, G. I. (1989). Informal organizational networking as a crisis-avoidance strategy: US Naval flight operations as a case study. *Industrial Crisis Quarterly*, 3, 159–176.

Rochlin, G. I. (1996). Reliable organizations: Present research and future directions. *Journal of Contingencies and Crisis Management*, 4 (2), 55–59.

Roe, E. and Schulman, P. R. (2008). *High Reliability Management: Operating on the Edge*. Stanford: Stanford University Press.

Roe, E. and Schulman, P. R. (Forthcoming). *Reliability and Risk: The Challenge of Managing Interconnected Infrastructures*.

Royal Society. (1992). *Risk Analysis, Perception and Management: Report of a Royal Society Study Group*. London: Royal Society.

Sagan, S. D. (1995). *The Limits of Safety: Organizations, Accidents, and Nuclear Weapons*. London: Princeton University Press.

Savage, J. (2004). *The 'Risk Analysis Tool'*. Chevy Chase: Global Aviation Information Network.

Schulman, P. R. (1993). The negotiated order of organizational reliability. *Administration and Society*, 25 (3), 353–372.

Sheffi, Y. (2005). *The Resilient Enterprise: Overcoming Vulnerability for Competitive Advantage*. London: MIT Press.

Smith, G. F. (1988). Towards a heuristic theory of problem structuring. *Management Science*, 34 (12), 1489–1506.

Smithson, M. (1989). *Ignorance and Uncertainty: Emerging Paradigms*. London: Springer-Verlag.

Smithson, M. (1990). Ignorance and disasters. *International Journal of Mass Emergencies and Disasters*, 8 (3), 207–235.

Snook, S. A. (2000). *Friendly fire: The Accidental Shootdown of US Black Hawks over Northern Iraq*. Oxford: Princeton University Press.

Snook, S. A. and Connor, J. C. (2005). The price of progress: Structurally induced inaction. In W. H. Starbuck and Farjoun, M. (eds), *Organization at the Limit: Lessons from the Columbia Disaster*. Oxford: Blackwell.

Standards Australia. (1999). *AS/NZS 4360-1999 Risk Management*. Strathfield: Standards Association of Australia.

Star, S. and Griesemer, J. (1989). Institutional ecology, 'translations' and boundary objects: Amateurs and professionals in Berkeley's museum of Vertebrate Zoology, *Social Studies of Science*, 19 (3), 387–420.

Suchman, L. (1987). *Plans and Situated Actions: The Problem of Human-Machine Communication*. Cambridge: Cambridge University Press.

Sutcliffe, K. M. (2003). Studying 'hard to see' things: Using organization theory to examine medical errors. Paper presented at the Academy of Management Annual Meeting, Seattle.

Sutcliffe, K. M. and Vogus, T. J. (2003). Organizing for resilience. In K. S. Cameron and Dutton, J. E. (eds), *Positive Organizational Scholarship: Foundations of a New Discipline*. London: Berrett-Koehler.

Svenson, O. (1991). The Accident Evolution and Barrier function (AEB) model applied to incident analysis in the processing industries. *Risk Analysis*, 11, 499–507.

Turner, B. (1971). *Exploring the Industrial Subculture*. London: Macmillan Press.

Turner, B. (1976a). The organizational and interorganizational development of disasters. *Administrative Science Quarterly*, 21 (378–397).

Turner, B. (1976b). The failure of foresight: An examination of some of the conditions leading to failures of foresight, and some of the institutionalised processes for accommodating such failures. Unpublished PhD thesis, University of Exeter.

Turner, B. (1978). *Man-Made Disasters*. London: Wykeham.

Turner, B. (1983). The use of grounded theory for the qualitative analysis of organizational behaviour. *Journal of Management Studies*, 20 (3), 333–348.

Turner, B. (1994). Causes of disaster: Sloppy management. *British Journal of Management*, 5, 215–219.

Turner, B. and Pidgeon, N. (1997). *Man-Made Disasters* (2nd ed.). Oxford: Butterworth-Heinemann.

van der Schaaf, T. V., Lucas, D. A. and Hale, A. R. (eds). (1991). *Near Miss Reporting As a Safety Tool*. Oxford: Butterworth-Heinemann.

Van Eeten, M., Boin, A., and de Bruijne, M. (2010). The price of resilience: Contrasting the theoretical ideal-type with the organisational reality. In Comfort, L. K., Boin, A., and Demchak, C. C. (Eds). *Designing Resilience: Preparing for Extreme Events*. Pittsburgh: University of Pittsburgh Press.

Vaughan, D. (1990). Autonomy, interdependence, and social control: NASA and the space shuttle *Challenger*. *Administrative Science Quarterly*, 35, 225–257.

Vaughan, D. (1996). *The Challenger Launch Decision: Risky Technology, Culture and Deviance at NASA*. London: Chicago University Press.

Vaughan, D. (2005). Organizational rituals of risk and error. In B. Hutter and Power, M. (eds), *Organizational Encounters with Risk*. Cambridge: Cambridge University Press.

Vincent, C. (2010). *Patient Safety*. Oxford: BMJ Books.

Vincent, C., Taylor-Adams, S., Chapman, E. J., Hewett, D., Prior, S., Strange, P. and Tizzard, A. (2000). How to investigate and analyse clinical incidents: Clinical Risk Unit and Association of Litigation and Risk Management protocol. *British Medical Journal*, 320, 777–781.

Wagenaar, W. A. and Groeneweg, J. (1987). Accidents at sea: Multiple causes and impossible consequences. *International Journal of Man-Machine Studies*, 27, 587–598.

Wallace, B., Ross, A. and Davies, J. B. (2003). Applied hermeneutics and qualitative safety data: The CIRAS project. *Human Relations*, 56 (5), 587–607.

Wastnage, J. (2005). Airlines get new ice alert. *Flight International*, 25–31 October, 12.

Weick, K. E. (1979). *The Social Psychology of Organizing* (2nd ed.). London: McGraw-Hill.

Weick, K. E. (1987). Organizational culture as a source of high reliability. *California Management Review*, 29 (2), 112–127.

Weick, K. E. (1989). Mental models of high reliability systems. *Industrial Crisis Quarterly*, 3, 127–142.

Weick, K. E. (1993a). The collapse of sensemaking in organizations: The Mann Gulch disaster. *Administration and Society*, 38 (4), 628–652.

Weick, K. E. (1993b). The vulnerable system: An analysis of the Tenerife air disaster. In K. H. Roberts (ed.), *New Challenges to Understanding Organizations*. New York: Macmillan.

Weick, K. E. (1995). *Sensemaking in Organizations*. London: Sage.

Weick, K. E. (1998a). Foresights of failure: An appreciation of Barry Turner. *Journal of Contingencies and Crisis Management*, 6 (2), 72–75.

Weick, K. E. (1998b). The attitude of wisdom: Ambivalence as the optimal compromise. In S. Srivastva and Cooperidge, D. L. (eds), *Organizational Wisdom and Executive Courage*. San Francisco, CA: Lexington.

Weick, K. E. (2001). Gapping the relevance bridge: Fashions meet fundamentals in management research. *British Journal of Management*, 12, S71–S75.

Weick, K. E. and Roberts, K. H. (1993). Collective mind in organizations: Heedful interrelating on flight decks. *Administrative Science Quarterly*, 38, 357–381.

Weick, K. E. and Sutcliffe, K. M. (2001). *Managing the Unexpected: Assuring High Performance in an Age of Complexity*. San Francisco: Jossey Bass.

Weick, K. E., Sutcliffe, K. M. and Obstfeld, D. (1999). Organizing for high reliability: Processes of collective mindfulness. *Organizational Behaviour*, 21, 81–123.

Wenger, E. (1999). *Communities of Practice: Learning, Meaning, and Identity*. Cambridge: Cambridge University Press.

Wildavsky, A. (1988). *Searching for Safety*. Oxford: Transaction.

Woods, D. D. (2005). Creating foresight: Lessons for enhancing resilience from Columbia. In W. H. Starbuck and Farjoun, M. (eds), *Organization at the Limit: Lessons from the Columbia Disaster*. Oxford: Blackwell.

Wright, D. A. and Lyons, J. E. (2001). Flight Data Monitoring: Its place within a Safety Management System. Paper presented at the 13th European Aviation Safety Seminar: Toward a Safer Europe, Amsterdam, Netherlands.

Zolli, A. and Healy, A. M. (2012). *Resilience: Why Things Bounce Back*. London: Headline Publishing Group.

Index

Printed and bound by CPI Group (UK) Ltd, Croydon, CR0 4YY